Tomb Raiders and Space Invaders

Tomb Raiders and Space Invaders

Videogame Forms and Contexts

Geoff King and Tanya Krzywinska

I.B. TAURIS

LONDON · NEW YORK

Completion of the project was made possible by a grant from the
Arts and Humanities Research Board

A · H · R · B

arts and humanities research board

Published in 2006 by I.B.Tauris & Co Ltd
6 Salem Road, London W2 4BU
175 Fifth Avenue, New York NY 10010
www.ibtauris.com

In the United States of America and in Canada distributed by
Palgrave Macmillan, a division of St Martin's Press
175 Fifth Avenue, New York NY 10010

ISBN 1 84511 108 7 hardback
EAN 978 1 84511 108 3 hardback
ISBN 1 85043 814 5 paperback
EAN 978 1 85043 814 4 paperback

A full CIP record for this book is available from the British Library
A full CIP record for this book is available from the Library of Congress

Library of Congress catalog card: available

Typeset in Bembo by Steve Tribe, Andover
Printed and bound in Great Britain by MPG Books Ltd, Bodmin

Contents

Illustrations

Acknowledgements

Thanks to Barry Atkins, Sue Morris and Marie-Laure Ryan for taking the time to read the manuscript before publication and for a number of helpful suggestions. We are also grateful to Philippa Brewster at I.B. Tauris for commissioning this book. Completion of the project was made possible by a grant from the Arts and Humanities Research Board.

Introduction

Space Invaders, Tomb Raiders

Ranks of sketchy white alien forms shuffle sideways across the screen. You move a small green turret along the lower edge, shooting at the alien 'invaders' and dodging for cover from their fire behind a row of protective blocks. Each time the aliens complete a movement from one side to the other, the ranks drop down closer. They start to move a little faster. An insistent electronic marching beat accompanies their progress, keeping time with their increased speed, winding up the tension. Try to take out vertical rows from the side, slowing their progress. Beware of any that get too low, giving you little time to avoid their shots. Hit aliens to clear the screen, scoring points as you go. Watch out for higher-scoring bonus aliens that move, periodically, across the upper edge of the screen. Keep hitting the buttons, watching, hypnotically, as it gets faster and faster. Your defences gradually get shot to nothing. Lose a life, but you might have another left. Clear the screen, gain another life, and they start lower, closer. Keep going and the pace quickens further. You stare at the screen, your eyes strain and your focus narrows; surrounding distractions recede from attention. How long can you survive? Eventually, always, you die, sooner or later. You cannot beat the machine, but you might hang on long enough to set a new high score.

After some time exploring the Paris ghetto and talking to various non-player characters, you eventually find the backstage door to the Serpent Rouge club where you must find a box to be traded for important information. Kill a guard lurking at the entrance, enter an office and spot a bunch of items on a desk; press 'action' to prompt Lara to pick up ammunition and a chocolate bar. On leaving, take the guard's gun – in case you get into a scrap later on. Follow a corridor and emerge onto the dance floor of the club. Dispatch a pair of guards and pull a switch that fills the space with fast-paced pumping techno music. More guards, prompting you to twist the in-game camera rapidly to get a good aim. More items to be collected. Climbing Lara up a gantry, you collect your thoughts; hit the save key just in case the jump you're about to make ends in death, and mentally go through the button presses needed to ensure success. Ready, steady – go! Lara's ponytail swishes as she jumps through the air and catches the edge of the gantry by her fingertips. She pulls up and stands still, awaiting your next command. But there's no respite. Tension mounts as you are assailed by more bullets, Lara's blood hitting the deck. Phew, you got through! Then more jumping, but this time the timing is wrong: Lara flails her arms and hits the ground below with a nasty crunch. Reload from the previous save; try again. This time it works. But more jumping leads to more deaths, the flow of the game interrupted as you're kicked out to the main menu. Back inside the game-world, you attempt frantically to find the 'sweet' spot from which to jump – and curse aloud at the precision demanded by the game. Several more jumps, some lever pulls in a particular order and the box is found. Exit Lara from the club, hitting the save key again with a palpable sense of relief.

Videogames[1] have certainly come a long way from the experience of *Space Invaders* (1978),[2] one of the breakthrough arcade games of the 1970s, to that offered by episodes of the *Tomb Raider* series such as *Angel of Darkness* (2003). *Space Invaders* restricts the player to a largely abstract and relatively unchanging form of play in which a limited range of fixed and immediate responses are required. The *Tomb Raider* games (from 1996) offer something much more like a virtual *world* with which to engage – a richer and more detailed series of spaces to explore and tasks to perform – through the third-person figure of Lara Croft. *Space Invaders* and *Tomb Raider* also have much in common, however. Each has a core gameplay dynamic on which much of the pleasure it offers is based, a particular kind of activity at which the successful player has to become proficient, largely through a process of extended temporal engagement: playing again and again – and again – until further progress is made, the player coming to a closer understanding of the underlying logic of the game. *Tomb Raider* requires the performance of a wider range of activities than *Space Invaders*, but these are reducible to a relatively limited set of moves. The principal difference between the two lies, perhaps, in the degree of material offered in support of, and around, the activities of core gameplay. *Space Invaders*, like other games of its era, is stripped back to the basics. *Tomb Raider* has more dimensions. It gives the player greater freedom, within the constraints of its basic mechanism, including freedom to explore the on-screen world to some extent beyond the immediate requirements of advancement through the game. It creates a stronger impression of occupying the game-world, even if at one remove. It provides more in the way of background context, in which to situate gameplay activities. It is also realized more fully and more 'realistically' at the level of audio-visual qualities. As a result of these dimensions, the *Tomb Raider* games appear to be more substantial social-cultural products, susceptible to more sustained readings in terms of their place in the wider cultural landscape in which they are played. How important these additional dimensions are to videogames more generally is one of the major questions addressed by this book.

Games have become a significant part of the recent and contemporary media/entertainment landscape. From relatively small and often obscure beginnings, videogames have become very big business, the stuff of rivalries between major transnational corporations such as Sony and Microsoft. They have also become a substantial component of popular culture, comparable to more established media such as film and television. Until recently, however, they have not received the kind and degree of analytical attention they merit. Academic studies of games date back to at least the 1980s, but in many cases have failed to address the specific nature and qualities of games considered as a medium or form in their own right. Early studies of games were dominated by quite different agendas, often hostile, sometimes as part of a wider 'moral panic' about videogames and their alleged influences or 'effects', especially on children. It is only in the last few years that 'game studies', as a discrete discipline, has begun to emerge, and even here it has struggled to gain recognition.[3]

The aim of this book is to contribute to the academic analysis of games, as media forms that need to be considered in their own right and as part of the broader environment of popular culture in which they appear. Our major point of focus is on key formal aspects of games – the ways games are structured and realized – and the kinds of experiences offered by the activities they require or encourage of the player. We also consider the contexts within which these experiences are shaped and deployed, including cultural and industrial dimensions. A central issue throughout is the nature of the pleasure offered by gameplay. Our argument is that games offer a range of different pleasures and experiences. It is often necessary to separate these out in order to analyze each in its turn, as we do as we move from one chapter to another. We start, in the first part of Chapter 1, by considering the nature of gameplay itself, the core quality that defines games as different from other media. We then consider how the experience of gameplay might be shaped or influenced by – or relatively independent of – sources of background contextual material such as narrative/story, genre or political-ideological resonances. This part of the book touches on, but also seeks to go beyond, what has in recent years been one of the more controversial debates in game studies: between those who argue for or against the significance of narrative as a dimension important to games or to which they ought to aspire.

A shift of focus occurs in Chapter 2, in which we consider games as spaces that can be explored or virtually inhabited to greater or lesser degrees. The second part of this chapter focuses on degrees of virtual 'presence' created by game-worlds, including analysis of the differences that result from shifts in in-game orientation such as those between games offered as virtual first or third person experiences. Chapter 3 examines qualities such as realism, spectacle and sensation in games. We consider the appeal not just of increased graphical 'photorealism', in many games, but also a functional variety of realism, founded on the attempt to model actions and reactions (as well as representational surfaces) in a manner that corresponds to some extent with their real-world (or other media) equivalents. This chapter also considers the spectacular qualities of game-worlds, including spectacle founded on claims made to the status of 'realism', before moving on to consider a variety of intense and impactful sensations that lie close to the heart of the appeal of some games. The final chapter shifts attention to the social, cultural and political–ideological dimensions of games, examining games as parts of the meaning-creating culture in which they are situated. Issues addressed here include ideological meanings coded implicitly into both background contextual material and core gameplay activities.

If dimensions of games and gameplay such as these can be separated out for analysis, our argument is that they also need to be put back together again. None operate in isolation. Exactly how they interact is subject to debate. Whether core gameplay activities should be privileged, above dimensions such as narrative context or standards of graphical representation, for example, is an issue to which we return on several occasions. Our argument, though, is that games offer multidimensional experiences. Which of these are foregrounded might vary from one game or game genre to another. Precisely which kinds of pleasures are taken also depends to a significant extent on the orientations of individual players. Even if some dimensions are seen as less *essential* to games than others, however, they can all contribute to the overall experience. If core gameplay activity is privileged, as some argue it should be, as the feature that marks games out from other popular entertainment media, it never occurs in a 'pure' form, unadulterated by some other dimension. Much the same can be said here as for other media. Film, for example, has been described as an essentially visual medium (especially before the full integration of sound into the basis of the medium). Film (or video) might still be considered to be a medium in which the visual is predominant, qualities such as camera movement and temporally sequenced editing being specific to the form. Even if considered secondary (against which some might argue), sound still plays a highly significant part in the film-viewing experience, however, often performing a central role in areas such as shaping the emotional coding of individual sequences. The same could be said of game dimensions such as the role of background contextual material or the level of graphical detail in which the game-world is rendered (although the latter can also have significance for gameplay itself, as we argue in Chapter 3): they may not be essential to what makes a game a game, rather than anything else, but they contribute to the overall experience offered to the player.

To consider these different dimensions, and their interrelationships, we draw on a range of critical perspectives and methodologies. Wider theories of play and games provide important insights on the nature of play, as a distinct realm of experience. Fields such as semiotics, narrative study and film theory help to inform the analysis of some formal features of games. Concepts drawn from sociology and from media and cultural studies aid in the analysis of the cultural and industrial contexts in which games are produced and consumed. The views of game designers offer another important point of reference. We use these critical perspectives in a heterogeneous manner, as analytical tools chosen to help understanding of particular aspects of games and gameplay, rather than from an allegiance to any single over-arching theoretical perspective. This emphasis on a plurality of approaches underpins the core claim of this book: that a full analysis of games requires not a privileging of one aspect of games over others, but consideration of the interplay between one and another. We do not claim to cover all possible aspects of games and gaming, however. In our predominant focus on games as part of popular culture, we do not dwell on issues such as the technical basis of games, or developments in gaming technology, other than briefly and in connection with other matters (such as improvements in graphics technologies in Chapter 3). This book does not include any empirical study of gamers themselves, either, which is clearly a dimension of more central importance to our perspective. Our emphasis is on what is *offered* to gameplayers rather than on exactly what aspects of the experience are taken up or enjoyed by particular gamers. The latter requires empirical study of gameplayers, either in general or in particular sections or sub-sections of the gameplaying population, an enterprise that can contribute significantly to our understanding of games but that lies beyond the scope of this book.[4] We have not attempted a taxonomy of game types, an issue that has concerned some interventions in this newly crystallizing field.[5] Neither have we paid as much attention to the industrial contexts within which games have been shaped as we would have liked, as a result of restrictions on space.

A word is also required on the games that feature in this study. We have sought to use a wide range of examples drawn from different game genres and platforms, but there are limits to how far this is possible. Playing games is a very time-consuming business, as any gamer will confirm. It can take dozens or in some cases hundreds of hours to complete a single game, which has forced us to be somewhat selective in the number of examples analyzed. In the majority of cases, we have restricted our analysis to games we have played ourselves, either in full or in part. A number of games appear regularly throughout the book, an outcome of practical necessity that also helps to underline the extent to which individual titles can be analyzed in a number of different dimensions. One problem with games, as objects of study, is their transience, especially given the rapid coming and going of successive platforms, which makes many older games less easily available for play. We have tried, therefore, to ensure a balance between games and game franchises that have gained 'classic' or canonical status and others that illustrate wider trends while being, potentially, more short-lived. In some cases, an individual title is used in a manner designed to be representative of a wider game-type, the principal example being the use of *EverQuest* in more general consideration of massively multi-player online role-playing games (even more time-consuming than others!). We have focused primarily on games played on home consoles and personal computers, rather than arcade games or the growing sector of games designed for an array of mobile platforms. There is also a tendency to lean towards games that fall broadly into the action-adventure category (including, in its widest sense, some role-playing and strategy games), to which we have tended to gravitate in our own play. Other kinds of games are also considered, however, at both the mass and niche market ends of the scale.

1

Gameplay
and its Contexts

A much discussed issue in game studies in recent years has been the relationship between the performance and enjoyment of the specific tasks associated with any particular game, or type of game, and the meaning-creating contexts in which these are set in the game-world. The relationship between gameplay and narrative has been the principal focus of this debate. To what extent are games a medium with a significant narrative, or story-telling, component? How far are game-specific tasks – such as running around in the on-screen world shooting, killing and trying to avoid being shot in a first-person shooter or marshalling and deploying resources in a real-time strategy game – affected by the narrative frameworks within which such activities are situated? Debate on this issue has, in some cases, been heated and polemical, the potential role of narrative being subject to both exaggeration and out-of-hand dismissal. The aim of this chapter is to open the question up more widely, to give detailed consideration to the nature and qualities of gameplay itself and its relationship with a broader range of contextual material. The latter includes associations brought to gameplay from narrative frameworks, but also from generic sources and wider resonances within its cross-media, social-cultural and political or ideological context. How, and how far, these are likely to 'play-into', or be 'in-play', during the performance of key gameplay tasks will be the subject of the latter part of this chapter. First, though, a close look is needed at the distinguishing characteristics of gameplay itself, including definitions of key terms such as 'game' and 'play'.

Gameplay

Gameplay, as experienced in videogames, might be defined along the following lines: the particular set of non-real-world tasks, goals or potentials set for the player's enjoyment within an on-screen arena, performed according to a set of pre-established rules and as a result of which a number of different outcomes are possible. Many such definitions have been offered by games developers and theorists.[1] The two most influential sources for definitions of gameplay, highlighting a number of issues central to our understanding of videogames, are the more general definitions of play offered by the cultural theorists Johan Huizinga (*Homo Ludens: A Study of the Play Element in Culture*, first published in German in 1944) and Roger Caillois (*Man, Play and Games*, first published in French in 1958). For Huizinga, the main characteristics of play are: that it is a voluntary activity, freely entered into as a source of pleasure and 'never imposed by physical necessity or moral duty';[2] that it involves a stepping out of 'ordinary' or 'real' life into 'a temporary sphere of activity with a disposition all of its own';[3] that this occurs in its own distinct time and place, ordered and rule-bound;[4] and that play tends to create its own communities, on the basis of particular shared activities.[5] Caillois' definition is broadly similar, building on Huizinga and adding some extra ingredients. For Caillois, as for Huizinga, play is essentially free, the activity of playing not obligatory for the player; otherwise 'it would at once lose its attractive and joyous qualities as a diversion.'[6] It is also, as in Huizinga, separate, an activity 'circumscribed within limits of time and space, defined and fixed in advance',[7] governed by rules, and make-believe, 'accompanied by a special awareness of a second reality or of a free unreality, as against real life.'[8] To these dimensions Caillois adds the suggestion that play is uncertain, the precise course and result not being determined in advance 'and some latitude for innovations being left to the player's initiative',[9] and unproductive, 'creating neither goods nor wealth'.[10]

[handwritten margin note: Player chooses to leave the rules of the real-world behind and enter into another world where their actions do not affect real life]

In addition to more general definitions of play and games, specific features can be attributed to videogames on the basis of their use of digital technologies. For Janet Murray, the representational power of computers 'enhances, intensifies and extends' various facets of play found in more traditional games.[11] Katie Salen and Eric Zimmerman suggest four characteristic traits of digital media that, working in combination, bring unique qualities to computer and video games: a form of interactivity that is immediate, although narrow in comparison with the activities involved in non-digital games (the use of mouse and keyboard or console joysticks and buttons, in comparison with a wider range of physical engagement in real-world gaming activities); manipulation of large quantities of information; the automation of complex procedural systems; and a capability for networked communication between players.[12]

PLAY VS. GAME; FREEDOM VS. RULES

It is widely agreed that videogames require rules. As Espen Aarseth puts it: 'Without rules to structure actions … we would have free play or other forms of interaction, but not *gameplay*.'[13] The balance between the establishment of rules and the creation of freedom for the player is highly variable, however, an issue that can be explored with the aid of two further concepts used by Caillois to distinguish between the meanings associated in English with the terms 'play' and 'game'. Caillois adopts the Latin terms *paidea* and *ludus*. *Paidea* is equivalent to 'play' in its most spontaneous and unstructured forms, 'a primary power of improvisation and joy'.[14] *Ludus*, closer to 'game', suggests the rules within which *paidea* is often contained. *Ludus* is the outcome, Caillois suggests, of a 'taste for gratuitous difficulty',[15] a term that might resonate with the players of the more fiendish elements of some videogames. Game rules are defined in similar terms by Bernard Suits as 'unnecessary obstacles' created purely to make possible the activity of play, forbidding more efficient means in favour of less efficient means (in a foot-race, for example, requiring runners to go the long way around a track rather than taking a short-cut across the middle).[16] A scale is offered that can usefully be applied to a wide range of games. At one end is free improvisation; at the other, the imposition of seemingly arbitrary rules. In between, many gradations and combinations are possible.

An attempt to take the meanings of these terms a stage further in the context of videogames is made by Gonzalo Frasca, who seeks to integrate Caillois' terms with the theory of play offered by the developmental psychologist Jean Piaget.[17] Piaget identifies three types of play, each related to different stages of growth in childhood: from exercise games (play involving sensory-motor activities) to symbolic games (involving make-believe and implying the representation of absent objects) and games with rules.[18] Exercise games and symbolic games, in this account, can entail 'regularities' – that is to say, repeated parameters such as throwing a marble from the same place or throwing it the same distance on each occasion – but not rules. Rules, in Piaget's usage, entail social or inter-individual relationships.[19] Frasca suggests something of a synthesis between Caillois and Piaget, in which *ludus* is taken to mean games that define a winner or a loser and *paidea* suggests games with 'regularities' rather than entirely unstructured play.[20]

The value of any of these definitions – those of Caillois or Frasca's synthesis of Caillois and Piaget – lies in their flexibility: the fact that they can be used to articulate the relative balance of qualities found in any individual game or game-genre. Some games fall in between the poles suggested by Frasca's definitions, for example: games that do not have a single winning or losing state, but in which the player might miss significant dimensions of the experience if particular tasks are not achieved. As Aki Järvinen, Satu Heliö and Frans Mäyrä put it: 'In a game there are definitions of winning or losing, or at least of gain and loss.'[21] A clear sense of gain or loss is established in massively multi-player online role-playing games (MMORPGs) such as *EverQuest*, for example, without reaching any defined point of overall victory or irredeemable loss. The player is encouraged to perform activities such as killing monsters and participating in quests to gain experience points and to increase the level of their character, gathering and selling resources in order to gain access to improved weapons, spells and armour. What can be gained can also be lost, once the early levels have been passed. The death of the character results in a loss of experience points and the possible forfeit of equipment if the corpse is not recovered within a given time-frame. Larger and more epic quests, adventures or raids can be achieved by more experienced players, increasing the satisfaction likely to be gained from gameplay. But, while adventures might depend on a mission being completed in an allocated time-frame, there is no overall definitive end point to the game

(margin handwritten note: Play is a part of child growth)

itself (hence the *Ever*Quest). At any one particular time, a limit is set on the maximum level characters can reach, but this has increased over time, the commercial imperative of a subscription-based game requiring continued expansion of such parameters rather than the possibility of achieving a state of final closure.

Even within its own open state, maximization of the achievement of the player's character is only one of a number of orientations available to players of MMORPGs. Other forms of gain and loss can be experienced, depending on the inclination of the individual. Richard Bartle suggests four dominant types of player in such games: achievers, for whom points gathering and level increasing are the main aim; explorers, who enjoy exploring the gamescape, both the virtual world and exploitable features of its construction; socializers, for whom the game is a backdrop to the pursuit of interaction with other players; and killers, whose pleasure comes from imposing themselves on or attacking other players.[22]

'Winning' in the sense of completing a game does not always exhaust its potential for pleasure, including play that entails a clear sense of gain. The more linear action-adventure game *The Lord of the Rings: The Two Towers* (2002), for example, can be completed quite quickly. The game is designed to encourage players to return to play again, however, with another of the three available characters, each of which has a different fighting style. Like many games, *The Two Towers* includes an emphasis on building the fighting skills of the player-characters, and the skill-ceiling of each cannot be reached in one playing alone. New weapons become available when skills are built over several completions of the game. Other titles encourage the player to return to completed games or levels, either to improve on the number of enemies killed or to gain access to hidden secrets. The player of *Primal* (2002), for example, can access previously played levels in search of hidden tarot cards. Concealed bonus features such as these, not necessary to completion of the game but a source of additional pleasure, are known as 'Easter eggs', special treats for the more dedicated player, especially in cases where their existence or possible location is not mentioned in the game manual. Players can also choose to broaden the challenge of a game that they have found pleasurable, such as setting out to win all the possible card layout permutations in *Solitaire*.

Some games with clear-cut win/lose structures give the player a say in how they are implemented. In *Civilization III* (2001), for example, the

In games with general rules there are multiple styles of play that depend upon the "inclination of the individual"

player can set the parameters according to which victory against non-player civilizations is measured. Victory can be gained by all, or a combination of, the following: by domination (conquering and controlling two-thirds of the world's territory), through diplomacy (by being elected Secretary-General of the United Nations), through overwhelming cultural dominance, by being the first to launch a spaceship or through military victory (eliminating all rival nations). It is also possible in many games to switch between *paidea* and *ludus*, between more immediate enjoyment of gameplay activities and play that is oriented towards the winning of the game in its larger parts or as a whole. Many simulation-based games are designed as environments for both *paidea* and *ludus*, Frasca suggests:

> For example, many flight simulators include different missions (particular goal-oriented activities where the player has to accomplish a certain task, such as bombing a city or landing under bad weather conditions). These *ludus* are hard coded within the program: the program includes a *ludus* rule and it will tell the player if she succeeded or not at the end of a session. However, this same mission-based simulator could also be used for *paidea*: the player could simply not follow the rule and would just play around with the airplane.[23]

The same can be said of games in other genres. Each mission in the real-time strategy game *Command and Conquer: Generals* (2003), for example, is framed by a clear win/lose equation. Explicit instruction is given on the conditions for military victory: destroying a particular enemy base, gathering a certain quantity of supplies, using air support to protect a set quota of friendly forces from attack, and so on. It is quite possible to ignore or depart from the primary goals of the mission, however. The player might decide simply to *play around* inside the game, one way or another. This might happen when a mission is going particularly well. Space can be created for less directed play when the player is confident that the mission objective is safely within reach of achievement. In one of the missions played as the United States, for example, the player is required to use the US forces to rescue three pilots shot down by the enemy. The last of the pilots, once rescued, has to be returned safely to the US base for the mission to be achieved. At this point the mission is close to completion, provided that the player has sufficient resources to be able to keep the pilot from danger. But it can be prolonged. The player can choose to finish off the remaining enemy units, creating additional troops and equipment if necessary or if funds permit. None of this is required for victory, but might be done for its own intrinsic satisfaction.

Something similar might happen in a more difficult mission, or when playing on a harder setting, when achievement of the victory object appears impossible. A player seeking optimal movement through game missions might choose to abandon and restart, while others might enjoy seeing how long they can hang on, or might take the opportunity to experiment with previously untried strategy or tactics. Both of these scenarios – assurance of imminent victory or hopelessness – can create a situation in which *paidea* is encouraged to take over: play for its own sake, within the same localized rules as the rest of the gameplay but extracted from the broader context of *ludus*. In each case, a trade-off is involved. *Paidea* when victory has already been achieved in everything but name or when it is impossible is something of an indulgence, with nothing at stake. But what it loses in one dimension (being part of a broader more meaningful challenge) it gains in another (the pleasure of play-for-its-own-sake). Freer or more experimental styles of play might also be used in the middle of a mission, depending on the orientation of the player. Players might choose to explore a game-world, for example, rather than to follow mission-critical objectives, an aspect of gameplay considered in detail in Chapter 2. Or the player of a first-person shooter or action-adventure might choose to go on a virtual shooting spree, killing more adversaries than necessary to the pursuit of a mission goal or shooting up parts of the on-screen environment, enjoying the experience for its own sake rather than as part of a goal-directed activity.

Some games are more responsive to this kind of free-form action than others, *Half-Life* (1998) being an example of a shooter in which widespread collateral damage can be caused for its own pleasure, as a mark of the player-character's agency in the on-screen environment (drinks machines can be shot up, for example, although no drinks can be obtained; drinks machines can also be shot up in *Max Payne* (2001), in which case drinks are obtained, although this remains in the realm as *paidea* as they are of no practical use in the game – they do not function as power-ups, which would have been possible). In the multi-player context of *EverQuest* it is quite common for groups of players to punctuate

[handwritten margin note: choosing to kill for one's own pleasure]

'serious' goal-directed play, which is often quite highly organized, with undirected playful activities such as having races, stringing together animated emotes, flirting, duelling but stopping before death ensues, or taunting each other with mild and amusing insults.

Players in any type of game might find ways to experiment or to push the boundaries of what can be achieved: steering deliberately off the track to see what happens if a car crashes into a river in a title such as *Colin McRae Rally 3* (2003), for example (in this case, the screen whites-out and the player is returned to the track if the water level reaches the top of the windscreen, but the car can be driven through the water, just for the hell of it, if it is kept below that point). Some games provide more scope for this kind of free-form play than others, one of the most celebrated examples being *Grand Theft Auto III* (2001), in which the player can choose to perform a range of random acts of exploration or violence instead of seeking to progress through the completion of missions. In the sequel, *Vice City* (2002), for example, it is possible to take a vehicle onto a long beach in which almost entirely free-form driving can be indulged, especially pleasurable at speed in a beach buggy or on a motorcycle (a voluntarily added *ludus*-goal can be to see how many sunbathers or other beach-users can be hit!). The player seeking a little more framework for

1. Freedom to 'play around': *paidea*, in a stylized third-person view, in *Grand Theft Auto: Vice City* (2002)

[handwritten in left margin: Seeing how far the game-world will let them go]

such activity can make use of a sandy racetrack provided at one end of the beach.

Many games offer quickly accessible modes designed to meet a demand for play that falls relatively closer to the *paidea* than the *ludus* end of the scale. First-person shooters often include 'quick' battle or skirmish modes as well as those which integrate individual battles into larger campaigns. Driving games usually have a 'single race' option, as do many other sports-based games, in addition to 'career' modes, in which each race counts in the player's progression in a league or ranking order. In *State of Emergency* (2002), in which player-characters are involved in anarchic rebellion against a corporate state, the player can choose 'Revolution' mode, pursuing sequences of missions linked together by storylines, or the quicker-fix 'Chaos' mode, which offers rapid bursts of frenzied against-the-clock action including fighting and acts of vandalism such as throwing litter bins through shop windows. Many beat-'em-up games are built around stand-alone individual fights, although these can in some cases be combined into 'story' modes in which a stronger degree of *ludus* is entailed. Side-games also feature in some titles. A number are found in *Dead or Alive: Xtreme Beach Volleyball* (2003), including versions of casino games and a game that involves platform-hopping across a swimming pool. These options are not entirely free from the demands of *ludus*. One-off races or games of tennis clearly have their own win/lose dynamics on a smaller scale, as does 'Chaos' mode in *State of Emergency*, in which the aim is to beat previous highest scores. Platform hopping or playing poker in *Xtreme Beach Volleyball* are ways of earning money that can be used in pursuit of the longer-term goals of a game based on the establishment of relationships with non-player characters. These activities are structured, confined and rule-bound in themselves, but can be played in a more casual, drop-in manner than is involved in the larger campaign-oriented components of the games, in which performance might be more strongly motivated but also restricted by consideration of its longer-term implications within the game.

Rules and freedom usually exist in a dialectical relationship, in videogames as in many other contexts. Rules restrict freedom, necessarily, but they also create it: that which is experienced as freedom in any meaningful sense in structured forms such as games is freedom *within* some particular structure of constraint. Simple rule-sets can, in some cases, generate complex possibilities of play, one of the defining characteristics of what Jesper Juul terms 'games of emergence', a concept to which we return below.[24] Videogame play can also be considered in terms of the potential for play *with* and beyond the rules. This ranges from practices defined unambiguously as 'cheating' to others that might be seen as a more creative bending or exploitation of the rules. Examples of cheating include the input of codes that render the player's character impervious to harm (playing in 'god' mode), that provide access to extra weapons or ammunition, or the use of 'no clip' codes that render the architecture of the game-world in a format in which player-characters can move through what would otherwise be experienced as solid structures. More ambiguously situated are sources of help officially sanctioned by the games industry, including published walk-throughs, strategy guides and telephone help-lines. Walk-throughs and cheats compiled by enthusiasts are also published through unofficial channels, principally on the internet. Exactly what constitutes a cheat is often a matter of interpretation. A player who obtains objects or money well beyond their character's means in a MMORPG, in the form of a gift or help from a more experienced player, might be considered to be gaining unearned and unfair advantage; alternatively, this might be seen as perfectly in keeping with the social dimension of the game. Some might consider taking advantage of a game flaw (such as trapping monsters in the corner of ramps in *EverQuest*) to be an unacceptable 'exploit'; to others it might be defensible in terms of the logic of the game-world (in this case, using landscape features, just as a real-world hunter might, to minimize danger).

Creatively bending the rules often involves taking advantage of unforeseen potential within the parameters of a game. One of the best-known examples is the phenomenon of 'rocket jumping' in *Quake* (1996), in which a rocket launcher fired downwards immediately after pressing the 'jump' command enables the player-character to reach otherwise unattainable heights. The discovery of such tricks can be a significant source of pleasure for players who reach an advanced level of competence. They can add an extra dimension to gameplay within the rules, although they can also 'break' the game, having the same impact as cheat codes, if they undermine rules or constraints of a fundamental nature. An example of the latter is the unintended use found for magnetic proximity mines in the third-person stealth game *Deus Ex* (2000). Some players learned to use them as stepping stones that could be placed up walls to gain access to areas that should remain off-limits, an unforeseen result of the determination of the designers to create a game in which players were given a greater degree of freedom than usual. The use of cheats, or devices that remain within the letter if not the spirit of the rules, is a contentious business among gameplayers. It can be seen, at best, as a second order of play, and fair game, especially when it involves the skill and initiative of the player who discovers a new manoeuvre. Some varieties of cheating are most frowned upon in multi-player games, where the gain of one player – a hack, for example, that enables a player to gain instant access to a high level weapon – is likely to be at the expense of others. Players who use cheat codes, walk-throughs or strategy guides are often looked down upon by those who resist such temptations. For others, though, these are important enabling devices in circumstances in which particular puzzles or tasks prove too difficult or time-consuming.

Playing innovatively with the game rules also extends to include game modifications, or 'mods', created by players, a process often encouraged, as in the case of the first-person shooter *Doom* (1993), the code for which was made freely available by the developer. The inclusion of modding tools has since become commonplace, although tension sometimes exists between freedom to play 'with' the game and limits the game industry seeks to impose on the process. As Andrew Mactavish suggests, officially sanctioned modding tools act as gatekeepers, restricting access to deeper levels of the game code. Players are free to innovate, but this level of meta-play also occurs within pre-established parameters and according to End User Licensing Agreements that define legitimate and illegitimate uses of modding tools.[25]

The desirability of potential for playing with the game rules depends largely on the kind of experience intended by the designer or sought by the player. Exploitation of unforeseen potential in the rules can reduce the immersive qualities of a game, as Sim Dietrich suggests.[26] It focuses attention on the surface level of the game *as* a game, with its own limited parameters and functionality to exploit, rather than encouraging a degree of suspension of disbelief that leans closer to an imaginary inhabitation of the role of the player-character. Dietrich's example is the feature in *Half-Life: Counter-Strike* (2000) that enables a player deliberately to buy a weak weapon in one round to save money to buy a stronger one in the next, the cash being retained even if the player dies. The procedure makes no sense within the logic of the fictional world of the player-character as terrorist or counter-terrorist. Its logic comes, instead, from that of the game-specific tactical and strategic demands of the title.

MODALITY: IT'S ONLY A GAME

One of the most obvious qualities of gameplay, as the above example suggests, is that it is, precisely, *play* – and play is a very particular realm of experience. Four of Caillois' six points of definition relate to this: that it is freely entered into and occupies a separate time and space; that it is unproductive; and, essentially, that it occupies a zone known to be one of make-believe and unreality. Play in general is best understood as a *mode* rather than a distinct category of behaviour, suggesting a particular attitude towards an activity and how it is situated in relation to what is taken to be the real world. Even in the animal world, Gregory Bateson suggests, the existence of play requires some degree of meta-communication – communication about communicative activity – a signal that says 'this is play' rather than something to be taken more seriously.[27] To play a game is to move into a special experiential arena, marked off (if not always entirely) from other activities; to enter a demarcated 'play-ground', as Huizinga terms it, which may or may not take physical form.[28] One of Huizinga's examples of the play-ground is the 'magic circle', a term adopted more widely by Salen and Zimmerman to suggest the domain in which gameplay of any kind occurs.[29] Within the magic circle of games a particular attitude towards experience exists, what Suits terms the 'lusory attitude', in which arbitrary rules are accepted simply because they make possible the forms of play that result.[30]

Markers of modality such as these are found in all forms of cultural communication, from everyday speech to commercially produced media products.[31] Distinctive framing routines and formal devices establish, for example, the claims to the status of reality made by television news and documentary or the fantastic qualities of speculative science fiction. The process of becoming media-literate is one in which we internalize these routines, attributing a different status and significance to different kinds of texts, and to social activities such as play itself. The modality of videogames is established at a number of levels, starting with the very application of the label 'game', with its existing cultural resonances;

"Play" has no effect upon what happens in the real world. It takes place in a world of its own

the fact that they are found in 'games' stores or the 'games' section of non-specialist shops and bought as sources of play. In their design and marketing, videogames are clearly located as commercial entertainment products. Their status, like that of most games produced and played in the industrialized world, is very different from that of more traditional games integrated into the central cultural ritual of societies, examples such as Roman gladiatorial games and the ballgame played by the ancient Maya that were, literally, a matter of life and death for those involved. From an anthropological perspective, as Brian Sutton-Smith suggest, games can be understood in some contexts as adaptive mechanisms that can serve to express and contain cultural tensions.[32] The demarcation of games as part of a separate sphere of 'leisure' is usually associated with the social orders resulting from the advent of industrialization, in which play and games tend to be separated out for the most part from the realms of ritual and/or overt social function.

Unlike cultural commentators who worry about the supposed 'effects' of games, players do not usually confuse the playing of videogames with activity outside the game, or even with the use of more serious simulators. Points of overlap can occur, even in games located clearly in the realm of fantasy. Two-way exchanges exist between games and simulations used in military training, for example, the best known being the licensing of a *Doom* variant by the US Marine Corps. Fears have been expressed that exchanges such as these have implications for the cultural significance of such popular titles. If a modification of *Doom* is used to train the military, does that imply that the commercial version also 'trains', in effect, certain kinds of behavioural responses that might not be considered positive in civil society (an issue to which we return in Chapter 4)? *Doom* was one of a number of popular cultural products associated with blame for the Columbine school massacre in Littleton, Colorado in 1999. What is missed out in such equations is precisely the effect of modality, the context-defining *frame* within which activity such as gameplay is performed.

Beyond its general situation as a game, more specific *formal* modality markers underline *Doom's* playful status. Cover and interface artwork immediately establishes a fantasy framework twice distanced from the material of external reality, a blend of neo-gothic and science fiction imagery. The backstory outlined in the manual is clearly the stuff of pulp

[handwritten margin note, left: a survival horror game is being used to train soldiers]

[handwritten margin note, right: Might train players as well]

science fiction, the player-character located as a marine sent into lone combat with an array of increasingly fanciful monsters drawn from a range of fantastic sources. Graphical representation of the in-game-world is crude and blocky, far more so than that of fictions produced in other screen-based audio-visual media such as film and television. Actions required by the player-character to survive are arbitrary and limited. Some map reasonably well onto what might be required in a real-world equivalent – moving and looking around the environment, aiming and shooting – but the moves to be performed, and the manner in which this is achieved through the interface, are limited and coarse-grained. All of these factors combine to communicate very clearly the status of the experience as one of play, bracketed off from the concerns of real life.

The balance of modality markers specific to individual games varies quite considerably from one to another. Similar basic dynamics of play can be garbed very differently at the local level, one of the ways the games industry offers product differentiation within the same underlying formats. If *Doom* gives the first-person shooter a distinctly fantastic neo-gothic SF impression, other entries in the genre have made claims to a much more 'realistic' level of representation. This is found in terms of both graphical realism and in details of setting, equipment and functionality, issues to which we return in detail in Chapter 3. Games such as the Second World War shooter *Medal of Honor: Allied Assault* (2002), located within very recognizably real-world-historical frames, make a significant investment in the 'authenticity' of details such as weapons and uniforms. The weaponry available in *Doom* starts with recognizable real-world referents such as pistol and shotgun before offering the destructive power of fantasy items such as the plasma rifle and the BFG9000. A scale of increasingly powerful weapons is also found in *Medal of Honor*. In both cases, the availability of particular weapons is a key factor in gameplay, more potent or specialized weapons being necessary to the performance of particular tasks. In *Medal of Honor*, however, all the weapons are based on real-world equivalents, the relative capacities of which are set out in what is presented as real historical detail in the manual and have an impact on their in-game functionality. Cover, interface and other artwork are also designed to signify a grounding in historical reality very different from the overt fantasy neo-gothic SF world of *Doom*. A mid-point between *Doom* and *Medal of Honor*, although closer to the position of the former, is marked by titles such as the *Doom* predecessor *Wolfenstein 3D* (1992) and its sequel *Return to Castle Wolfenstein* (2001), in which real-world historical referents (Nazis, a Second World War setting) are mixed with those of more *Doom*-like fantasy (experiments in the creation of a superhuman zombie army, Nazi witches and necromantic archaeology).

Games whose localized modality markers lean towards the realism/authenticity end of the scale are, on balance, more likely to become subjects of controversy in debates about real-world issues. By making claims to authentic representation of Second World War contexts, in some respects, *Medal of Honor* opens itself to potential criticism about the adequacy of the simulation it offers of aspects of an historical experience. It loses, to some extent, the insulation provided by the modality-invoking statement that it is just a work of fantasy. It remains a game, however, something very far removed from any directly consequential real-world activity of the kind it represents and asks the player to perform. The relative distance between more or less realistically coded games is vastly shorter than the large ontological gap that exists between the most authentic-seeming of games and any part of the historical/real world to which they are related. This is not to say that play is not a significant activity; merely that it is significant as a very particular kind of activity that occupies its own distinct realm. Play is usefully understood by Sutton-Smith, as 'a paradoxical form of communication and expression'; to play at an activity is both to perform and *not really* to perform it, a fact that helps to explain the conflicts and controversies that often occur at its boundaries with the 'real' world.[33] The realm occupied by gameplay is separate from that of the rest of the world, although not entirely so. In its very distinctness – the way it is defined as apart from other realms – gameplay remains part of the wider social universe in which it is located. In multi-player games, for example, the added dimension of a social reality within the game-world can blur the modal framework. More generally, meanings with real-world resonance or potential implications can translate across the boundary, as argued in the second half of this chapter and in Chapter 4. The fact that they have to move across a boundary to come into play underlines the fact that an initial state of separation exists.

ACTIVITIES, TASKS, GOALS

Each type of game, and each game within a genre, creates a particular set of gameplay activities, tasks and goals. These tend to combine to constitute what Craig Lindley terms a gameplay *gestalt*, 'a configuration or pattern of elements so unified as a whole that it cannot be described merely as a sum of its parts.'[34] From the point of view of the player, a gameplay gestalt establishes a particular group of 'perceptual, cognitive, and motor operations' required for successful gameplay.[35] More concretely, these present themselves as a combination of gameplay *hooks*; a hook being described by Geoff Howland as any activity performed by the player 'for the purpose of furthering their playing'.[36] Gameplay hooks are distinguished by Howland from marketing hooks, 'designed to attract the player to buy the game, or from the style or gimmick hooks that may entice initial play'.[37] They constitute what might be termed the core gameplay experience, the basic pattern of operations and considerations with which the player is concerned once any initial novelty or gloss has worn off. Different forms of gameplay hook identified by Howland are as follows: *action hooks*, requiring the player to move controls, characters or pieces around the game-world, or interacting with the game explicitly in other ways such as talking to a non-player character; *resource hooks*, involving issues such as ammunition and health in a shooting or combat based game, or finance, raw materials and available technologies in a strategy game; *tactical and strategic hooks*, such as decisions to be made about the use of particular moves or resources in pursuit of goals; and *time hooks*, involving anything focused on future events in the game such as waiting for an item to be spawned or completing a mission, level or race under time constraint.

In every game, as Howland suggests, 'players spend the majority of their time on a small set of actions', the *key* hooks that often define its genre.[38] These comprise what Katie Salen and Eric Zimmerman term the 'core mechanic', 'the essential play activity players perform again and again in a game'.[39] Alongside these are found *supporting* hooks used to differentiate one game in a genre from another. In a first-person shooter, for example, key hooks found across the genre include action hooks such as the navigation of the player-character through space, shooting at enemies and taking cover. These are combined with resource hooks, principally the monitoring of ammunition, health and the supply of weapons and other necessary equipment, and with tactical and strategic hooks – how to combine shooting with taking cover or which weapons to use to maximum effect in particular circumstances. Examples of supporting hooks found in particular examples include the introduction of a stealth mode in *Return to Castle Wolfenstein* and the higher than usual premium put on the need to remain in cover to avoid being hit by often unseen enemies in *Vietcong* (2003), an attempt to map into the game one of the distinctive features of the American military experience in Vietnam.

Key hooks in the third-person action adventure genre are similar in some regards, although with a stronger emphasis on action hooks such as exploration, the performance of tricky climbing or jumping manoeuvres and finding objects, and tactical/strategic hooks such as the solving of puzzles. Supporting hooks would include the specialized forms of movement permitted in some individual titles: the 'bullet-time' mode in *Max Payne* that slows down the action, giving the player-character extra capacity to avoid being shot; the variety of special moves, including walking along walls and shooting at enemies while performing cartwheels, that can be performed in 'focus' mode in *Enter the Matrix* (2003). In role-playing games (RPGs), key hooks are usually provided by fighting and/or casting spells, exploration and the pursuit of quests in order to gain experience points and increase the capabilities of the player-character, with a strong social dimension involving interaction with other players in massively multi-player online variants. Resource hooks tend to loom large in strategy games, much of the activity in which revolves around processes such as constructing buildings and equipment, developing sources of raw materials and/or finance and deploying such resources in whatever kind of procedure is foregrounded by a particular title. Examples of secondary hooks include the use of a 'creature' to do the bidding of the player in *Black and White* (2001), and the choice of 'good' or 'evil' moral alignments offered to the player. Both *Black and White* and the real-time war strategy game *Ground Control* (2000) also offer a distinctive free-moving camera effect that can be used to shift from the genre's usual top-down overview to more close-up detail of the action.

COMPELLING AND IMMERSIVE

Each of these activities offers its own particular potential to create pleasure for the player, a number of aspects of which are investigated in detail in different parts of this book. A feature of many games, however,

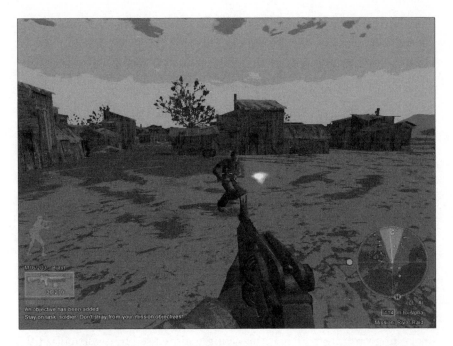

2. Multiple demands on the attention of the player of a first-person shooter in *Delta Force: Black Hawk Down* (2003). Note gauges to be monitored for health and ammunition on lower screen-left and inset map showing enemies and direction of objective on lower-right.

across generic boundaries, is that they require the performance of a simultaneous *combination* of activities, the balance of which varies from one example to another. It is the imposition of numerous different demands that helps to account for both the challenge offered by many games and their compelling and immersive qualities. A typical game situation requires the player to attend to a multitude of tasks while moving forward, incrementally, through a particular mission, level or stage of development. In a first-person shooter, this means gradually gaining ground through dangerous terrain, attention divided between attack, defence and the monitoring of vital statistics. In a strategy game, it involves monitoring progress (or setbacks) on multiple fronts, keeping a large number of balls in the air. In games such as *Civilization* (1991), *Age of Empires* (1997) and *Command and Conquer* (1996), this involves management of resource production and its deployment, the latter often including ongoing action at different ends of the game map. The demand is particularly high in real-time strategy games (such as *Age of Empires* and *Command and Conquer*) in which the player has to respond to the simultaneous moves of opposing forces, without the space for reflection afforded in the turn-based variant (such as *Civilization*) in which players are allowed time to complete their moves before facing any response. In MMORPGs the sense of having to attend to different actions simultaneously is at its strongest in group actions such as attacks against difficult adversaries, during which players have to concentrate on their own health and that of other group members, some of which might need protection or the help of healing spells while others move in to take the brunt of the attack – at the same time as keeping a look-out for other potential threats.

The incremental nature of gameplay tasks helps to explain its compelling nature (an aspect of play emphasized by Huizinga), the urge it creates to keep playing. In games such as first-person shooters and third-person action-adventures, players are confronted with tasks that often have to be repeated before success is achieved, the degree of repetition depending on factors such as the saving regime used by a particular title, the player's ability and the difficulty setting on which the game is being played. Enforced repetition can be frustrating and off-putting and might, in some cases, lead to the abandonment of the game. But, short of that point, it can also create a strong impulse to keep trying, especially when it is a case of finishing off a particular component before the end of the current playing session. The compulsion to 'just have one more try' – and then 'just one *more*' and another, and another – can be a strong one, even when it requires back-tracking and repeating a sequence of tricky manoeuvres. The urge to keep playing can also be felt at the point where a much-repeated section has just been completed. The temptation is offered of a fresh, new situation – usually the ringing of a few changes within the same basic scenario – the immediate appeal of which can be strong, as a reward for persistence. The same cycle can easily repeat itself: extended periods of being stuck or forced into repetition followed by periodic breakthrough and the opportunity to move forward until the next point of difficulty, a structure of experience described by Aarseth as one of *aporia* followed by *epiphany*.[40] Games that have few or widely scattered 'save' points can be particularly difficult to stop playing. A strong incentive is created to continue to the next 'save' option because of the loss of progress that results if play is halted between one save and another. A particularly notorious example is found in some of the *Tomb Raider* games, in which players cannot quick-save at will and 'save' crystals are often located at the end of a series of tricky manoeuvres. In *Buffy the Vampire Slayer: Chaos Bleeds* (2003) a whole level has to be completed before the game can be saved, creating potential for high levels of frustration and/or greatly extended periods of play.

In real-time or turn-based strategy games, a similar urge to keep playing can be created by the desire to see what happens next, how one of many localized scenarios might play out. The fact that operations are usually ongoing on multiple fronts, and that they include both those initiated by the player and moves by non-player rivals, can create a self-perpetuating momentum the default tendency of which is to keep going until marked breaks such as those created by victory or defeat. In a game of *Command and Conquer: Generals*, for example, in which the player chooses the side of the Global Liberation Army (GLA), the player might send out an attacking force against United States positions. Battle ensues, its outcome a function of both automated calculations by the game engine and micro-management by the player (pulling back damaged units to prevent their destruction, sending in reinforcements, and so on). During the thick of this action, the GLA base might face aerial attack from the US, including the use of devastating fuel-air bombs that create an urgent need for repairs to essential resource-building infrastructure and air defences such as stinger missile sites. On top of this, US ground forces might launch an assault and the player might be in the process of constructing a force of scud missile launchers with which to strengthen the attack on the enemy base. Events such as these overlap, but occupy their own time-frames. They develop at different rates, giving the player the chance to turn from one to another, and always, in mid-game, inviting the player to keep going, to see what will happen next. In a turn-based strategy game such as *Civilization*, the incremental nature of play is institutionalized. The number of turns required to achieve any new move is openly advertised across the territorial map, some development usually temptingly close to fruition, while the option to keep playing for just one more turn – and another – is as explicit as the pressing of a button.

In role-playing games, the urge to keep playing is often stimulated by the desire to achieve the next level, to keep fighting beasts or embarking on quests to gain those few more experience points required to gain the satisfying 'ding' that greets levelling-up in *EverQuest* or its equivalent in other titles; and then, once that is achieved, to set out on the path towards the next level and the new competencies and abilities to explore the game-world that it brings. In multi-player games, an added pull can be created by involvement in group play activities that cannot easily be delayed or put on hold: the player usually has to keep going, maybe for an agreed period of time, or be forced to disband in a potentially hostile area, with a consequent loss of benefits and the risk of gaining a reputation for unreliability. Regular visits to a MMORPG world enable players to keep up contacts with friends made in the game, but also create pressure to keep playing or risk being left behind as others advance in capability.

The potential to create an immersive effect, in which the player is absorbed into the game, is an important aspect of gameplay. Immersion in the sense of establishing an illusion of quasi-physical sensory *presence* in the on-screen world of the game is considered in greater detail in Chapter 2. But immersion can also be created at the level of gameplay activities, through the establishment of combinations of ongoing perceptual, cognitive and motor demands sufficient to engage a high proportion of the player's attention. Games focused on action, hand–eye coordination and personal identification between player and on-screen character seek to create immersion through sensory input, as François Laramée puts it: through 'realistic visuals, positional audio, force-feedback, dramatic acting, and so forth.'[41] Strategy games offer what Laramée terms 'intellectual immersion', in which the player is required to make a constant stream of abstract decisions: 'In both cases, the designer's job is to create a *closed environment*, a set of perceptions that are sufficient to represent an experience and to absorb the conscious mind.'[42]

Terms such as these, used to describe the immersive quality of a wide range of games, have much in common with the notion of 'optimal experience' outlined in numerous studies by the psychologist Mihaly Csikszentmihalyi. Optimal experience, identified by Csikszentmihalyi in a wide range of work and leisure activities, results in the creation of a state of *flow*, 'the state in which people are so involved in an activity that nothing else seems to matter.'[43] The connection between games and the concept of flow is far from accidental, Csikszentmihalyi having turned to play theorists including Huizinga, Caillois and Piaget at an early stage

[handwritten margin note: All of these factors are present and important in survival horror]

in his work.[44] The particular relevance of play to the understanding of flow lies in its quality of intrinsic motivation: the fact that it is engaged for its own sake, as a source purely of pleasure, regardless of any extrinsic significance it might have (as a beneficial learning or adaptive process, for example). To understand the gameplay of videogames, it is necessary to begin with a focus on the intrinsic dimension, the specific pleasures of gameplay *as* gameplay, rather than as a sublimated form of some other aspect of experience. As Brian Sutton-Smith suggests, even if play in general is considered to serve adaptive purposes in humans (teaching certain activities or capacities such as flexibility), its adaptive function might itself be intrinsic. Its adaptiveness 'might centre on what play does for a sense of well-being, as ecstatic play, rather than what play does as work or as adaptation.'[45]

[handwritten margin note: Play is used as a mechanism of learning]

Csikszentmihalyi's concept of flow is offered as a phenomenology of enjoyment, an outline of eight major components identified in analysis of the ways individuals describe their most positively heightened experiences.[46] The fit between these components and the experiences offered by videogames is remarkably close. The eight components are: challenging activity that requires skill; clear goals and feedback; a merging of action and awareness; concentration on the task at hand; loss of self-consciousness; the paradox of control; the transformation of time; and what Csikszentmihalyi terms 'autotelic experience', the end of which lies in itself. The first of these components could be a description of most videogames, leaning towards the *ludus* end of the *paidea/ludus* scale: challenging activities that require skill, usually rule-bound and goal-oriented. To create the potential for a flow experience a balance is required between the challenge posed by the activity – in this case, the game – and the skills possessed by the player. A game, or part of a game, that is too challenging for the player is likely to cause anxiety; one that is too easy is likely to create boredom. In between lies what Csikszentmihalyi terms the 'flow channel', in which the skills of the player are just sufficient to meet the challenges of the game.[47]

The flow channel is not static, either in the illustration used by Csikszentmihalyi (tennis) or in videogames. A player starting with a low level of skill will require modest challenges initially, but these will need to be increased, incrementally, to match the increasing skill gained with practice by the player. This is precisely what is offered in many videogames.

In early arcade games such as *Asteroids* (1980) and *Space Invaders* the rate at which enemies appear and the threat they pose to the player increases, steadily, as progression is made from one stage to the next. Opening missions in a first-person shooter, an action-adventure game or a strategy game often serve an introductory purpose, pitched at an easier level and/ or accompanied by on-screen help features that give guidance on how to perform the basic moves. In some cases, these functions are performed in what are framed as training modes, in locations such as the indoor and outdoor obstacle courses at the palatial home of Lara Croft in the *Tomb Raider* games. The availability of a range of challenges appropriate to player skills, and earned player-character capacities and equipment, is built very clearly into a MMORPG such as *EverQuest*. An assortment of creatures and monsters populates the various landscapes of the game, each being labelled explicitly in terms of the level of challenge it would present if engaged in combat by the player. Colour-coding is used to indicate the relative status of a potential adversary: green 'looks like a reasonably safe opponent' for non-player characters (NPCs) well below the level of the player; blue 'looks like you would have the upper hand' for NPCs one or a few levels lower than the player; white 'looks like an even fight' for an NPC of the same level as the player; yellow 'looks like quite a gamble' for NPCs one or two levels higher; and red 'what would you like your tombstone to say' for more than two levels higher. These gradations are not fixed but relative to the level attained by the player-character. Creatures that offer a reasonably safe and useful source of experience points in the early stages are barely worthy of notice once a few levels are gained (unless they possess something required in a particular quest), a pleasurable sense of progression being created by the gradual ability of the player to take on opponents that are more challenging and bring greater rewards as they level-up.

In this case, what is involved is the level of skill embedded in the player-character more than that of the player hm- or herself. The same factors enable the player-character to embark on increasingly elaborate quests and to become a more valuable resource to others in group activities. In genres such as shooters and action-adventures, progress through the game is generally accompanied by a steadily increasing level of immediate difficulty for the player in the form of tougher opponents or more complex and difficult manoeuvres, puzzles and other challenges.

Examples include the increasing difficulty of dispatching game bosses in *Quake* or *American McGee's Alice* (2000), among many other titles, or the increasingly more tricky (and often fatal) jumping required in the *Tomb Raider* series and towards the end of *Buffy the Vampire Slayer* (2002). The aim of the designer is to maintain an appropriate learning curve, to increase the level of difficulty in step with the anticipated increase in the skills of the player, a process that involves balancing both the difficulty level of individual activities and the total number of demands placed on the player. An increase in the number of gameplay hooks makes the game more complex and demanding. Too many hooks can become overwhelming, as Howland suggests; too few, and boredom is likely to set in once the initial novelty of a new title is exhausted.[48]

A crucial factor in the balancing of activity and skill, in games as elsewhere, is identified in another of Csikszentmihalyi's components: the existence of clear goals and feedback. To engage effectively in challenging activity, matching skill against challenge, it is essential that a clear sense is established of what has to be achieved. This is the case in both the short and longer terms: immediately, killing or avoiding a particular opponent or solving a particular puzzle; or, at the *ludus* end of the scale, in the pursuit of larger-scale victory in a level or across the length of a game (in *Buffy the Vampire Slayer: Chaos Bleeds*, for example, the player must defeat hordes of vampires and demons, and solve puzzles, to collect disparate parts of a body needed to defeat the First Evil, the game's definitive boss). Unambiguous feedback is also required: a clear sense of the extent to which any activity by the player succeeds or fails. Many games offer instant feedback. For the player-character that fails to negotiate a space in a first-person shooter, immediate feedback comes in the form of the character's death and the need to restart the level or return to a previous save point – or at least a significant reduction in health clearly registered through sound effects (grunts, groans) and a marked downward shift in the health bar on the game's interface. The centrality of shooting to a wide range of games might be explained as much by its suitability for the provision of action that creates an immediate feedback response as by any broader cultural factors, as Marie-Laure Ryan suggests.[49] Feedback can be dramatized on-screen – the spectacular death of an enemy blasted with a powerful weapon, for example – or accompanied by dry textual information such as 'x hits y for 120 points' or 'you gain experience' on defeating a suitable opponent in *EverQuest*. In some types of games, especially strategy games, the fruits of action are delayed into the future – the time it takes for a particular resource to be developed – but instant feedback is usually provided to signify that the process is underway and some indication is given of how long it will take to be completed. Without a framework of clear goals and feedback, gameplay is liable to be confusing, which can be the case, especially for new players, in extremely open-ended games such as MMORPGs or largely non-directive games such as *Animal Crossing* (2002).

A third component of flow identified by Csikszentmihalyi, the merging of action and awareness, one of the primary sources of the term 'flow' itself, is also applicable to the pleasure generated by the most satisfying examples of gameplay. The right balance of challenge and skills can create a state in which the player's attention is completely, or very close to completely, absorbed in the activity. Humans have a finite attention capacity, which limits the number of involving mental tasks in which we can engage at any time.[50] Sufficiently demanding and engaging (i.e. well balanced) gameplay can go a long way towards filling that capacity, creating a state of perceptual and cognitive immersion that leaves little space for consideration of anything else. 'People become so involved in what they are doing,' Csikszentmihalyi suggests, 'that the activity becomes spontaneous, almost automatic; they stop being aware of themselves as separate from the actions they are performing.'[51]

In the early stages of playing a new game or a new type of game, players are likely to be distinctly aware of themselves as separate from the activity of play. A new interface may have to be mastered and a new configuration of keyboard or joypad. The commands and controls used in some games are more intuitive than those of others, seeming to map with more intrinsic logic to the action they cause in the game-world on-screen: the use of a joystick to move an avatar in the same direction as the movement of the stick, for example, as compared with some of the complex combinations of abstract button pressing required in beat-'em-up games such as the *Mortal Kombat* (from 1993) or *Tekken* (from 1995) series. Some control systems and interfaces take longer to get used to than others, a time factor reduced in many cases by the emergence of familiar patterns of controls used across a range of titles (the PC keyboard convention of using the 'w' key for forward movement, the 's' for backwards and the 'a' and 'd' for sideways, for example). More complex interfaces can provide greater functionality, however, than those which are most rapidly grasped. With sufficient time and practice, most systems can become familiar. At a high level of habitual use, the control/ interface system can become close to invisible, in the same way that an experienced typist no longer has conscious awareness of the process of reaching for each of the keys required to type a sentence such as this. Repeated usage results in the creation of customized neural pathways in the brain, reducing the amount of processing required for reaction to on-screen events. As the game designer Chris Crawford puts it: 'The difference between a beginner and a skilled player is that the skilled player has learned to build shorter, faster neural pathways from the visual cortex to the cerebellum.'[52] When controls and interface are effaced, through a combination of more intuitive design and familiarity, the player is given a stronger sense of acting *in* the game-world, an illusion of more immediate (i.e. less apparently mediated) participation.

Corollaries of the merging of action and awareness are two other components identified by Csikszentmihalyi: concentration on the task at hand and loss of self-consciousness. One of the potential pleasures of immersive absorption in activities such as gameplay is the opportunity they provide for other preoccupations and anxieties to be forgotten. A strong focus of attention on the tasks at hand leaves little or no room for anything else. Gameplay, like other sources of leisure and work that require sustained concentration, can provide an orderly arena into which the player can move to escape the multitude of disorders and uncertainties often characteristic of everyday life.[53] As Huizinga says of the ordered realm of the playground more generally: 'Into an imperfect world and in the confusion of life it brings a temporary, a limited perfection.'[54] This narrowing of focus can also include a loss of consciousness of self; not a loss of *self*, and certainly not of consciousness, as Csikszentmihalyi stresses, but a loss of consciousness *of* the self as a separate entity.[55] The player can feel 'at one' with the game or 'in the zone', an experience described by many gamers of the most heightened and absorbing periods of play.

Another dimension of this kind of experience is the sense of control gained by the player. Or, as Csikszentmihalyi puts it in other contexts, 'the *possibility* rather than the *actuality* of control.'[56] The game-world is an arena set off from the rest of the world, one in which special rules obtain that, in most cases, give the player the possibility of gaining a level of control generally unavailable in ordinary life. What people enjoy 'is not the sense of *being* in control, but the sense of *exercising* control in difficult situations.'[57] The paradox of control, in this sense, is that its exercise requires the absence of a situation where control can be guaranteed. This fits very well with the structure of many videogames in which the player faces a combination of being both in and out of control. The player is granted a certain scope for controlling agency in all games, yet this is determined by the particular rules and parameters of any individual game. The pleasure of playing lies, often, in a particular combination of freedom and determination, control and lack of control. The sense of control is strongest when the player has freedom to complete tasks in more than one way, but this, itself, is determined by the game. Successful moments of gameplay, such as getting through a difficult challenge in a shooter or an action-adventure game or levelling-up in a role-playing game, create an impression of control or mastery. This is largely illusory, however, given that the player usually has no control over the challenges set or parameters such as those determining the requirements needed to attain a higher level. In multi-player games, the sense of accomplishment and control felt by experienced players can be increased by the practice of helping new players; much of the in-game chat revolves around the comparison of strategies and skill levels, including frequent boasting about achievements. Processes such as learning new in-game skills or discovering new ways to achieve goals are likely to further the player's sense of gaining control but this is almost always pre-structured by the controlling power of the game itself, the exception being cases of unanticipated player innovation such as 'rocket jumping' and other examples detailed above.

An experience often reported by gameplayers is the sense that time passes differently during anything other than short periods of gameplay, particularly that it tends to pass more quickly, that hours can disappear in what seem like minutes. This kind of transformation of time is another component of the flow experience as documented by Csikszentmihalyi. Intense levels of absorption or immersion in the game, and the closing out of the external world, imply a move into its rhythms and timescales rather than those of the real-world clock. This is another dimension in which games can create a pleasurable escape from the routines and constraints of daily life, although it can also have a negative impact, in the sense of time that seems 'lost', appointments missed or real-world tasks postponed or left unfinished (is that the sound of the bath overflowing?).

The concept of flow, and its various elements, applies very well to optimal gameplay experiences, although it is important to recognize that this is an *optimal* state, far from always attained. A number of specific factors can contribute to its achievement or, often, prevent such a state from being achieved. The balance between challenge and skill can easily go awry for reasons ranging from poor game design to a lack of sufficient investment of time, patience and effort on the part of the player. Frustration created by the need for repetition of a difficult manoeuvre or inability to find the route to the next stage of a level is likely to reduce any impression of immersion, although it also increases the satisfaction pay-off that results when success is finally achieved. How much frustration can be contained within this experience, without creating alienation for the player, is likely to vary from one example to another. Many games give the player the opportunity to adjust the balance, principally through difficulty-level settings, ranging through categories such as 'easy', 'normal', 'hard' and 'heroic'. In shooters such as *Doom* and *Halo* (2001), for example, the number of enemies decreases on easier settings. *Silent Hill* (1999) and a number of other titles include an 'auto-lock' weapons feature. When it is switched on, enemies can be hit merely by shooting in their general direction rather than requiring more accurate aiming, a change that can make all the difference in the heat of the action and when subject to panic-induced button fumbling.

Players who find a game, or parts of a game, too challenging can also resort to devices such as cheats and walk-throughs. These shift the balance in favour of the player but are in themselves liable to disrupt any strong sense of flow, requiring a halt in play while the cheat is enabled. Cheats such as the use of 'god' mode in a shooter or action-adventure game, or constant reference to a walk-through or strategy guide, can tilt the balance too far in favour of the player, taking much of the edge out of play and reducing its absorbing qualities. Used more judiciously, cheats can enable players to get back closer to the flow channel, however, during especially difficult periods of play: indestructible 'god' mode might be used briefly, and then left, in a game such as *Medal of Honor*, for example, to help the player-character get across a particularly broad expanse of open ground without being shot; extra ammo or health might serve a similar purpose, temporarily, before normal play is resumed. From an industrial perspective, it is important for some flexibility of capability to be built into titles that seek to appeal to a mass market as well as more dedicated or 'hardcore' gamers.

Game design of a more or less intuitive variety can also affect the degree to which players are likely to gain optimal experiences of flow or immersion, or the ease with which they are likely to be obtained. Consciousness of the existence of relatively arbitrary game devices is likely to reduce immersive potential. Hit-point systems, for example, used to calculate the relative strength of characters and to chart their state of health during combat, have a number of advantages, Jonathon Schilpp suggests, including their ease of use, versatility and familiarity to players.[58] But they tend to draw attention to the device itself, as a mechanical process, rather than embedding it in the fictional qualities of the game-world, even if players can become sufficiently habituated to particular devices for this to become less noticeable over time. Hit-point systems lay bare the numerical models used by game software, especially when their dynamics are presented explicitly to the player, as is the case in the on-screen information supplied during combat in examples such as *EverQuest*. A more immersive effect can be created by the use of hidden hit-point systems or, as François Laramée suggests, by turning mathematical calculations into 'symbolic, qualitative, or fuzzy representations that make more intuitive sense to the player'.[59] If the measurement of health is mapped more directly onto the appearance and behaviour of the player's character, for example, Schilpp suggests, the focus is not on abstract hit-points, but directly on the character's health, strengthening the suspension of disbelief, tightening the emotional bond between player and character and helping to draw the player more deeply into the game-world.[60] A somewhat crude example is the use of an insert image of the avatar's face, instead of a linear health bar, in the *Doom* interface, increasingly bloodied as the player-character's health deteriorates. Many subsequent games map health status onto the appearance, behaviour and capacities of the player-character. In *The Getaway* (2003), for example, gunshot wounds create dark blood-stain patches on the clothing of the avatar and cause him to groan, limp and generally move more slowly, affecting functionality for the player as well as signifying a lower state of health (a precedent set by

Silent Hill and *Resident Evil* [1997]).

Numerous other factors can also intrude on the gameplay experience, reducing the likelihood of reaching anything like an optimal state. Inadequate equipment might make gameplay too slow and frustrating (a dated graphics card or slow connection speed causing 'lag' when playing online) while an unsuitable playing environment might create too much scope for distraction. Gameplayers often seek a private space in which outside interference can be minimalized, using devices such as headphones where necessary to increase separation from the surrounding world,[61] but it is not always possible to prevent interruption.[62] Real-world concerns, demands or timescales might also be too pressing to be kept from consciousness, depending on the situation of the player. A variable balance exists between the relative strength of demands posed by real and game-world activities. The latter exert sufficient attraction to counterbalance some of the former, but only within limits: the bath might overflow, on occasion, during a 'quick' nip into the game-world (or the phone might go unanswered), but the house is unlikely to be allowed to burn down. The qualities of flow identified by Csikszentmihalyi are useful as an *ideal type* of the state that might be produced by the most absorbing gameplay. They can also be located more broadly in a particular kind of cultural framework, fitting into one of a number of rhetorics underlying theories of play identified by Brian Sutton-Smith. The concept of flow can be understood in the context of what Sutton-Smith terms the 'rhetoric of the self', established in theories that interpret play in terms of the subjective experiences of the player. Such theories can be seen as products of a particular social, economic and cultural conjunction, dominant in contemporary western society, in which an emphasis is put on notions of individual freedom.[63] Concepts such as flow and intrinsic motivation make no sense in the context of different notions of the self found in many other cultures, as Sutton-Smith argues. This does not make such concepts of any less use in the understanding of contemporary videogame play, but suggests that they should not be elevated to the status of universals.

Gameplay Contexts: Narrative, Genre and Beyond

If it is important to start with analysis of the nature and pleasurable effects of gameplay in its own right, a full understanding of games also requires consideration of the contextual material within which gameplay is situated in any individual game or game-genre. Gameplay does not exist in a vacuum, any more than games do as a whole. It is situated, instead, within a matrix of potential meaning-creating frameworks. These can operate both at a local level, in the specific associations generated by a particular episode of gameplay, and in the context of broader social, cultural and ideological resonances. The extent to which contextual material or associations are likely to come *into play* during play is variable, according to factors relating to the nature of the game and the manner in which it is played in a particular gaming context. In some situations, quite commonly at the height of the gameplay action, contextual material is likely to recede from view. But games, like other cultural products, always contain potential for the creation of extrinsic as well as intrinsic meanings. Some of these are considered in greater detail in Chapter 4, in which we focus more broadly on the social and cultural dimension of games and gameplay. The remainder of this chapter considers the role of contextual frameworks, principally those established by narrative and genre associations. We start by analyzing aspects of narrative and genre that can be identified in the design of the game-text: the fixed parameters of the game as it is offered to the player, or the narrative and genre reference points within which it might be situated. In the last part of the chapter, we consider more closely the relationship between gameplay and contextual material: the extent to which such dimensions are likely to be *in-play*, rather than relegated to a position in the background, during particular sessions of gameplay.

NARRATIVE

The narrative potential of videogames has been one of the dominant concerns for a number of theorists, including some coming to games from a background in literary studies. Games have often been included in studies of interactive fiction, along with non-game forms such as hypertext fiction, in which computer-mediated texts typically offer a number of different pathways for the reader. The narrative dimension of games tends to be seen in this context as somewhat crude and debased. Hypertext fiction is located by George Landow as part of a more elevated literary tradition, modernist and/or postmodernist, including the work of novelists such as James Joyce, Robert Coover and Jorge Luis

Borges.[64] A recurrent concern in the work of some commentators is with the future *potential* games might have to aspire towards something more sophisticated, in narrative terms, than their typically existing form. Henry Jenkins has suggested, for example, that in terms of narrative depth and meaning, contemporary games are at a level of development equivalent to that of early cinema, in the first decade of the twentieth century, yet to achieve anything like their full potential.[65] A similar focus on the narrative dimension of games, combined with a sense of its greater unrealized potential, is found in the work of Janet Murray, Barry Atkins and the designers Peter Molyneux and Randy Littlejohn.[66]

Counter-arguments have responded on at least two levels: that narrative is not central to games or that it exists essentially in opposition to gameplay, and that it is misguided or unhelpful to conceive of games in terms of what they might become sometime in the future rather than what they currently are. One of the main reasons for objections to any emphasis on the narrative components of games, where they exist, is that the narrative dimension itself is not usually interactive, and therefore lacks the quality seen as the most distinctive element of videogames as compared with other media. Narrative structures in most games are fixed in advance and, generally, unchanged by the activity of the player. On occasion, debate in this area has descended into a hyperbolic dismissal of the role played by narrative in games, most notably in Markku Eskilinen's injunction 'to annihilate for good the discussion of games as stories, narratives or cinema'.[67] In Eskilinen's oft-quoted view, perhaps overstated for polemical effect, 'stories are just uninteresting ornaments or gift-wrapping to games, and laying any emphasis on studying these kinds of marketing tools is just a waste of time and energy.'[68]

Narrative is entirely absent from some games, especially abstract puzzle games such as *Tetris*. Aspects of narrative are present in many others, but they often play a marginal role. Little more than a minimal backstory is created in some cases. More substantial overarching narrative frameworks are developed in others, along with localized narrative components. Exactly how narrative is mobilized where it is present, and of what importance it is likely to be to players, is variable – and its operation has to be considered in the specific context of games, a context very different from that of historically more established narrative-oriented forms such as novels, plays or feature films. Games should not be discussed simply *as* stories, as Eskilinen suggests; even the more story-oriented games cannot be reduced to their narrative dimensions. But stories in games can be a good deal more than just 'uninteresting ornaments or gift-wrapping' and even where these are used as marketing tools, that itself is a subject worthy of consideration.

A useful starting point here is Jesper Juul's distinction between 'games of emergence' and 'games of progression'. Games of emergence, as suggested above, are those in which a number of simple rules combine to form a wide range of interesting variations. This, for Juul, is 'the primordial game structure … found in card and board games and in most action and all strategy games'.[69] In games of progression, a series of separate challenges are presented to the player in serial form, the player having to perform 'a predefined set of actions in order to complete the game'.[70] The designer controls the sequence of events, making this the arena 'where we find games with cinematic or story-telling ambitions'.[71] Progression is identified as a historically more recent structure, coming into videogames in the form of the adventure game, and is the kind of game structure on which narrative-oriented commentators tend to focus.

Narrative frameworks are found in some games that fit Juul's category of emergence, including large-scale role-playing games in which players have a great deal of scope to explore the world on their own terms. Such frameworks play a far less directing role, however, than is usually the case in games of progression. The player of an example such as *The Elder Scrolls III: Morrowind* (2002) can choose whether or not to pursue activities related to larger plot elements, such as the reason why the player-character is released from Imperial custody at the start or the machinations of various factions struggling for control of the fictional universe. Substantial advance can be made through the game – exploration, combat, the pursuit of quests, increasing the experience and skills levels of the player-character – without any more than passing engagement with this kind of narrative background. In *EverQuest*, the choice of whether or not to worry about narrative is made explicit in the form of a control that can be used to turn on or off a story mode in which narrative updates are provided. Players can also choose to invest more strongly in narrative context by reading books in which a mythic background is elaborated or by visiting new areas that might be opened up temporarily in line with a new story arc. Localized forms of progressive, pre-structured gameplay are also found embedded in games of emergence such as this, principally in the form of quests.[72] Quests take the form of narrative fragments, either very brief one-off story-contexts for a particular rewarding action by the player (a non-player character who has been abandoned in the wilds by his protector in *Morrowind*, for example, and needs escorting to the nearest town) or sometimes combined or intersecting in larger mini-narratives. Narrative material can be realized within the play of games of emergence more than is originally anticipated, as was the experience of the designer Peter Molyneux with *Black and White*: 'We thought it would sit quietly behind the game, but the story came alive and started to draw the player through the game in a way none of us, apart perhaps from the scriptwriter James Leach, had envisaged.'[73]

A form of narrative that is itself emergent can also be identified in game genres such as role-playing, simulation and strategy. Relatively undirected play from initial rule-sets can create an implicit narrative that emerges from the particular choices made by the player: the experiences of a player-character in role-playing games such as *Morrowind* or *EverQuest*, the developing relationships in a game of *The Sims* or the assorted 'counter-factual' historical narratives that emerge in each playing of *Civilization*. These are likely to be less tightly structured than pre-programmed narrative, but, as Henry Jenkins suggests in the case of *The Sims*, 'they are not as unstructured, chaotic, and frustrating as life itself.'[74] Relatively unstructured forms of progression are written into many such games: the progressive development of the player-character in a role-playing title, for example, which implies a process of forward-moving character development that has something in common with the development found in other forms of character-centred narrative. Character generally plays a smaller role in games than in more traditional narrative-centred media because the central character tends to become 'our complete surrogate ego', David Joiner suggests, with little or no intrinsic personality of its own: 'As such we are less interested in the protagonist and more concerned with the external environment in which it is embedded.'[75] Distinctive character features can be built into gameplay, however, shaping dimensions such as the goals to be pursued by players/player-characters and their particular in-game capabilities.[76]

Players are likely to have a stronger investment in character in role-playing games than in other genres, given their responsibility for choosing from a range of initial character attributes and the manner in which these are strengthened as the game proceeds. In online role-playing games, this investment is likely to be increased because players interact with others in the guise of their chosen characters: the attributes of character to some extent frame the manner in which players regard one another. As Chris Crawford suggests, however, the kind of character development that results is different from that found in more traditional narratives: 'This emphasis on character development tends to work against the needs of dramatic development – dramatic twists and turns clash with the prevailing tone of steady advancement.'[77] The player-character can face setbacks, in the form of the loss of experience resulting from death, but only in a rather mechanical manner. The player can choose to avoid the process of ongoing character-development, but not without severely limiting the scope for other forms of emergent gameplay (an increase of character experience being necessary if freedom is to be gained to roam the game-world in relative safety and to embark on a wider range of activities). The implicit emergent narrative 'lived' through the game can also become explicit, especially in its more dramatically heightened sequences, generating retrospectively 'tellable' events, as Lisbeth Klastrup suggests, in cases such as higher level 'epic' quests in *EverQuest*.[78] The experience might be understood as one of 'story-living' rather than story-telling, Klastrup suggests, although the telling itself has an appeal, as a secondary form of activity, evidenced in the prevalence of players' stories sections on MMORPG websites.[79] Here the journey through the game-world might be retrospectively understood as having a narrative arc, representing a kind of gestalt of the experience of gameplay, but this depends on the extent to which players actively reflect afterwards on their play, or the degree to which a game is played through to the end.

If players of games of emergence can, among other activities, generate a variety of emergent narratives or tellable stories from the initial parameters, one of the tasks set by some games of progression is to realize a narrative structured in advance into the gamescape. This is not the case with all games of progression, some of which have little substance in the narrative dimension. Many first-person shooters, for example, including popular classics such as the *Doom* and *Quake* games, supply a single minimal backstory scenario that is not developed during progression through the different levels of the game. Progression entails a movement from one location to another in which progressively tougher opponents are faced, progressively more powerful weapons can be obtained and players are expected to increase their skills through practice, but in which little if anything is experienced in the way of further narrative development. The basic dynamic is one of repetition of gameplay activities at increasingly higher levels within a context that remains essentially static after being established at the start: reiterations of the same types of actions. Other games, including the first-person shooter *Half-Life* and many third-person action adventures, including *Max Payne, The Getaway* and *The Thing* (2002), are more plot oriented. Narrative material is developed during the course of the game, often interspersed with gameplay activities in which the dynamic is much the same as that suggested above: broadly similar assortments of tasks to perform but often more testing, and with access to more resources, as the game proceeds.[80]

A number of narrative devices are deployed in the opening sequences of *Half-Life*, for example, as the scientist player-character Gordon Freeman goes to work at the high-security Black Mesa research facility. On-screen text provides basic information about Freeman's identity and background, also serving to establish initial points of narrative enigma. His administrative sponsor is listed as 'classified', implying a secretive motive the player can expect to be revealed at a later stage. Comments by non-player characters in the early stages build expectations that something is amiss, creating an explanatory context for subsequent events. A security guard refers to 'some problem' in the chamber of the 'anomalous materials laboratory'. A number of messages await Freeman but cannot be accessed because the computer system is down – narrative information that is missing, in other words, increasing the overall impression of suspense. Two scientist non-player characters standing outside the laboratory comment about the 'purest' or 'most unstable' sample they have yet seen, one giving the reassurance that 'nothing will go wrong' – a clear foreshadowing, according to genre or narrative convention, that it will. After everything does indeed go wrong, a 'dimensional breach' resulting in alien infestations, another scientist asks why the authorities did not listen to his warnings, further implying that the situation is not merely the result of innocent accident. A number of plot twists impact on gameplay as the game proceeds. Security guard non-player characters aid the player on a number of occasions in the early levels, during which the goal established for the character is to survive and to reach the surface. A twist occurs, however, when the player first encounters a group of soldiers. Sounds of shooting accompany the player-character into the space in which the soldiers are located, which might, at first, be assumed to be the soldiers engaging the alien enemy. It soon becomes apparent that they are shooting at the player-character, however, although maybe too late to prevent the character being killed and the player having to return to the last save-point. Why the troops are shooting at the player-character, here and subsequently, becomes another source of enigma, background to the immediate task of having to deal with another hostile force. The player-character's goal also has to shift when he subsequently reaches the surface only to be forced to return underground on finding it overrun with hostile troops.

The carefully crafted narrative of *Primal* pivots around the fact that chaos and order are no longer in dualistic equilibrium. The main player-character, Jen, is plunged inadvertently into a mythical realm and charged with the task of rebalancing these primal forces. A central enigma relating to her origins is established, raising questions about the nature of her true identity and the source of demonic attributes that transform her body into a lethal fighting machine. A number of different devices are used to supply this kind of narrative material. Some, such as cut-scenes, entail a break out of the main gameplay arena. When Jen transforms into demon form for the first time (complete with an impressive set of horns and damage-inflicting claws), the player has just completed a fight with the first boss of the game. Exploiting the post-fight lull, a cut-scene ensues in which the camera tracks in slow motion around Jen's transforming body as it is visibly wracked by a supernatural force. When the time- and body-bending effect fades, Jen asks her fighting partner what is happening to her. He imparts a little information about the power given to her by the transformation but noticeably withholds any full explanation of the cause, a device that serves a narrative purpose – increasing the player's motivation to continue, in search of an answer – at the same time as urging the player to make more immediate use of the character's new-found fighting skills.

Narrative reliance on cut-scenes and other 'out-of-game' devices, as they are termed by the designer Richard Rouse, is one of the main reasons why the narrative dimension is often seen as essentially opposed to that of gameplay.[81] Cut-scenes can create a narrative-oriented framework within which subsequent sequences of player activity are situated, however, as Rune Klevjer suggests, as illustrated by the above example from *Primal*. The cut-scene, for Klevjer, 'is a narrative of *pre-telling*, paving the way for the mimetic event, making it part of a narrative act, which does not take place after, but *before* the event. The cut-scene casts its meanings forward, strengthening the diegetic, rhetorical dimension of the event to come.'[82] Narrative material can also be provided by 'in-game' devices, more seamlessly integrated into the game-world. Examples include written materials such as signs or notes in the game-world that can be read without switching out of the scene into a separate screen filled with text, dialogue with non-player characters, the behaviours of non-player characters and the design of level settings.[83] *Half-Life* marked a notable development in this direction, avoiding cut-scenes or other information that has to be accessed outside the main game-space. Scenes important to the plot of *Half-Life* remain fully interactive, allowing the player to move around while information is relayed by non-player characters and other integrated devices.

In games such as these, the challenge offered to the player includes realizing the pre-existing narrative structure and making sense of the narrative context in which gameplay occurs. It involves an experience described by Julian Kücklich as akin to 'the hermeneutic process of reading a literary text, by challenging the player to make predictions about what is to come, or to reconstruct the events that led up to the present situation'.[84] In *The Thing*, for example, the player often comes upon scenes of death and destruction. Damaged, blood-spattered interiors and the remains of carcasses from which shape-shifting aliens have emerged provide both evidence of recent events, as constructed in the narrative past, and warning about the likely kinds of events to come. This invites a process of hermeneutics of the kind suggested by Kücklich, even if rather limited and obvious in the conclusions it supports. The game also includes more fleeting and potentially intriguing elements, including appearances of the non-player character Whitley, a figure who turns up on several occasions in the margins of the gameplay and exposition and turns out to be a primary source of central plot events.

Narrative development of this kind can play an important role in establishing qualities such as variable pace, drama and suspense – to give added depth to gameplay that might otherwise become one-dimensional. This is an issue not just for academics, especially those disposed favourably towards narrative as a culturally sanctioned form that can enable games to be taken more 'seriously', alongside forms such as novels and films. It also matters to many game designers, an important point given the tendency of some commentators to treat narrative as essentially a concern brought to games from outside, principally from those seeking to impose on games study perspectives more relevant to other media such as literature and cinema.[85] Narrative still remains in the background a great deal of the time, however, even in the more story-oriented games of progression. The provision of narrative material can be seen as a reward for successful gameplay. The unveiling of a new plot development often comes after the completion of a series of gameplay tasks. For Kücklich: 'Typically … the player is presented with tasks to be completed and puzzles to be solved, which serve as retarding elements, or "narrative barriers", as it were, against the players' impulse to unravel the "plot" of the game.'[86] A judgement is made here about the relative investment of the player in either side of the gameplay/narrative-progressive dynamic, but it is not possible to say with any certainty that players *play for* the narrative, as such, rather than enjoying the gameplay as much as, or more than, the access it gives to narrative progression. The balance of pleasure might change from one game to another – depending on the relative quality of both gameplay activities and narrative development – and from one player to another, depending on individual preferences.

Whatever the preference of the player, however, or the particular narrative development offered in any individual title, the bulk of the playing experience of most videogames that have narrative dimensions occurs *in between* the moments of narrative elaboration. Narrative usually functions to string together sequences of gameplay activities of the kinds outlined in the first part of this chapter, making contextual sense of smaller, more local cause-and-effect-based actions. Games with overarching and developing narrative frameworks such as the examples cited above might be reduced to a basic three-act structure of beginning, middle and end, but, as Craig Lindley suggests, with a highly extended second act in which gameplay activities dominate over narrative development.[87] A recursive structure is identified by Lindley, in which the same model is applied to the game as a whole, to individual game levels and to individual game tasks within each level. In each case, the core gameplay experience occurs in the extended second act, framed by introductory or climactic material that does most of the narrative work, often through the use of out-of-game devices such as cut-scenes.

Factors determining the degree to which narrative material is likely to remain in-play throughout the game include the pace at which movement through the game is allowed or encouraged. A faster pace, other things being equal, is likely to increase the proximity of narratively loaded components, creating a stronger sense of linear continuity, of narrative binding, across sequences of gameplay activity. A slower pace, or larger gaps between narrative devices (or more widely spaced play sessions), is likely to reduce any impression of narrative continuity or progression, creating a more episodic experience. Likely speed of progression can be increased through the use of devices such as navigational aids that steer the player in the direction necessary for progression, encouraging a more linear passage through the game-world in which narrative continuity is more likely to be sustained – an issue to which we return in Chapter 2. In *Enter the Matrix*, for example, player-characters can move at a helter-skelter pace, faster than usual for third-person action-adventures, and are constantly provided with orientation by a directional arrow at the top right-hand corner of the screen. The effect is to create a strong impression of momentum, very different from the exploratory wandering in search of the right route through the more puzzle-like gamescape characteristic of titles such as the *Tomb Raider* games. Forward-driving momentum is often halted, of course, by more difficult gameplay activities – a tricky series of rooftop jumps to perform, for example, or engagement with a large number of well-armed enemies – but only as long as it takes to reload and try again, giving the game a clear sense of directed progression, even if this is often performed in fits and starts. The length of a given game might also affect the experienced coherence of a narrative arc: in shorter games, the impression of coherence might be enhanced while longer games often place emphasis on the more general experience of being in the world of the game (especially in subscription-based MMORPGs). Generally, narrative is delivered and experienced in games in a more fragmentary and drawn-out manner than in more narrative-centric forms.

Narrative does not only exist in games in the form of the larger, overarching frameworks within which gameplay is sometimes situated. Many smaller or more fundamental narrative components are often found, starting at the level of basic cause/effect relationships. Linear narrative implies an ordered sequence of events in which one factor influences another in a chain of causes and effects: factor *a* causes effect *b*, which goes on to be the cause of effect *c*, and so on. Cause/effect processes of this kind are an essential characteristic of the action/feedback structure of all games, at a local level, whether or not they build up to a more substantially narrative-oriented framework. Particular actions can affect the player's broader relation to aspects the game-world, in addition to their more immediately apparent consequences. If players choose to kill certain guards in *EverQuest*, for example, they might find it more difficult, subsequently, to enter or exit areas policed by guards of the same faction (and they will not be able to use them as shields against other enemies). If players of *Half-Life: Blue Shift* (2001) choose to shoot unthreatening NPCs they receive a warning from inside the diegetic universe that they have violated their contract of employment and are thrown out of the game. More generally, players are likely to understand that if they ignore various cues provided during the course of a game they are less likely to achieve goals or to achieve them in the most efficient manner.

Games often use narrative-oriented components such as individuated characters and fictional settings in which actions are performed in pursuit of particular goals. Marie-Laure Ryan argues that ingredients such as these are not used for their own sake but as means towards another end, that of luring players into the game-world. For Ryan: 'Narrativity performs an instrumental rather than a strictly aesthetic function: once the player is immersed in the game, the narrative theme may be backgrounded or temporarily forgotten.'[88] How far this might be the case, and in what circumstances, is considered in the last part of this chapter. Even seen Ryan's way, however, as strictly secondary, the role of narrative components remains significant, given the importance usually attributed to the creation of an impression of immersion. Basic narrative elements or dynamics can also be linked more closely to core gameplay activities. If the *agon*, or contest, is one of the fundamental types of game, as suggested by Caillois, it is also, Janet Murray reminds us, a basic narrative unit:

By pulling a player into the game world using character and narrative you pull them into the consciousness of the character

The Greek word *agon* refers to both athletic contests and to dramatic conflicts, reflecting the common origin of games and theatre. A simple shoot-'em-up videogame, then, belongs to the extremely broad dramatic tradition that gives us both the boxing match and the Elizabethan revenge play.[89]

Many games also draw on long-established traditions in their use of narrative models such as the quest and the heroic journey, formats found in a wide range of cultural mythologies and folk tales (including blueprint action-adventure tales such as *The Odyssey* and *Beowulf*). Quest frameworks, in which characters are sent on missions (often to exotic places) to perform heroic actions, form the basis of many games, especially in the action-adventure and role-playing genres, obvious examples including *Primal*, *EverQuest* and the *Tomb Raider* series. Quests are also found as more locally embedded mini-narratives within the more open structure of games of emergence, as suggested above. The quest format and the hero's journey, a narrative archetype identified by Joseph Campbell in a wide range of myths and stories, lend themselves particularly well to the requirements of action-adventure and role-playing games, providing the ideal framework within which to set the tasks to be performed by the player-character.[90] In the hero's journey the central character is forced to leave behind the ordinary world, entering another realm in which a series of tests and ordeals have to be overcome. The format is offered by Troy Dunniway as an ideal narrative template for game design, its facility being based largely on the simplicity and familiarity of the form.[91] Structures such as these, with their roots in oral story-telling, have always allowed for a loose, episodic structure of a kind particularly suited to games. The emphasis tends to be on the journey itself, and the assorted experiences encountered *en route*, rather than on the end-point or destination, much the same as could be said for games that have overarching narrative frames but in which the majority of attention is devoted to the performance of the particular gameplay tasks required for progression.

In Campbell's account – which has influenced narrative theorists and practitioners, the latter including *Star Wars* creator George Lucas – the hero's journey is comprised of 25 separate plot components, from 'The Call to Adventure' to 'Final Victory'. Many of those in between, such as 'Monster Combat', 'The Enchanted Forces & Helpful Animals' and 'Descent into the Underworld' can easily be imagined as game ingredients or levels. A simplified and updated version by Christopher Vogler includes as an early stage 'The Reluctant Hero', a device used in games such as *Max Payne, The Getaway, Primal* and *Buffy the Vampire Slayer* to provide moral justification for the actions of the player-character.[92] In both *Max Payne* and *The Getaway*, the central figure is forced by circumstances, against his will, into a series of extremely violent encounters with both police and criminal forces. In *Primal* and *Buffy* the central characters have their heroic destinies foisted upon them by metaphysical forces. A similar set of plot components is found in the literary theorist Vladimir Propp's earlier study of Russian folktales, a large body of which is reduced to variations on a series of basic plot 'functions'.[93] Games, as Janet Murray suggests, tend to be quite simple and crude in their use of such components, compared with the complex range of substitutions and rearrangements available in the folk tale.[94] A small number of elements are usually repeated with only limited variation: typically, in many cases, using Propp's typology, 'The hero is given a difficult task', followed, eventually, by 'The hero successfully performs the task', and so on. The fact that the narrative dimension of games is often crude and simple should not be confused, however, with claims that narrative is of little or no significance. The one does not follow from the other, as is sometimes implied. Existing videogames may be disappointing to some critics in their lack of narrative subtlety or sophistication, but the narrative dimension still exists and needs to be understood, both in its own terms and its interaction with gameplay. Relatively crude narrative material is, in fact, probably best suited to the job, in existing game formats, providing a few strong hooks on which to hang gameplay activities and well-matched to the protracted and multi-levelled engagement of most games.

The familiarity of archetypal narrative frameworks such as the quest or the hero's journey is such that they can be drawn upon without the need for extensive elaboration in any particular manifestation. The notion of a central character being sent off on a quest or a series of missions, usually involving a shift out of more recognizably everyday routines, is sufficiently well-established as a narrative convention to be accepted usually without question. This is particularly useful in forms such as videogames in which narrative elaboration is often likely to be experienced as a distraction from the more active playing of the game. Briefly sketched, familiar conventions provide a frame within which focus can be directed to the more immediate demands of gameplay. This is the case with broadly archetypal formats and with more specific pre-established narrative frameworks such as those provided by intertextual reference. An important point, sometimes overlooked, is that the narrative dimension of gameplaying is not limited to the function of narrative material that can be located explicitly within the individual game-text itself. Games can also *play into* the context of narrative material elaborated elsewhere. This is most obvious in games designed as spin-offs from other media forms, such as games based on film franchises, but it can also apply more widely.

A good example of this phenomenon is suggested by Henry Jenkins in his response to Jesper Juul's analysis of the arcade game *Star Wars* (1983). The game, Juul reports, comes in three phases, each involving the control of a spaceship engaged in different combat actions. In the third phase, a version of the climactic assault on the Death Star, some similarity with scenes from the film might be detected, Juul argues, 'but you would not be able to reconstruct the events in the movie from the game. The prehistory is missing, the rest of the movie, all personal relations'.[95] *Star Wars* the game, Juul concludes, 'can not be said to contain a narrative that can be recognised from Star Wars the movie ...'[96] This is true, as far as it goes, but it rather misses the point. The narrative context for the action performed in the game is established in advance, in the movie and, especially in this case, as a result of the prominent position it attained in the popular culture of its time. The game does not need to repeat any of this material to be able to play into a context in which it can be assumed that players will be able to fit it into its narrative place, either directly, in the case of a scene based on one from the film, or more generally, in the sense of locating action in the broad framework of rebels vs. empire established by the film and its sequels. This is the case both in this individual example and in the wider economy of which it is a prominent manifestation, in which an important emphasis for large media conglomerates is on the production of franchise properties that can be exploited across a range of different media forms. As Jenkins puts it: 'Increasingly, we inhabit a world of transmedia story-telling, one which depends less on each individual work being self-sufficient than on each work contributing to a larger narrative economy.'[97]

The value of franchise operations for media corporations is that the familiarity of successful properties in one realm, such as cinema or television, can be used to sell a range of spin-off products, including games. Games are themselves the source of spin-offs in some cases, including films, but the dynamic tends to work more often in the opposite direction. It is easier, generally, to adapt more narrative-centred forms such as film and television to games than it is to do the opposite. Popular films or television series provide well-established characters and scenarios that can be mobilized in games without the need for extensive narrative elaboration in the game itself. Narrative frames established elsewhere provide contexts for gameplay more readily than gameplay – within its own limited narrative parameters – lends itself to cinematic adaptation, because games are usually weaker in the development of dimensions such as plot and character that are important to films. Film-to-game adaptations are often greeted with scepticism by gameplayers who suspect, not unsurprisingly, that they are less than usually likely to have been developed with their distinctive gameplay features in mind. Licensed properties can be attractive to developers, however, and not just for the commercial reasons associated with the advantage of higher levels of awareness from which they can benefit in a crowded marketplace. As designers Daniel Tanguay and Brent Boylen suggest: 'A licensed property can provide an immediate universe of references to help the team focus on gameplay instead of ancillary content.'[98] The constraints imposed by licensed properties can restrict the freedom of developers, but they are freed from the need to create their own narrative context from scratch.

The *Buffy the Vampire Slayer* franchise, for example, has a high brand-recognition factor, spanning a range of media and including several game versions. The television show ran for seven series from 1997 to 2003, building a loyal audience for its protracted construction of a coherent fantasy world: the 'buffyverse'. With an emphasis on action – fights against various vampires and demons – and a tough good-looking action heroine, the format lends itself well to the action-adventure game genre. The games locate themselves temporally at various points in the story arc established by the series. *Buffy the Vampire Slayer* is set during Season Two (*Buffy* is still going out with vampire Angel) while *Buffy the Vampire*

Slayer: Wrath of the Darkhul King (2003), only available on the Gameboy Advance, is located in Season Four (when *Buffy* is in a relationship with the unsuitably human Riley). *Buffy the Vampire Slayer: Chaos Bleeds* makes more general allusions to events throughout the whole series.[99] These games spend very little time establishing characters, assuming that players are already familiar with the events of the series. As a result, there are relatively few expository cut scenes (or the static picture and text equivalent in the more resource-restricted context of the Gameboy). The *Buffy* games all draw heavily on the pre-existing 'buffyverse', with its particular metaphysical order, created by the show and other spin-offs such as comics and novellas. Various in-jokes and narrative resonances are expressly addressed to *Buffy*-literate players.

Useful comparison can be made between the *Buffy* games and *Primal*, a free-standing game that is similar in some significant respects but that has to do more work to create its own world and characters. An unusually large number of expositional cut-scenes are required, both at the start and throughout the game. Extensive marketing was needed to sell from scratch the central character, Jen, and the world she inhabits. The advertising campaign was much bigger than that used for the *Buffy* games, including expensive television spots. Competing for the same target market as the *Buffy* games, *Primal* makes use of various codes to identify the nature of the game, creating points of recognition for fantasy-literate gameplayers (including, as the voice of Jen, the actor Hudson Leick, who played a tough woman warrior character in the television series *Xena: Warrior Princess*). A more risky venture than the *Buffy* games, the pay-off for *Primal* is the creation of a game that stands out from many others by having a well-developed storyline of its own in which emphasis is placed on character development, a dimension unusual in games.

For players, the existence of a pre-established narrative framework can create added resonance to the gameplaying experience, a sense of being able to occupy and explore story-worlds created elsewhere. The player of one of the many *Star Wars* spin-off games might, for example, gain an extra dimension of pleasure from the impression of inhabiting a part of the *Star Wars* universe, either one closely connected to the events of the films or one that exists on the margins of the multiple narrative lines of the series. For enthusiasts of the franchise, playing the MMORPG *Star Wars Galaxies* (2003) is likely to be a significantly different experience from that of otherwise broadly similar games in the genre. A close connection exists in many such cases between narrative and the particular spaces in which it unfolds, or for which a narrative context has been created elsewhere. The narrative dimension of games, as Henry Jenkins suggests, can be understood in the context of a tradition of 'spatial stories', the principal dynamic of which is the creation of fictional worlds through which the protagonists travel – another point of connection with the quest, the odyssey and the travel narrative as well as more recent works of science fiction and fantasy. Games consoles can be viewed as 'machines for generating compelling spaces', an aspect of games to which we return in more detail in the following chapter.[100]

Game spaces can be imbued with narrative meaning in a number of ways. Spaces such as those of the *Star Wars* games evoke established narrative associations. Others contain what Jenkins terms 'embedded narratives', in which narrative material is built into the space itself, a process termed 'environmental story-telling' by Don Carson, a designer of theme park attractions cited by Jenkins, who suggests a number of techniques that can be adopted by game designers.[101] The story element in theme park rides and other attractions is 'infused into the physical space a guest walks or rides through', a process that can also be applied to games. Narrative clues can be distributed throughout the environment, Carson suggests, including the use of 'cause and effect vignettes', staged areas 'that lead the player to come to their own conclusions about a previous event or to suggest a potential danger just up ahead'.[102] The effect sought by Carson is similar to that identified in narrative-oriented games by Kücklich, encouraging a process of narrative reconstruction and projection by the player. Players can also be pulled through the story by following a trail of 'breadcrumbs', indicators of the passage of a previous fictional character, the kind of role performed by Whitely in *The Thing*. A similar concept suggested by Murray is what she terms 'the story in the maze', in which the development of narrative is again tied to, and emerges through, the navigation of space.[103]

GENRE

Game spaces can also play on established genre frameworks such as those of horror, science fiction or fantasy. Genre associations take numerous forms, as do definitions of genres themselves (we use the term here in the sense in which it is commonly used in reference to different thematic, narrative and other types in media such as film and television – to refer to categories such as horror, science fiction and fantasy rather than game-specific types such as first-person shooter or role-playing game). Some genres are defined at least partly according to their settings, the alternative worlds of science fiction and fantasy, for example, which makes them readily available for the provision of spatial-contextual material in games. Genres or sub-genres can also be defined in narrative terms, according to the particular scenarios with which they are associated: *Doom*, *Half-Life* and *The Thing*, for instance, as examples of the 'alien invasion' variant in science fiction. Developers and academic commentators agree on the important role genre can play in providing a context for the pursuit of gameplay activities. Designers of game-worlds should focus initially on thematic and narrative genres rather than gameplay conventions, Joshua Mosqueira argues, 'because genres like fantasy, sci-fi, cyber-punk, and even the Wild West are more evocative and offer a better starting point for both story *and* gameplay'.[104]

World-building in games, as Mosqueira suggests, is about the creation of context as much as the creation of an entire, detailed universe. Context provides answers to key questions such as: the identity of the player-character, what they are trying to do, how they might win or lose, where the action is happening, and why: 'Why is the player crawling through corridors? Why is she gathering resources to build armies? To win, yes, but for the game to be an experience, the *why* needs to be less about game mechanics and more about interaction and, yes, story.'[105] Or just some mixture of the two. Genre is a particularly useful source of such context because of its familiarity, in much the same way as broader narrative archetypes or licensed properties. This is the case in all popular media, established genres offering an instant source of identification of the kind of experience likely to be offered by a particular text. It is especially useful to games, however, as media not so well suited to the articulation in any depth of their own contextual background because of their participatory status. Genres, like other archetypes, offer instantly recognizable frames of reference that allow gameplay to proceed with only minimal elaboration of the specific scenario offered in any particular example. The main reason why only a brief page of background text is sufficient in titles such as *Doom* and *Half-Life* is that so much of the work

3. Generic territory, instantly recognizable: scientist and futurist/laboratory setting in *Half-Life* (1998)

in establishing their contexts is done at the level of genre associations built into aspects of the games ranging from titles and cover art to the design of the in-game world – the high-tech/gothic combination in the former and the archetypal secret research laboratory of the latter.

Genre 'helps to bind a game's elements into a cohesive whole', as Mosqueira puts it, 'while at the same time it provides a basic underlying structure and even suggests gameplay mechanics'.[106] Genre can influence gameplay options themselves, not just the background against which they are set, especially in the case of the supporting gameplay hooks. The ability of the player-character to teleport from one place to another, for example, is generically motivated as part of the repertoire of science fiction in *Doom*, or as part of the magical-fantasy quality of the world of *EverQuest*, in which it can be of great value to players seeking a rapid means of transit in the extensive landscape of a MMORPG. The ability to 'gate' or 'port', as the process is known, is a significant factor in *EverQuest* gameplay. As a gameplay device, it might seem arbitrary and intrusive if it were not for the broad generic motivation. This is a good example of the way contextual background tends to work, not necessarily drawing attention to itself greatly for its own sake, but providing a context in which otherwise arbitrary gameplay actions make some kind of sense. An activity such as teleportation would be incongruous in games such as *Grand Theft Auto III*, *Max Payne* or *The Getaway*, for example, in which player-character actions have to approximate not so much to reality as to the conventional limits of the thriller genre.

Genre often 'scripts the interactor', as Murray puts it.[107] In an interactive horror story, as she suggests, the player always knows to enter the haunted house, because it is a well-established convention of the genre. In a game, the player might have little choice. Not much happens, for example, if a player stays outside in the relatively uninteresting garden and does not dare enter the Old Dark House of *Clive Barker's Undying* (2001). Genre provides a context that makes the action meaningful, within an established frame of reference, rather than arbitrary – a factor that strongly increases the immersive and pleasurable potential of the experience. A similar point is made by Petri Lankoski and Satu Heliö, drawing on the scheme of narrative codes established by Roland Barthes.[108] One of the codes identified by Barthes is the 'hermeneutic code', which deals with the creation and resolution of narrative enigma – as applied to games by Kücklich and, implicitly, by Carson. Another is the code of 'narrative action', termed by Barthes the *proairetic* code, a code that takes on an added dimension in games, when much of the action is to be performed by the player-character. Understanding of the code of action 'is the basis for decision making in a game',[109] as Lankoski and Heliö put it, and particular codes of action – actions that are conventional and expected – are found in particular genre frameworks. The cut-scenes of *Grand Theft Auto III* speak to the player, Rune Klevjer suggests, and they speak in a particular way: 'A recognizable rhetoric meets you; the voice of a genre.'[110]

Genre conventions are widely used to provide motivation for the actions required of player-characters, to supply contexts in which activity such as the rampant shooting sprees required in many first-person shooters and third-person action adventure games does not appear entirely gratuitous. War and gangster genre conventions serve this purpose for conflict against human enemies; horror, science fiction and fantasy for the destruction of the alien and otherworldly. In *Grand Theft Auto III*, the sub-generic context is that of the new recruit to the gangster world making his way up the underworld ladder, a context that involves the performance of a variety of missions, most of which involve violence against others. A broad intertextual media context is established in the opening titles, resonating particularly with the contemporary rediscovery – as 'cool'/'cult' objects – of 1970s iterations of this kind of landscape: a laid-back jazz-influenced theme evocative of period crime/car-chase movies, accompanied by drop-in fragmented images and typeface-design suggestive of television cop/crime series of the time. In *Max Payne* and *The Getaway*, the familiar scenario is that of the outlawed anti-hero, forced to demonstrate his capacity for violence against his will. In horror-based games, and some science fiction and fantasy, the contextual framework tends to be more black-and-white, the player-character established as a protagonist working in the interests of good against evil forces, overtly in the *Buffy the Vampire Slayer* games, less overtly in the *Resident Evil* cycle (1996–present) and slightly more ambiguously in *Silent Hill 2* (2001). *Blood Omen 2* (2002) strikes a different metaphysical and moral chord by putting the player on the side of the glamorous blood-drinking bad-boy vampire. These are all relatively simple, clear-cut contexts. They have the virtue, for games, of being both familiar from other products of popular culture and lending themselves to the production of extended variations on the main theme in the shape of whatever activities are foregrounded by the type of game in which they are used.

Contextual frames such as those provided by genre and narrative can be morally loaded, as many of the above examples suggest, providing not just popular-culturally meaningful association but value-judgement. Story or genre frameworks often seek to *justify* the kind of behaviour required of the player-character if progress is to be made through the game. Max Payne, as operated by the player, does not just indulge in orgies of violence, but is a put-upon character left with no choice if he is to survive; Mark Hammond in *The Getaway*, likewise, is forced into violent activities by gangsters who have kidnapped his young son. James Sunderland in *Silent Hill 2* is looking for his wife. In each of these cases, sympathy for the plight of the protagonist is sought through the melodramatic device of violent intrusion into their domestic life. In science fiction or SF/horror hybrids, the player-character's task is often to save the world or humankind, sometimes single-handedly, from the onslaught of alien forces: John Dalton, for example, in *Unreal II* (2003) and the Master-Chief, 'bred for

[margin handwritten note: Does that justification actually change anything?]

combat, built for war', in *Halo*. War games tend, with some exceptions, particularly in the real-time strategy format, to put the player on the side defined – from the perspective of creators and principal target market, at least – as 'the good guys'. Favourite enemies are the Nazis in the Second World War, their primary attraction being their widely accepted status as adversaries beyond the acceptable pale, and thus worthy of any mayhem inflicted by the player (exceptions include the *Close Combat* series, in which the player controls Nazi forces in a number of Second World War scenarios); this strategy is given its fullest expression in *Return to Castle Wolfenstein*, in which the Nazi/demonic equation is made literal.

In some cases, morally coded reference points have been imposed on games specifically to make them more acceptable, to regulators if not necessarily to potential players. The classic example is *Carmageddon* (1997), in which figures to be knocked down by the player were at one stage during a regulatory debacle turned from human pedestrians (even if little more than bunches of fuzzy pixels) into zombies, a shift signified by changing their blood from red to green, to provide an apparent framework of moral justification for killing. Whether moral frameworks such as this, and other contextual associations, have a more than superficial impact on gameplay is the subject to which we turn in the remainder of this chapter. If narrative, genre and other resonances provide contexts in which gameplay occurs, are these dimensions really *in-play*, or just somewhere in the distant background, during gameplay?

Gameplay in contexts/contexts in gameplay

A potentially wide variety of associational meanings can be attached to the materials through which gameplay is engaged in any individual game or game-genre. These include associations from broadly generic contexts, from particular genre-oriented narrative themes and from specific narrative products such as individual films, television shows or other cultural materials. Broader socio-cultural values can also be encoded into the game-world, from the kinds of moral oppositions cited above to more overtly political-ideological implications. But how far are these dimensions likely to be *in-play* in games? It is one thing to identify elements such as narrative, genre or ideological significance, but quite another to suggest exactly how operative they are likely to be during game-specific activities such as those outlined in the first part of this chapter. A number of factors can be suggested that might shape or determine the extent to which contextual associations are in-play in any particular game or any particular playing situation. A useful starting point is to focus on games that have relatively explicit or contentious political-ideological dimensions, a situation in which the impact of contextual associations might be drawn more sharply to our attention (an issue to which we return more generally in Chapter 4). Two examples from different game genres that can serve as illustrations, alongside some of the examples used earlier in this chapter, are the real-time strategy game *Command and Conquer: Generals*, already cited in a different context above, and the first-person shooter *Delta Force: Black Hawk Down* (2003).

Both games offer material typical of the kind expected in their respective game genres. The main gameplay concerns for the player of *Command and Conquer* are resource development, management and deployment. Barracks are constructed and managed to produce troops; war factories or their equivalents to produce armoured and other vehicles. More advanced buildings are used to develop more specialized technologies and capabilities. Resources are built up and/or deployed in the field against enemies and for defensive purposes. An eye has to be kept on strategic factors such as the development of any particular offensive campaign, the availability of sources of revenue and the potential for enemy attacks. *Black Hawk Down* calls for familiar first-person shooter tasks such as rapid but careful passage through the on-screen space of the game, avoiding and/or shooting enemies, taking cover, trying not to shoot figures marked as innocent civilians, taking advantage of the help offered by non-player character comrades, monitoring ammunition and health levels (while seeking to replenish both) and completing the requirements of individual missions.

In both cases, these generic features are situated within ideologically and geopolitically loaded contexts. *Command and Conquer: Generals* contains many points of reference uncomfortably close to geopolitical issues that were pressing and current at the time of its release, most notably the supposed 'war against terrorism' proposed by America in the wake of the attacks on the World Trade Center and the Pentagon in September 2001 and the invasions of Afghanistan and Iraq led by America in 2002 and 2003. The player has a choice of playing as the United States, China or the Global Liberation Army (GLA). The latter is identified as a 'terrorist' organization, making key strategic gameplay use of underground tunnel networks and equipped with weapons including scud missile launchers, anthrax shells and suicide bombers. A number of signifiers are thereby put into play that had acute real-world resonance when the game appeared: scud missiles as a previously favoured weapon of the Saddam Hussein regime in Iraq, anthrax being among the biological weapons feared by America and its allies (and having gained renewed saliency after deaths caused by spores sent through the US mail from a domestic source in 2001), suicide bombers being common currency of Islamic militants in the Middle East and elsewhere, and tunnel networks featuring as the favoured base of operations used by the al-Qaeda network in Afghanistan. The GLA of the game is not meant to be a representation of al-Qaeda, being more akin to a conventional army in some respects. Its representation in the game – troops and vehicles – is distinctly cartoon-like in style, an important element in establishing *Command and Conquer's* modality as a game rather than any more serious geopolitical simulation. But, within this arena, the game includes numerous *semantic elements* – units of meaning – capable of playing strongly into its contemporary geopolitical context. *Black Hawk Down* is more explicitly based on actual geopolitical events, its missions being located in a specific historical and geographical conjuncture: the operations of US forces in support of the United Nations in Somalia in 1993, another context freighted with ideological implications.

How far, then, are these contexts likely to be in or out of play? One way to address this question is to construct an axis of possibilities with extreme positions at either end and a large grey area in the middle. At one extreme would be a purely abstract process of gameplay, entirely free from any extrinsic associations or motivations. At the other would be a notion of gameplay fully saturated with extrinsic contextual material of one kind or another. Neither extreme is likely to be fully applicable. Gameplay is always situated somewhere in between, a number of factors influencing the relative degree to which it might approach one or other end of the scale. The two extremes offer a useful starting place, however, from which to understand the extent to which each needs to be qualified.

At the fully saturated end of the scale, the geopolitical or ideological dimension of a title such as *Command and Conquer: Generals* would be very strongly in play at every moment. When each particular, detailed gameplay task was performed, it would be done with full consciousness of the contextual association. When a scud missile launcher was developed and moved into position by the GLA, for example, it would resonate strongly as a representation of the real-world equivalent used by the regime of Saddam Hussein in recent history. It might be experienced in the context of a real threat posed to the anti-Saddam forces – or, for the opponent of action against Iraq, as a vicarious equivalent of hitting back at US neo-imperialism. The powerfully symbolic real-world status of 'scud missile' would loom large, in other words, rather than the weapon being experienced as just one among many provided in the repertoire of a game. In an action–adventure title such as *The Getaway*, the equivalent would be the experience of every gameplay task through the imaginary lens provided by the generic context and the particular situation faced by the player-character. Every driving, shoot-out or stealth mission would be woven tightly into this frame, the player identifying closely with the fictional character.

Such associations can come into play, sometimes quite strongly. But they are never likely to reach a point approaching that of total gameplay saturation. They are bound to recede from consciousness, probably very often, during the implementation of basic gameplay tasks, and in the formulation of broader tactical and strategic approaches in a game such as *Command and Conquer*. There is a *routine* dimension to gameplay of all kinds that cannot entirely be displaced. In *Command and Conquer*, this involves the minutiae of tasks such as keeping up a steady production of resources, as well as larger considerations about the best combinations in which they should be deployed, what future capabilities should be researched, how to restrict the enemy's access to resources, and so on. The cognitive demand imposed by these processes is such that they often become the focus of attention in their own right; it is not practicable to imagine them being weighed down, always, moment by moment, by the available contextual associations. The same goes for games such as *Half-Life* and *The Getaway*, in which the game-generic dimension is also almost certain to come to the fore much of the time; in which Gordon Freeman or Mark Hammond, and their game-fictional plights, recede and the player's own interaction with the game-world *as* the world of a game, with all of its particular pleasures and frustrations, becomes the focus of attention. It

4. Scud missiles launched in attack on a US base in *Command and Conquer: Generals* (2003): loaded with real-world resonances, or just abstract counters in a game repertoire?

is quite possible to spend an entire session of play stuck repeatedly in a particular phase of a mission in *The Getaway*, for example – shooting the player-character's way through a building and/or attempting a driving mission, the two kinds of activity often linked together with no save point in between – without making any progress that activates even limited developments in the narrative concerning Hammond's efforts to locate and rescue his son. The landscape of *Half-Life* teems with references to the particular narrative/genre context, in both visual iconography and a sound design filled with atmospheric music and creepy sound effects, including the off-screen noises of aliens yet to be encountered. The environment, a network of seemingly endless corridors, ventilation ducts, stairways and laboratories, is heavily coded according to genre. All of this, however, can be reduced to something closer to the status of an abstract puzzle-maze, especially in longer or repeated periods of gameplay uninterrupted by the presentation of fresh narrative material.

What, then, of the other extreme? If contextual associations can never always be fully in play, does the routine implementation of gameplay tasks reach a point at which contextual associations recede entirely? For the player of *Command and Conquer* as the GLA, does the production and use of scud launchers or anthrax weapons become a purely abstract feature of gameplay, in which the loaded nature of their connotations falls out of view? Does the game, as Caillois suggests, have 'no other than an intrinsic meaning.'?[111] This may sometimes be the case during gameplay, but the possibility of extrinsic, contextual meaning is never entirely absent. Much of the time, the scud launcher might just be experienced as another weapon, merely a counter in an abstract game; one more item to be produced, moved up into position, defended from attack and used against the enemy. But it remains a signifier whose very particular connotative potential is always available to be mobilized in particular circumstances. In the same way, 'Gordon Freeman' or 'Mark Hammond', as fictional characters, might well disappear from view quite often for the player of *Half-Life* and *The Getaway*, but character, milieu and narrative development remain potentially in-play, to varying degrees, at one moment of gameplay or another.

Even the most abstract game contains such potential, including perhaps the most often discussed example, *Tetris* (1989). The gameplay of *Tetris* consists of repeated attempts to fit abstractly geometric descending blocks into a pattern. Janet Murray has been criticized, quite sharply, for reading into this an associational meaning. For Murray, in an often-quoted passage, the game, although it was developed in the Soviet Union, 'is a perfect enactment of the overtasked lives of Americans in the 1990s – of the constant bombardment of tasks that demand our attention and that we must somehow fit into our overcrowded schedules and clear off our desks to make room for the next onslaught'.[112] As Eskilinen suggests, what Murray does is to project her own interpretation onto the game, an act of 'interpretative violence', as he terms it, rooted in 'the determination to find or forge a story at any cost' in order to constitute *Tetris* as an object worthy of study.[113] Nothing is learned of the specific features that make *Tetris* work as a game. This is true, but what is needed here, to escape the polemic that sometimes exists between positions constructed as those of 'ludologists' versus 'narratologists', is an appreciation of gameplay characteristics, the *potential* they carry for interpretive association, and analysis of the likely balance between the two in any particular situation. It is in the nature of cultural products, including abstract-seeming games, that they can *take on* metaphorical or associational meaning of the kind Murray finds in *Tetris*. Similar readings of *Space Invaders* and *Pac-Man* (1980) are made by Chris Crawford, for example, from the perspective of a game designer fully cognizant of the game-specific qualities of each.[114] To suggest that such metaphorical readings can legitimately be made is not the same as *reducing* games to such meanings or suggesting that they are primarily defined by them. The distinction is an important one. The same can be said of narrative context. David Myers, for example, argues strongly against the value of backstory in games, suggesting that it is often imposed on games for commercial reasons but likely to interfere with, rather than to support, gameplay. It is difficult, Myers suggests, 'for any single and self-consistent backstory to contain the great barrage of meanings generated during play'.[115] This is true. Narrative is often offered as a source of context within which play can be located, but its hold is always likely to be limited by factors such as the nature of the particular gameplay experience involved and the orientation of the player.

If we exclude the extremes of purely abstract gameplay and gameplay totally saturated by associational meaning, we are left with a large middle ground within which specific arguments can be made for the extent to which contextual material might or might not be in-play in any particular example. What is required here, as generally in the study of games, is analysis of the game-as-playable-text – the material offered by the game itself – and consideration of a number of different ways in which the same game text might be experienced from one occasion to another.

It is important to stress that exactly how the balance operates between gameplay-for-its-own-sake and gameplay-in-context is hard to determine in other than an approximate fashion. This is not a question that lends itself to an exact science of understanding. A number of factors can be identified, however, that might influence the extent to which contextual associations are in play, including: different moments of play *within* any individual game or game genre; the *mode* of play, including factors such as difficulty settings and the use or otherwise of cheats or walk-throughs; the volume of explicit reference to contextual material in any individual game; the degree of contentiousness or contemporary resonance of contextual associations; and, crucially, the orientation of players, including their emotional or intellectual investment in character, genre or other aspects of contextual background.

Material extrinsic to the performance of core gameplay tasks is likely, on balance, to recede from view as gameplay proceeds within any particular game. Specific framing materials are usually foregrounded most strongly at the start, in materials such as the backstory provided in the manual and opening cut-scenes. A substantial chunk of the manual for *Black Hawk Down*, for example, is devoted to an account titled 'Somalia: A Troubled History', including a map and graphical representations of statistical data on issues such as population density, ethnic divisions and natural resources. The opening video sequences make stronger than usual claims towards verisimilitude, mimicking the format of a television news broadcast to provide basic context for the missions in which the player takes part. Actuality footage and date-stamped captions that refer to real historical moments are used to ground the game in a real-world context. Like many other shooter games, this also serves to establish some illusion of a moral context for the action. The player is situated as a cause for good, fighting against militia forces that are undermining UN humanitarian relief efforts. Reminders of this context are also supplied at the start of each individual mission, several of which involve the rescue of UN relief convoys. As each mission progresses, however, the emphasis is likely to shift to the more generic, and at least relatively value-neutral, performance of conventional shooter tasks.[116]

The mission titled 'Besieged' in *Black Hawk Down*, for example, begins with text informing the player that the task is to rescue a group of Pakistani UN troops protecting a supply convoy who have come under siege in an urban area, the road ahead blocked. The player-character drives into the area in fixed 'rail-shooter' mode, using a machine gun mounted on a vehicle to fire at enemy snipers, technicals and militiamen armed with rocket propelled grenades, dismounting when the convoy is reached. The task is then to deal with snipers in surrounding buildings and enemy forces on the ground, negotiating streets and bombed-out interiors before eventually placing charges on a truck that has been used to block the road, at which point the missions ends in success. Care has to be taken, especially at the start, to avoid shooting Pakistani troops by mistake (killing too many 'friendlies' or 'innocent civilians' leads to mission failure and a requirement to start again). Initially, the specific scenario, in the 'US humanitarian mission in Somalia' context, is quite visible and in the foreground, graphics contributing by evoking a reasonably concrete sense of grounding in a particular place. As the mission proceeds, however, the basics of shooter gameplay come increasingly to the fore.

A game-specific decision has to be made about where and when to save the game, a limited number of saves being permitted in each mission (in this case six). Too early and profligate use of saves is liable to make the latter stages of the mission more difficult to complete without larger portions of repetition. Saving comes into play, as in so many games, because of the constant likelihood of the player-character being killed and having to start again. Every time the player has to save and restart from an earlier point, any notion of immersion in association-specific context is likely to be reduced, as gameplay mechanics intrude further into the experience. Other shooter game specifics also come rapidly into play, such as the need to monitor available levels of ammunition and health. In an early pass, the player might be too profligate with bullets from the character's main weapon (an M16 rifle) and struggle, later, when reduced to fighting first with a pistol and then with just a knife. A return to an earlier save, or to the start of the mission, might be used to correct the balance, to use M16 bullets more judiciously. Reduction in the characters health level creates a similar dynamic, maybe requiring more careful use of cover. The player also has to be on the lookout, as in all shooters and many action-adventures, for health boosts (one, at least, is available) and further supplies of ammunition (no, can't find any, so might have to backtrack).

Contextual associations are likely to slip furthest from view in extreme states of play, at its most heightened and, equally, at its most potentially tedious. Little perceptual or cognitive space may be left for awareness of context when gameplay is at its most fast and furious: when the player has to move fast to shoot and avoid being shot, especially when ammunition or health are low (the latter being when the stakes are highest, especially if a long stretch of the mission will have to be repeated in the event of death). Attention has to be paid, simultaneously, to navigation, the interface providing a map that indicates the direction of the objective, the direction of enemy fire and the location of friendly and unfriendly forces. Similar levels of demand are imposed in the most heightened periods of action in a real-time strategy title such as *Command and Conquer: Generals*, when attention has to be paid to simultaneous ongoing developments on multiple fronts. If contextual associations often occupy a place in the background, this is likely to be increased under these conditions, in the case of the geopolitical-ideological dimensions of *Black Hawk Down* and *Command and Conquer* or the narrative/genre resonances of the more intensive exchanges in games such as *Half-Life* and *The Getaway*.

A heightened state of play might involve self-conscious concentration on game-specific tasks or something closer to Csikszentmihalyi's concept of flow, one of the defining characteristics of which is, precisely, to shut out everything other than an intense focus on the immediate task at hand. Regimes of saving-and-repeating can add to the intensity of the experience, especially in games such as *Max Payne* that permit an extremely rapid resumption of play. They can also create frustration, however, and sometimes boredom, when a player is forced into multiple repetitions. This is another situation in which contextual background is likely to be reduced to the more distant background, the gameplay situation taking the shape of an abstract problem to be overcome rather than one that retains much in the way of contextual depth. Games often build elements of variation into repeated attempts at missions, in an effort to maintain interest and reduce the likely alienation of the player. These can, in some cases, help to some extent to maintain contextual awareness. In *The Getaway*, for example, scripted comments made by the player-character change to a degree from one attempt at a mission component to another. The effect is to create a slightly stronger sense than would otherwise be the case of the experience being mediated by a character, in a narrative-oriented situation, rather than just an abstract task to be performed (again) by the player.

The extent to which contextual associations are in play can also vary according to the particular *mode* in which a game is played: whether on 'easy', 'normal' or 'difficult' settings, or whether cheats or strategy guides are used. In easier modes, or with the use of aids, the player can move more swiftly through the game. This might tend to increase likely attention to contextual material, creating a greater impression of progressing through the specific milieu established in an individual title, rather than becoming bogged down in more abstract tasks. The act of implementing cheats, or consulting a guide, might also have the opposite effect, however, directing attention to the dimension of gameplay-task-to-be-achieved rather than that of performing in a particular milieu.

The volume of explicit reference to contextual material can also vary extensively from one game to another, as has already been suggested in the case of narrative. Even with its highly contemporary geopolitical resonances, *Command and Conquer: Generals* is rather vague in terms of backstory, the supposed roots of its conflict not being explicitly stated. Players are, presumably, expected to bring to bear their own broad real-world familiarity with actual and potential conflict between the United States, China and the GLA. *Black Hawk Down* is much more explicit and detailed. Differences can also be found in the extent to which reminders of context are provided in the thick of the gameplay. *Command and Conquer* contains many details that highlight the real-world geopolitical context within the imaginary space of the game. The missions unfold in versions of real places, including some directly involved in recent or contemporary conflict at the time of the game's release. In one GLA mission to destroy a US air base, for example, it is notable that the base is named as Incirlik in Turkey, one of the key bases from which US planes flew in the 1991 attack on Iraq. And the first mission played by the United States sees US troops stationed outside Baghdad, much as real US troops were shortly after the release of the game; in the game-fiction, the GLA use anthrax in an attack on US troops who move into the city, the kind of anticipated use of biological weapons that was feared but failed to materialize in the real thing.

The US and GLA gameplay options of *Command and Conquer: Generals* also resonate to a significant extent with the real-world equivalent: the importance, especially, of air power to the US and the strategic use of tunnel networks to the GLA. Its exclusive access to air power often seems to give the US a considerable advantage, if not as great as the overwhelming superiority enjoyed in the real world. Playing as the GLA, the player faces the constant prospect of bombings that inflict severe damage on bases or advanced forces. These can be countered, the player learns, through the development of sufficient numbers of air defences. Playing as the US, life is sometimes made easier through the use of air power, not always involving any action on the part of the player. Towards the end of the mission set in and around Baghdad, for example, when the task is to destroy a GLA scud facility, the player might assemble a large force ready to take on a defensive line of GLA tanks. As the US force approaches, however, an automated radio call is made for air support; a fuel-air bomb is dropped, wiping out the defensive force without the player needing to lift a finger. Snippets of dialogue also act as reminders of real-world discourse, even if reduced to the status of comedy quips. 'American cowards; fight on the ground, like men', is one, related to the use of air power. Another declares: 'The arrogance of the USA cannot go unanswered.'

The contextual resonances of *Command and Conquer: Generals* are more likely to come into play than most because of their particularly contentious and contemporary nature, another factor in the gameplay/ context equation. Explicit connection with events in the forefront of public attention at the time of release is likely, on balance, to increase the extent to which associational material remains in focus. The real-historical-political background setting of *Black Hawk Down* was some years in the past when the game appeared, a factor likely to lower the impact of such resonances (earlier games in the *Command and Conquer* series include counter-factual versions of Cold War conflict between the Soviet Union and western Allies, as well as more fanciful extrapolations). The game also locks the player into the perspective of the US military, a factor likely to make it less contentious for many, except those opposed to US military interventions overseas. *Command and Conquer: Generals* combined timeliness with the strategy game convention of allowing the player to play the 'other' side; factors likely to make it more contentious, to bring associational material relatively more strongly into play, regardless of whether the 'other' side is defined here, for one player or another, as the US or the GLA. Played just before, during or immediately after the American-led attack on Iraq in 2003, the game entered an extremely heightened context in which its associational meanings might be more than usually likely to be drawn to the foreground of attention. An extended version of this kind of grabbed-from-the-headlines experience, including the same theatre of operations, was subsequently offered by the subscription-based online Kuma\War series of games, launched in 2004, providing a number of squad-based shooter games, regularly updated, based on real-world missions from very recent history.[117] Initial options included a re-enactment of the operation in July 2003 that resulted in the death of Saddam Hussein's sons, Uday and Qusay, and other anti-insurgency missions in post-invasion Afghanistan and Iraq, including response to an attack on an Iraqi police station in Fallujah that occurred only weeks before its conversion into the game. In each case, Kuma\War is designed to keep the real-world referent closely in the player's mind, mission gameplay being supplemented by news-style video sequences, text and other sources of reference in which detail is given of the events on which it is based (including comment on exactly how real-world missions have been reflected or heightened in the transition into games). Elsewhere, the more generic-seeming the associational context – the more familiar and generally uncontested a background it might constitute – the less likely it may be for its contextual material to come strongly into play. The Second World War, for example, is sufficiently distanced in time and, in most cases, sufficiently uncontentious (assumed generally to be a simple moral crusade, even if the reality was more complex), to have gained largely unproblematic generic status, as a familiar and comfortable context that can remain primarily in the background.

Another crucially important factor in determining the extent to which associational material is likely to be in play or not is the receptivity, and particular orientation, of the individual player. In the case of geopolitical or ideological context, especially, some players are far more likely to be attuned to such material than others – or more concerned about such matters, making them likely to play into the gaming situation. For the player opposed to the American interventions in Somalia or Iraq, playing *Black Hawk Down* or *Command and Conquer: Generals* is likely to be an experience in which contextual associations cannot be kept at bay. An anti-war protestor might find it difficult to bring themselves to play *Command and Conquer* as the US, especially in the spring and early summer of 2003, and might experience playing the GLA as a form of imaginary-symbolic response. A keen supporter of the attack on Iraq might be equally attuned to contextual resonances, if from an opposing perspective. For a player less informed about or exercised by the issue, many points of contextual association might be missed or ignored, in favour of a concentration on material specific to the game-genre. A contributing factor might be the familiarity of the player with the particular genre involved. To a fan of the first-person shooter genre *per se*, for example, a game such as *Black Hawk Down* might be just another variation of the formula, recognized as such, in primarily game-generic terms, the particular garb in which it is produced taking the form of relatively superficial veneer.

Player interest, familiarity and expertise can also be a factor in the potential for the mobilization of resonances provided by narrative, genre or particular franchises. To the fan of *Star Wars* or *Star Trek* a greater dimension of contextual association might be experienced in any of the many spin-offs from the two franchises – a sense of occupying a space within a particular world, within which gameplay tasks are to be performed, rather than a more neutral or game-genre-specific arena in which to do the same. The sense of the presence of a fictional character, as opposed to just the player-playing, is also likely to be stronger in such contexts. To the fan of *Buffy the Vampire Slayer*, playing as a central character in which emotion is invested in one of the *Buffy* games, their own performance – good or bad – might be measured against that associated with the character. A fan of science fiction or fantasy more generally might pay extra attention to genre-specific contextual detail found in any title that fits into those categories. Player orientations such as these can affect gameplay decisions and outcomes. Playing as a Jedi knight in the *Star Wars* tie-in game *The Phantom Menace* (1999), for example, the more highly attuned player might choose an approach based on the minimal use of force, in accordance with the Jedi code established more generally in the franchise. The result, in a particular engagement, can be different from that experienced by a player who acts in the more direct and forceful manner characteristic of many other titles in the third-person action-adventure genre to which the game belongs.

Depending on the orientation of the player, the balance between gameplay as a more abstract task and gameplay that takes on associational resonance can shift, sometimes in what might be unexpected directions. Some of the missions in *Black Hawk Down*, for example, culminate in a dash on the part of the player-character to the point at which the US troops are to be extracted. This usually entails fighting off enemy forces on the way. In the mission 'Radio Aidid', a considerable distance has to be covered, across open ground and behind the cover of buildings, before escape is achieved. Played with few if any saves left, this can be quite demanding, requiring a number of repetitions. The primary emphasis, then, tends to fall on repetitive core gameplay activity that involves disposing of numerous largely abstract figures. In this case, geopolitical-ideological context can come back into play *through* the process of abstraction. For a player sufficiently attuned to the issue, it is precisely

[handwritten marginal note:] When a story of character is strong enough the player will act as if they actually were a part of that world

the notion of having to kill hordes of abstract figures that has potential to resonate with the real world context, in which racist-ideological frameworks cast the alien 'other' as a faceless and disposable mass. This is a dynamic built strongly into the film from which the game takes its title, in which strong emotional emphasis is put on the fate of a small number of American servicemen during operations in which large numbers of enemy deaths are presented as no significant cause for concern.

If the extent to which contextual associations are in play is likely to vary according to a number of factors, as we have suggested, can any broader conclusions be made, any tendencies that override differences found from one moment of play to another? In general, the balance between gameplay and meanings created by associational context is likely to favour the former over the latter. An instance such as playing *Command and Conquer: Generals* at the height of the attack on Iraq in 2003, with contemporary resonances hard to escape, is an extreme case; and, even here, the routine, game-genre-specific demands of gameplay are often sufficient to occupy all or most of the attention of the player, even if the player is highly receptive to the contextual dimension. If gameplay activities and contextual background impose rival demands on the cognitive resources of the player, as Lindley suggests (in his case, the emphasis being on gameplay vs. narrative gestalts), something might have to give. What gives is always most likely to be richness of contextual background, for the simple reason that gameplay can proceed without any noticeable attention to background while the opposite is not the case. When it comes down to it, gameplay is more likely to operate as the primary frame that contextualizes and at times obscures extrinsic referents.

Specific contextual detail is less essential to games than basic gameplay activity, and it is often located in the background. That is not to say that it does not still perform an important role in the overall experience offered by many games, even if it might shift in and out of focus during gameplay. Familiar background, such as that provided by genre frameworks or geopolitical assumptions, establishes a ground from which gameplay can proceed, drawing on established cultural competences that do not need overtly to be activated at all moments to be 'in play' in a broader sense. The great majority of games, in fact, draw on some kind of basic real-world, human or socio-cultural context, reproducing some version of a recognizable world within which gameplay proceeds, even in the highly stylized close-to-abstract universe of a title such as *Pac-Man*. Inessential qualities of games – like inessential qualities of other media products – can also contribute significantly to the distinctive impression created by any particular title, either in the total gameplay experience itself or in establishing commercial grounds for product differentiation.

As we argued in the Introduction, games study requires the analysis of a number of different dimensions of games, including both gameplay and the meaning-creating contexts in which it is situated, even if the latter are often relegated to a secondary position at the height of the gameplaying action. The two cannot entirely be separated, even for a commentator such as Lars Konzack, for whom one is clearly privileged over the other. The semantic meanings of a game are secondary to its primary ludological structure, Konzack argues:

> The signs conveying meaning are indeed superficial, but they still help in putting the game into perspective. Two games may have exactly the same gameplay, but by having different ornamental signs and narratives (such as pictures, sounds and/or text) they convey different meanings of what is happening in the text.[118]

The term 'ornamental' implies a more dismissive attitude towards contextual material than seems to be suggested by the conclusion that different meanings are being conveyed. There is some empirical evidence to suggest that the garb in which gameplay activities is clothed can have a substantial impact on the playing experience. In one study involving children aged 11 and 12, two structurally identical games were offered to groups divided on gender lines.[119] Each was set in a different imaginary context: a quest to recover a king's crown and a quest to find bears' missing honey. The former contained overtly male-gendered characters while the latter used representations designed to be as neutral as possible. Boys performed much the same in each version but the performance of girls was greatly increased in the gender-neutral version, an outcome that suggests the potential significance of contextual background: 'Despite the constraints and demands of the task being identical in both versions of the software, the images and metaphors used to "carry" the task had a crucial bearing on girls' interaction with the software.'[120]

Many games offer gameplay tasks and activities very similar to others

[Margin annotation: A game that includes violence but portrays it as a bad thing will lead the player to regret using force, while a game that portrays the use of violence as helpful or accepted will cause a player to embrace violence]

in the same game genre, as suggested in the first part of this chapter. These activities are the most distinctive aspect of games, *as* games, and need to be identified and analyzed as such. Contextual background material might often appear to be a relatively superficial source of product differentiation. It can have considerable impact on the overall experience offered to the player, however, as indicated by the example cited above and many others outlined in this chapter. A complete study of games needs to take both levels into account, along with a number of others.[121] The pleasures offered by games are complex and multi-layered. Gameplay has its own intrinsic appeals. It might be said that these can be heightened by the location of gameplay within recognizable contexts, but this presumes that more than a very rudimentary gameplay can ever exist outside some kind of legible contextual framework. If gameplay is often to the fore, it might be argued that this is only possible as a result of the existence of the contexts – broad and more specific, crude or subtle – within which it makes any sense.

Gamescapes

Exploration and Virtual Presence in Game-Worlds

The exploration of game-worlds, and the creation of a sense of presence in the virtual on-screen environment, can be related to dimensions such as narrative and the generic resonances of games considered in the previous chapter. Exploration of game-space, as we have seen, can be a way of realizing pre-structured narrative design. The creation of impressions of presence might also increase the extent to which contextual material remains in play, generating a sense of immersion in the specific game-world as well as in more abstract gameplay tasks. Exploration and the sense of presence that results from the creation of sensory immersion in the gamescape can also be central to the accomplishment of gameplay tasks in many games. Both exploration and the creation of a sense of presence are important aspects of games in their own right, however, with their own intrinsic dynamics and appeals. Even where exploration is closely linked to the pursuit of goals or missions that advance the player through game levels, for example, it can include scope to move more freely within and through a variety of on-screen landscapes, a pleasure that can be indulged for its own sake. More than simply a background setting, the world of the game is often as much a protagonist, or even antagonist, as its inhabitants. The 'defining element' of videogames is spatiality, according to Espen

Aarseth, who argues that games are 'essentially concerned with spatial representation and negotiation',[1] issues that have often been neglected in debates between those styled as ludologists and narratologists.[2]

This chapter is organized around two principal dimensions of space in the gamescape. We start by considering the degrees of freedom offered by different games, from the most restrictive to those which offer maximum potential for spatial exploration, including consideration of issues such as modes of navigation and locomotion within the game-world. We then look at the degree to which games create for the player an impression of virtual presence within the gamescape, a mediated sense of spatial immersion within the on-screen world. Our focus will range from the large scale – the way entire game-worlds are structured spatially and rendered navigable – to closer textural detail that seeks to fabricate an impression of virtual embodiment, immediacy and presence.

Degrees of Freedom

At the most restrictive end of the spectrum are games that afford no scope for spatial exploration. In classic examples such as *Pong* (1972) and *Tetris*, a single fixed screen-space constitutes the entire game arena, within which the player has very little room for any activity other than that required by immediate response to the central game task. A modicum of freedom is provided by *Pac-Man*, but within extremely limited single-frame confines and heavily constrained by the need to avoid enemies. A greater impression of movement through space is provided by side-scrolling games, such as *Defender* (1980) and *Super Mario Brothers* (1985), but this also remains entirely restricted. Greater scope for exploration is usually associated with games that produce more detailed three-dimensional worlds through which the player-character moves, although the principal gameplay tasks of many 3D games are such as not to encourage a design that affords great scope for exploration. The main action of sports games, for example, is often confined to fixed tracks or arenas. In racing games, the track defines the path to be taken. Even in off-road rally games, such as the *Colin McRae Rally* series, the scope to venture off the track is usually very limited. Spatial restriction is also an integral feature of many beat-'em-up and wrestling games in which fighting takes place in localized arenas, keeping combatants in close proximity to one another.

In some games the player-character is carried through the game-world in much the same manner as the occupant of a theme park ride, as if on rails, hence the name given to the rail-shooter format used as the basis for games such as *Star Fox* (1993) and the arcade-style *The House of the Dead* cycle (1998–2002). On-rails type restriction is also found in some cases in other first-person shooters, including the *Medal of Honor* series (from 1999) in which the player-character is occasionally rooted to a position such as operating a machine gun fixed in the back of a truck. In many cases, lower degrees of freedom to explore are associated with older games designed for platforms with fewer processing resources than those of today. This correlation is far from absolute, however, as suggested by the fact that the rail-shooter format is still used in otherwise innovative examples such as *Rez* (2002), a third-person game in which freedom of movement is restricted to left/right and up/down motions (to acquire power-ups and shoot enemy viruses and firewalls) within a predefined trajectory through the simulated space of the interior of a computer. Restriction is also fundamental to gameplay in the updated 3D equivalents of earlier 2D platform-based games, examples such as *Super Monkey Ball* (2001), in which the player is required to keep a rolling ball (containing a monkey) on various tilting, angled and moving platforms. Restricted on-rails movement is also used in some cases to move the player from one space to another, creating the impression of the existence of a larger game-world than that which can be explored by the player while avoiding the use of a transitional cut-scene; examples include the roller-coaster-style mine-cart ride used in an early level of *American McGee's Alice* and the opening train-ride sequence of *Half-Life*.

Capacity for exploration also remains limited in many graphically rich 3D game-worlds, for at least two reasons. Resource management is one factor, even with ever-increasing processing power, because of the demands made by other game components such as graphics rendering or the implementation of particular gameplay options. The designers of *The Lord of the Rings: The Two Towers*, for example, chose to limit exploration in favour of filling the game with resource-intensive movie clips and detailed, high-resolution graphics. While the franchise lends itself to the exploratory freedom associated with a role-playing game (of which there is a version, *War of the Ring* [2003]), *The Two Towers* emphasizes the digital recreation of battle scenes from the first two films in the trilogy, into which the player-character is placed to fight through massed enemy

5. Spatial restriction as basis of gameplay: *Super Monkey Ball* (2001).

hordes or do battle with a boss. Scope for exploratory freedom is tightly constrained throughout, the emphasis of the game being on the building and honing of player-character fighting skills.

Restriction should not be understood only in negative terms, however. It is also the basis for many key gameplay effects that result from channelling the player or player-character in particular directions. Much of the fun of a restrictive game such as *Super Monkey Ball* lies precisely in manoeuvring within a spatially designated path. Restriction is also integral to games that offer greater margins for freedom of exploration. This is especially true of Juul's 'games of progression', in which the player's primary role is to realize a pre-existing structure of events.[3] Limiting and directing the movement of the player-character is essential to the creation of pleasurable effects such as fear and suspense in horror-based games, for example, or creating a linear narrative framework of some kind within which gameplay activities are situated.

Many 3D action-adventure or first-person shooter games occupy a space between the extremes of restriction and freedom to explore. A pre-set path is often combined with degrees of freedom to explore around the margins. The player-character is often required to move through and investigate the game space, to progress and also to find objects such as ammunition and health power-ups helpful or necessary to progression. This often involves periods of exploration that are not necessarily fruitful, but that may be enjoyable (or in some cases frustrating, or a balance between pleasure and frustration) in their own right. Many game spaces are designed specifically to provide scope for exploration, often including excessively convoluted structures (large or small), the primary motivation for which is to facilitate spatial investigation. Examples include what the designer Ernest Adams describes as the 'strange and wasteful design' of one building complex in *Quake*,[4] the complex cave systems encountered in the first *Tomb Raider* and the gothic grandeur of the 'old dark house' in *Clive Barker's Undying*.

Invitations to explore take various forms in such games. The tempting glint of a possibly useful object might lure players from their chosen path, a device often used in the *Tomb Raider* series. The vista of a new area glimpsed through a window or appearing between features of the immediate environment might also distract the player from a more immediate goal, especially when presented in an aesthetically striking or attractive manner – an aspect of game design considered in detail in the following chapter. A dynamic interchange is often found between concealment and revelation of space, a spatially oriented device that bears comparison with those used to structure information and events in more narrative-led media. The pay-off for successful exploration is often the revelation of new spaces that offer further challenges of the same or different kind. Inducement to explore spaces thoroughly can also make sense from a commercial perspective, increasing the amount of play that can be generated within a single gamescape. Some horror-oriented games, such as *Legacy of Kain: Soul Reaver* (1999) and *Silent Hill*, invite the player to explore the same space more than once, in different dimensions. In *Silent Hill*, a shift occurs between the worlds of the ostensibly 'ordinary, everyday' and of the fantastical nightmare. Switching from the material to the spectral plane in *Legacy of Kain* reveals new features that must be explored and investigated if the player is to gain access to certain parts of the game-world.

Encouragement to explore can also be more direct. Players of *Unreal II* are invited by a non-player character to explore the home-base spaceship when they first enter it, a small space in this case that, once mapped, becomes a base to which to return to receive missions and equipment. Cues that promote exploration are often provided, sometimes in a teasing manner, as in *American McGee's Alice*. When Alice asks one non-player character if he can help her become very small, to access a tiny entrance, she is told: 'The Fortress of Doors holds such secrets. But you will need more than a wish to get inside.' Game-worlds are often designed to obscure from view important features such as entrances to new spaces, requiring players to explore in a more than cursory manner if progress is to be made, even in games in which progression is favoured over exploration for its own sake. Exploratory deviation from primary goals is also encouraged by the inclusion of secrets, 'Easter eggs' or other pick-up materials not directly related to the main goal of the game – the exploration required to find the tarot cards planted in *Primal*, for example, some of which are quite well hidden and easily missed if players do not take time to explore the available space thoroughly. Some helpful power-ups in *Tomb Raider* are also obscurely placed, their status signalled by the on-screen message 'you have found a secret'; a similar feature is found in *Quake II* (1997). Enticements to explore can also come from out-of-game sources such as game reviews or communication with other players. The producers of *EverQuest* at one point offered the following message-hint in the game's 'tip' window: 'no peeking over the big hole in Paineel. That really is a deep, dark hole, and if you fall in, you will most likely die, and don't think your levitation will save you'; a warning, yes, but also perhaps a tantalizing invitation to the more intrepid player.

The balance between freedom and restriction varies from one game to another, as is the case with the distinction between rules and freedom in gameplay more generally. Most games can be characterized, at various levels, by the balance offered between the constraints created by rules and goals and the scope allowed for 'playing around' more freely within the game-world; between *paidea* and *ludus*, as suggested in the previous chapter. In *Half-Life*, for example, restriction predominates. The gamescape consists of seemingly endless sequences of corridors, ventilation ducts, stairwells and laboratories, through which the player is encouraged to move in a primarily linear fashion.[5] Some scope is given for *paidea*, primarily in the form of non-essential destruction of the environment, but relatively little in the way of freedom to explore. The *Tomb Raider* games, by contrast, offer larger traversable spaces in which, on balance, much more time is likely to be spent in exploration. Somewhere between the two lies *Unreal II*, which switches between what might be termed the 'corridoring' of player movement (often literally, sometimes metaphorically) in *Half-Life* and the freedom to explore of *Tomb Raider*. In some games, the player can only move a relatively short distance from the pre-structured path, often little more than a narrow passage of navigable space. Appealing vistas often exist that cannot be explored. In others, wider latitude is allowed, as in *Silent Hill 2*, in which quite large areas of the mist-shrouded town in which the game is set are open for general exploration at any one time. Early sequences require the player to explore the space available in search of clues, but the environment can also be explored for its own sake. From an industrial perspective, increasing the extent to which the game-world can freely be explored can be a useful source of product differentiation, as in the case of *Far Cry* (2004), a first-person shooter notable at the time of release for both the detail of its graphics and the freedom given to the player to move around its tropical island setting.

Limits to exploration can be characterized as 'hard' boundaries, absolute restrictions in the gameplaying arena, and 'soft' boundaries that act as temporary barriers but that can be traversed under certain conditions (a key needed to open a door, for example; hard boundaries can also be rendered soft in special circumstances such as the use of 'no-clip' cheat codes to enable the player-character to traverse otherwise solidly rendered structures). Both types of boundary can function to control the movements of players. Soft boundaries, a product of obstacles set for the player, are usually given justification through the fictional-world activities in which the player-character is involved. Hard boundaries are also given plausible motivation, as far as is possible, to avoid impressions of arbitrariness that are likely to reduce the immersive qualities of a game. This is easiest in interior settings, as Ernest Adams suggests, in which real-world spaces are also relatively small and confined by walls. In exteriors, artificial constraints are often naturalized though the use of settings such as islands or the use of impassable terrain such as mountains and swamps.[6] Ice cliffs and chain-link fences rationalize the borders of the external playing area in the first level of *The Thing*. Yawning holes in the ground that delimit the playing space of *Silent Hill 2* operate more enigmatically, signifying the destruction created by some strange force.

In *The Getaway*, the outer boundaries of the game-world are marked by realistically motivated road-closure barriers.

Hard boundaries are not always given such visual legitimation, however. In some cases the horizontal equivalent of a glass ceiling is encountered, halting player-characters in their tracks. This is a frequent occurrence in *Unreal II*, in which the player can see spaces into which movement is impossible for no reason that is given legitimation by the existence of a physical obstacle in the game-world. Where transgression of spatial limits is arbitrary, this is sometimes represented in terms that remain consistent with the particular fictional construction of the game-world. If the US military player-character strays too far from the main field of action in *Black Hawk Down*, for example, he is declared AWOL and the mission is failed. Hard perimeter boundaries can be avoided altogether in some cases. Limited, single-screen game-worlds can use a wrap-around format, in which objects leaving the screen on one side reappear on the other, a feature that dates back to the first commercial arcade game, *Computer Space* (1971).[7] The edges of game-worlds could also be extended potentially to infinity through the use of what Richard Bartle terms 'implicit terrain', generated on the fly. The content produced would not be very compelling, as Bartle suggests, as it is only likely to repeat a limited number of characteristics, 'but it removes the problem of clichéd boundaries.'[8]

Soft boundaries include the many environmental obstacles to the progress of the player-character found in games such as third-person action-adventures and first-person shooters: the precarious ledges, unstable floors and tricky jumping routines of the *Tomb Raider* series, for example. Progress through the game is also necessary to the opening up of space in strategy games such as *Civilization* and *Command and Conquer*, in which exploration is dependent on the movement of the player's resources across the game map. As with many strategy games, *Civilization* begins with most of the world in darkness, the contours of the gamescape and the deployment of rival powers revealed only gradually as the player sends figures out to explore by land or sea. The unveiling of new terrain has an appeal of its own, satisfying a sense of curiosity about what lies beyond the currently visible border, even in an example such as *Command and Conquer* in which it serves highly instrumental purposes in revealing the location of enemies, resources and key mission objectives.

A number of navigational devices are used to provide orientation for players during the process of exploration, some more overt than others. Obvious examples include the provision of maps of the gamescape, located both inside and outside the game-world itself. Maps are often available in games in which relatively large spaces are available to the player at any time. In the Paris section of *Tomb Raider: Angel of Darkness*, for example, a map within the game-world can be visited and inspected, as is also the case in some examples of the *Myst* series (from 1994), among others. An out-of-game-world map in *Silent Hill 2* shows the road layout of the zone occupied by the player, providing an important aid to navigation and indicating scope for exploration. Key buildings are identified, encouraging players to visit areas likely to prove important to progress, although access is often restricted until particular tasks have been accomplished. Out-of-game-world maps of this kind are probably more common (often because fine detail is hard to see on in-game varieties), the fiction often being (implicitly or explicitly) that they are provided to player-characters as part of their itinerary. Players can in many cases switch to a map that fills the screen. Such a move usually puts the game into 'pause' mode, permitting time for leisurely examination of the map, although in some cases, including *EverQuest*, switching to the map involves a loss of attention to ongoing events in the game-world that can be hazardous. Maps accessed outside the main space of the game can have the advantage of being more flexible than those found on location, however, often providing a range of scales from micro to macro view of the gamescape. In *Primal*, for example, players might switch from a micro view that shows features of the immediate environment to a wider view that helps them to find the way to a new area. Further out of the game-world, some games provide printed maps of the gamescape, from the single sheet fold-out maps accompanying *Grand Theft Auto III* and *Vice City* to the extensive maps that can be purchased in various printed and downloadable guides and atlases to assist players of MMORPGs such as *EverQuest*.

Smaller on-screen map inserts are provided to aid navigation in many action-adventures or shooters, often located in a corner of the game screen and showing only the immediate vicinity of the player. Game-world features such as the outlines of buildings are depicted, along with elements such as the positions of friends and enemies. Maps of this scale are geared more towards progression than free exploration, covering only restricted parts of the gamescape and oriented towards the provision of information required for onward movement through the game, including the presence in many cases of arrows signifying the direction of mission objectives. These can be arbitrary impositions on the screen, as in *Grand Theft Auto III* and *Vice City*, in which the map-insert marks features such as the character's home base, the places from which missions can be obtained and the objectives of current tasks. They are realistically motivated in some cases, however, particularly in science fiction oriented game-worlds, in which the map insert can be justified diegetically as part of a heads-up display. In the more expansive outdoor levels of *Halo*, a 'nav' point appears at times, a small icon that informs players how far in metres they are from the current objective, a device motivated by the establishment of the cyborg nature of the player-character. *The Getaway* offers a neatly integrated navigational system during driving missions, the path to be taken being signalled by vehicle indicators designating which way to turn.

Other forms of guidance can be projected onto the figure of the player-character itself. If the player of *Silent Hill 2* wanders the character too far from the main features of the gamescape, for example, written help is provided in the form of an on-screen caption, the content of which is motivated by the previous experience of the character, as in: 'This is the road I came in on. There's little point in going back.' In third-person games, in which the player-character can be seen by the player, character movements can be pre-orchestrated to indicate in certain directions at particular moments in the game. The inclination of James Sunderland's head in *Silent Hill 2* suggests that something of value lies nearby in that direction, a device also used occasionally in other games including some of the *Tomb Raider* titles and *Buffy the Vampire Slayer*. Such devices are used primarily in games that provide large traversable spaces, much of which is superfluous to progressive game tasks and in which the design of the environment itself is not overly directive. In the case of *Silent Hill 2*, the large number of directional cues of this kind is also compensation for the lack of clear visibility provided in a world enveloped in fog. Non-player characters can also function as directional guides. In *Unreal II* guidance, including advice on how to negotiate obstacles, is provided via an in-helmet radio from a female colleague in a spacecraft orbiting above. A similar device is used in one level of *Max Payne 2* (2003) and in a more aggressive and taunting form in *Manhunt* (2003). In some missions in *Vietcong* the player-character, Sgt. Steve Hawkins, is part of a patrol that includes a scout or point-man, characterized as a local trained by US advisers. The point-man, when employed, usually leads the way through gamescapes such as jungle and paddy fields.

Literal signposts within the game-world are also used to provide orientation in some cases. Signposts at junctions between paths are one of the most important sources of directional guidance in *The Elder Scrolls III: Morrowind*, for example, offering an in-game-world alternative to the option of switching into a separate map mode. As well as working more effectively to maintain a sense of immersion than the map option, signposts are also a more reliable guide to the route to be taken if the player wishes to stay on the relative safety of the beaten track, the winding nature of which means that crude compass direction – as provided in the map – does not necessarily ensure taking the correct route. In some cases, on-screen navigational aids lack any realistic motivation, any logic established by the fictional world of the game. A good example is the large directional arrow provided in *Enter the Matrix*, as mentioned in the previous chapter. Players of the game have some freedom to spend time in what might prove to be fruitless exploration of blind alleys, but they are strongly encouraged to move (rapidly) in a particular direction.

Directional guidance can also be provided by less overt devices. The locations of enemies or resource pick-ups often function as navigational crumb-trails, cueing many of the movements of the player towards a goal. These can also lead down blind alleys: the path mapped out by pursuit of an enemy or in search of a power-up might not always be the one required for progression through the game, although pickups found en-route might be important to survival. Auditory features, including the triggering of music at certain points, can also operate as pathway cues or indicate that the player is on course towards an objective. Some third-person games use predetermined shifts in camera angles and framing to indicate goal-related pathways. When the game engine of *Silent Hill 2* initiates a shift from long-shot to a mid-shot or close-up, for example, the player is informed that the area or object in question should be investigated more fully.

The scale of the gamescape, and the kind of perspective offered, also play roles in the form and function of navigational aids, as well as affecting the type and degree of exploration encouraged. Strategy games tend to provide an aerial view of the game-world, with directional cues designed to be visible at this scale. In *Black and White*, for example, key buildings in the landscape send a column of light up into the sky that can be seen when the player is operating in 'god' mode. When the point of view is scaled to that of characters on the ground, directional cues are more likely to be found in the immediate environment. These may be apparent at a glance, or be revealed only on closer inspection. In *Unreal II*, interactive features of the gamescape only become apparent as the player-character walks up to and investigates them; it is only at this point that a graphical interface appears that enables the player to perform a given action such as opening a door or pressing a switch to heal an ailing NPC. Encountering individual features of this kind for the first time provides reassurance that the player is on the right path. Some exploration is usually required in advance, before closer investigation of particular objects or surfaces. The detailed nature of the graphics of *Unreal II*, scaled dynamically to character point-of-view, encourages the player to investigate space closely; scope for such detail, in terms of processing resources, is created by the relatively narrow corridors within which the gameplay is confined, a trade-off between detail and extensiveness.

The existence of navigational devices can encourage players to explore gamescapes in ways other than those oriented towards progression through particular game tasks or the larger arc of the game itself. They tend to channel movement around the game-world, however, sending the player-character off in particular directions, even if these are not in pursuit of immediate progression. Maps can be important sources of orientation for any kind of play, including the most free-form modes of exploration. They can help to overcome the *dis*orientation that is a common feature of gameplay, particularly in relatively featureless or unvarying environments, and especially in situations in which bearings can be lost, such as after combat in a previously unvisited area in a game with a large and open terrain such as *EverQuest*. Maps can indicate areas that simply appear interesting to visit, at any given stage in a game that offers relatively large scope for movement, without the anticipation of any other immediate pay-off. Navigational devices aim to lead the player strongly in particular directions in many cases, however, even where some scope is provided for more exploratory movement. Their function very often is to encourage the player not to explore very far, which might often be an effort to disguise the extent to which scope for exploration is limited.

While following directional indicators along a relatively narrow corridor, players can agree to participate in the illusion that the surrounding environment is more navigable than is really the case; that the traversable route is part of a larger world of equally realized status. The moment the player departs from the designated path – where this is possible, especially in outdoor spaces without clearly motivated boundaries – the illusion can easily be broken. During a jungle mission in *Vietcong*, the player-character is encouraged to follow the point-man. Exploring off to the sides of the designated route, the player will quickly discover the existence of very narrow confines, in some cases motivated by rocky cliffs but often seemingly arbitrary: a wall of foliage that is impenetrable while foliage closer to the path can be negotiated. The point-man device provides contextual motivation for staying on track, however, justified by the plausible fiction that he is an expert in the terrain and in spotting signs of enemy activity. If the player-character pushes ahead of the point-man, ignoring the stipulated mode of play, he is liable to be punished by walking into a booby trap of one kind or another, as might be expected to have been the case in the real-world equivalent of jungle warfare against an often unseen enemy. Contextual association, in this case, supports the spatial limitations of the gamescape. A deliberate decision can be taken to ignore directional indicators in any game, however, to test-out or explore spatial limits for its own sake. This might be a form of *paidea* likely to take place when the player is stuck or repeating a task on numerous occasions, as relief from goal-directed play; but it might also be a pleasurable strategy in its own right.

Exploration of gamescapes can also be categorized in terms of the types of locomotion available within a game. These can determine the types of navigational cues available, as is the case with the use of vehicle indicators in *The Getaway*. Modes of locomotion are also central to the relative balance between restriction and freedom. Many games offer a range of modes of movement. The player-character's ability to run, drive, fly, jump, crawl, crouch, climb, shimmy or swim is usually tailored to the size and contours of the gamescape, permitting various types of terrain or obstacles to be traversed. This process can strengthen the sense of spatial freedom and exploratory agency, although the degree to which movement appears to be measured precisely to the shape of the gamescape does evidence the extent to which the potential for movement or exploration, in general, has been orchestrated in advance. Exactly how the player-character moves in the *Tomb Raider* games is often strictly controlled, for example. Many spaces cannot successfully be negotiated unless the player resorts to shimmying, jumping or swimming. 'Walk' mode, as opposed to the default running motion, is expressly designed to prevent Lara Croft falling from the many precarious ledges that have to be traversed. Low ledges that cannot be climbed can only be reached in *Legacy of Kain: Soul Reaver* in a flying motion achieved by the character sprouting rudimentary wings while jumping. Combinations of jumping and flying are also central to progression in games such as the *Spyro the Dragon* series (1998–2004).

In some cases the mode of locomotion itself operates as a restrictive device. This is particularly the case with the jumping manoeuvres that have to be performed in games such as *Tomb Raider*, in which very precise positioning is required if the death of Lara is to be avoided. A shift of locomotive mode is sometimes required if the player is to traverse particular soft boundaries, such as the use of a motorbike and a speed-boat in two cases in *Tomb Raider III*. Taking flight in a one-person banshee aircraft in *Halo* allows entry to new spaces situated high on cliff faces that cannot be accessed in any other manner. In these cases motorized transport is available only at certain specific points, and for particular purposes. In contrast, games such as *Grand Theft Auto III*, *Vice City* and *The Getaway* offer access to a large variety of vehicles at any one time. Part of the pleasure of these games is trying out different examples, both to explore their cityscapes and for the fun of cruising around in anything from a low-slung motorbike (*Vice City*) to a London bus (*The Getaway*). Using motorized transport is a source of pleasure in its own right, but, given the scale of the gamescapes, it is also essential to the accomplishment of missions in which time is a factor. Walking and running is also an option in these games, of course. Too slow for the efficient coverage of larger distances, locomotion on foot remains another mode in which territory can be explored, especially if a closer examination is sought. It is also essential for activities such as interacting verbally or violently with non-player characters.

Spatial constraint is often used to create or heighten emotional responses in games that offer a mixture of restriction and latitude for exploration. In games that otherwise offer relatively open spaces, close constraint might be imposed in situations such as when the player faces a boss character. Fighting difficult opponents in limited space – with no exit, no place to hide, rest or take advantage of power-ups – can create a heightened impression of urgency and danger. In *Primal*, for example, exits from the battle arena at certain points in the game are blocked until the fight is won. The elation likely to be experienced by the player when victory is achieved is partly a function of the subsequent opening up of new space. Pleasurable release follows temporary constraint, a dialectical experience typical of many of the more intense experiences of gameplay. The greater the initial constraint, and the greater the delay before success is achieved, the more potent the effect is likely to be – unless, of course, the process is protracted to the point at which the player gives up in frustration or resorts to cheats such as the implementation of 'no clip' codes. In conditions of frustration, exploration and close spatial investigation can become an intensive, localized effort to overcome a particular obstacle or to find a particular exit or entrance. Eventually gaining access to a coveted new space can create a heightened impression of player/player-character agency and of personal achievement. An oscillation between control/loss-of-control is characteristic of the experience of many games, at various levels, including the shift between spatial restriction and greater freedom of manoeuvre. It works to a particularly pronounced and generically resonant effect in horror-oriented games.

Restrictive devices are used to create a palpable sense of fear and claustrophobia in horror-related games such as the *Silent Hill*, *Resident Evil* and *Doom* series. These include enclosed spaces and/or limits to the range of vision of the player-character, the latter the result of insufficient light or, in the first two iterations of *Silent Hill*, the presence of enveloping mist. Restricted visibility imbues exploration with an increased sense of danger, the uncertainty of what might be lying ahead in wait. This can also be created by fixed, pre-determined camera positions that prevent the player from seeing areas from which threats might come, removing the freedom of looking otherwise usually provided in third-person games. Suspense can be created by pre-determined cuts to spaces other than those currently occupied by the player-character; spaces in which threats are identified that will soon be faced by the player, a device used in titles including the *Resident Evil* series and *The Thing*.

The greatest scope for exploration is usually found in role-playing games, which often create large gamescapes across which player-characters are considerably free to roam at will, the largest game-worlds being found in massively multi-player role-playing games such as *EverQuest*, *Anarchy Online* (2001) and *Star Wars Galaxies*. Exploration for its own sake can be a substantial source of the appeal of such games, along with the central process of developing the capacities of the player-character and the opportunities provided for interaction with other players. Constraints still exist, however. Exploration can be enjoyed for its own sake, but only up to a point. Player-character development and/or collaborative action with other players are essential if many parts of the game-world are to become navigable in any safety. Any of the wild regions of *EverQuest* are home to monsters that pose a threat to the novice player, for example, while the 'Planes of Power' regions are accessible only to characters of level 46 or above. The size and mode of implementation of the *EverQuest* world of Norrath is also such that it is broken up into separate zones, each of which has a limited number of points of entry and quite narrow confines, the boundaries of which often seem arbitrary – yet another set of mountains that cannot be scaled, for example. The structure is close to that of the 'rhizome', a non-hierarchical organization that can be explored in many different directions, a favoured image in poststructuralist theory used by Janet Murray as an alternative to the more progressively oriented 'story in the maze', although in Murray's case it is used in reference to hypertext fictions.[9]

The impression of uninterrupted freedom of exploration in *EverQuest* can also be hampered by the time lag that occurs when the player-character moves between one zone and another, the extent of which depends on the computing resources available to the player. This is the result of the manner in which the different geographical spaces of the game are implemented, each zone running on a separate computer as part of the cluster that comprises each of the servers on which the game can be played. In this respect *EverQuest* suffers in comparison with the less commercially successful *Asheron's Call* (from 1999), which adopted a different system of load-balancing in which responsibility for geographical areas is divided among sub-servers, the result of which is the creation of what presents itself as a more seamless world that establishes a greater sense of unencumbered freedom of movement, more akin to that found in the large but less extensive landscape of single-player RPGs such as *Morrowind*.[10] In *Morrowind*, entirely hard boundaries are found only around the outer edges of the game-world, although many soft boundaries, such as cliffs and lava streams, can only be negotiated with the aid of spells such as those creating the possibility of levitation. Gameplay strategies adapt to shortcomings such as the separation of zones in *EverQuest*, however. Pursuing monsters are escaped in the passage from one zone to another, which can prompt a strategy of embarking on dangerous combat from the relative safety of a position close to a zone boundary. Zones also offer convenient sub-divisions within which players can identify who else is playing in the same locality.

Players of games such as *EverQuest* and *Morrowind* can choose to emphasize exploration over other activities, but not absolutely. Some engagement in processes such as fighting enemies and taking on quests is required if the capabilities and equipment necessary for survival are to be obtained. If players of *EverQuest* are to continue to gain the experience points required to advance to higher levels, they are required to keep travelling farther afield. The gamescape is designed with this in mind. Players begin in an assigned home town, the location of which depends on the race of their character. As a character begins to level-up, it loses the ability to gain experience from killing monsters in the immediate home environment. New areas must be explored if further experience is to be gained. Encouragement to explore and to gain acquaintance with new spaces is provided by quests available in the early stages of the game, including missions to deliver mail to unfamiliar places; in many cases these will prove to be locations in which experience necessary for levelling-up will be available at a later date. Access to new areas is often a source of pleasure, as suggested above, although new spaces can also bring new anxieties: new types of terrain, with consonant threats and dangers to be mastered. To thrive, the player moving into a new zone needs to pace out the terrain, noting areas of safety, geographical hazards (such as chasms) and places in which monsters spawn. The in-game chat facility might be used to seek guidance from others more familiar with the space; in single-player games, a walk-through or other sources of external advice might be consulted. The learning curve is usually not too steep, however, and here, as in other aspects of gameplay, anxiety can soon turn towards a pleasurable sense of mastery. The establishment of knowledge of a given space, and how it connects with others, is often more important in large multi-player games than in single-player games, in terms of both the spatial extensiveness of MMORPGs and their group dynamics. Knowledge operates as a significant form of cultural capital in such games, demonstrating Michel Foucault's thesis that (spatial) knowledge is power.[11]

Ease of exploration does not equate unequivocally with advancement of level, however. It is easier and less hazardous, in one respect, to explore the large game-world of *EverQuest* before the player-character reaches level 10, after which character death becomes of greater consequence (the body has to be found if its possessions are to be retrieved, which is not always easy). As another player advised one of the authors: 'when you get to level 8–9, see the world, as there is no real cost involved if you die in the course of exploration then.' Certain spells also facilitate greater exploration, giving advantages in this respect to particular classes of character, one of many devices that encourages cooperation between players. 'Spirit of Wolf' enables characters to run faster, which makes exploration quicker and safer, as most monsters cannot catch characters moving at this speed. Various '(tele)porting', 'gating' and 'binding' devices also aid the process of travel, reducing the often considerable time required to journey across the world. Not all places are accessible in this way, however, and while porting can save the player from having to re-tread familiar ground it can also reduce the extent to which new terrain is actually explored en route to a destination. As Eddo Stern suggests, the use of such 'magical' portals in *EverQuest*, *Ultima Online* (from 1997) and *Asherson's Call* permits 'the condensation of a sprawling Cartesian virtual space into a compact non-Cartesian data space ... allowing nonlinear navigation that takes advantage of instantaneous Random Access Data Retrieval, a "right" many post-industrial consumers demand being accustomed to navigating freely through their CDs, DVDs, Databases, Internet sites, Hypertexts and Television channels.'[12]

Exploration looms larger in the equation in *EverQuest* and other large-scale MMORPGs than in games with more restricted geographical scope, but the design encourages a balance of activities rather than any exclusive focus of attention. It is probably the case that most players of

6. Explorable and recognizable game terrain: crossing a virtual Westminster Bridge (illegally!) in *The Getaway* (2003).

EverQuest spend more time fighting in groups and focusing on levelling-up than they do on spatial exploration for its own sake, which is more likely to be the preserve of newer players. Travel is very often undertaken to gain access to experience points or to acquire items needed in their own right or for use in spells, alchemy or trade, rather than for the sake of exploration itself. The same kind of balance is offered by games such as *Grand Theft Auto III* and *The Getaway*. Each offers a progressive, mission-based structure located within an extensively explorable contemporary urban gamescape. In *The Getaway*, players are given freedom to roam, to walk or drive around the virtual cityscape, but not at all times. In a time-based driving mission, for example, failure to keep pace or to keep on track leads to mission failure and the need to start again. During a shooting or stealth-based task it is possible simply to walk out, hijack a car and indulge in free-form driving, until or unless the actions of the player-character result in death (if the car crashes to the point that it bursts into flames) or arrest, after attracting the attentions of the police. Free-range activities such as these can be a valuable source of release from the frustrations that can arise from being stuck in or repeatedly failing a particular mission component.

Grand Theft Auto III offers a wider choice of activities: the acceptance of missions given to the player-character by crime bosses, the successful achievement of which leads to the advancement of the character, or the option to engage in freelance activities such as random acts of exploration, driving, vehicle theft or violence. Players of both *Grand Theft Auto III* and *The Getaway* also have freedom to break spatial rules such as driving on the wrong side of the road (subject to the risk of crashing) and through pedestrian and other off-road areas. *The Getaway* offers a single game-space within which soft boundary restraints come and go, depending on the nature of the latest mission. Soft boundaries play a more fixed role in *Grand Theft Auto III*, restricting access to different parts of the Liberty City setting depending on the state of the player's progress through the game. At the start, for example, access is restricted to the island of Portland, a limitation given diegetic motivation by the destruction in the opening sequence of the Callahan Bridge that leads to the next zone, Staunton Island, and signs announcing that the subway is closed. Driving onto the bridge is prevented by road-closure barriers. It is possible to walk much of the way across the bridge, but then a large and impassable fissure is encountered, a barrier justified by the fictional explosion that occurred during the previous incident on the bridge. A substantial number of missions have to be completed in Portland before access to Staunton Island is permitted. Similar boundaries in the sequel *Vice City* are experienced more arbitrarily. A number of bridges are initially closed to the player, restricting access in much the same way as in the original. Barriers prevent vehicle access but gaps exist through which it would clearly be possible to pass on foot if this were permitted; it is not possible, however, which is experienced as an unmotivated restriction.

The pleasure of exploration is closely tied up with many other features of gameplay, as we have suggested throughout this chapter so far. Different kinds of pleasure – and, in some cases, un-pleasure or frustration – can result from freedom to explore at will and the restriction that results from a more choreographed gameplay experience. Many games offer a balance between the two, seeking to give the best of both worlds: a world that players can navigate for themselves, up to a point, and one into which a number of specific activities have been orchestrated by the designers. The pleasure of exploration separated out from other aspects of gameplay, as far as this is possible, might be understood in terms similar to those that apply to spatial exploration in the real, external world. There might be a pleasure intrinsic in the fresh stimulation offered by movement into new spaces, especially when this follows extended periods of time spent in terrain that is familiar to the point of becoming stale. How we might make sense of this in broader cultural terms remains open to question. It is also worth pointing out that 'new' spaces often resemble those from which they are entered more than might be suggested by concepts such as freshness and novelty; the re-use of similar terrain features, with only slight changes, can usually be explained in terms of resource management. In some games, to move into a new space is to find one much the same as the old, or just the ringing of a few relatively minor changes (yet another series of corridors or ventilation ducts in the likes of *Half-Life*, for example, or still more warehouse-type spaces full of boxes in many shooter and action-adventure titles).

A genuine sense of freshness and difference is experienced in some cases, however: the move in *EverQuest* from a region of grassy open ground and woodland to one of desert or frozen waste, for example. It is tempting to invoke, in this context, a widespread human drive towards, or pleasure in, exploration for its own sake, as a satisfaction of curiosity or an expression of growth or restlessness. Such tendencies are liable to be culturally specific rather than universal, however. They have been expressed historically in movements such as the European exploration and colonization of the globe in earlier centuries, a process given its nearest game equivalent in titles such as *Civilization* and *Age of Empires*. Real-world imperial ventures of this kind have often sought legitimation in claims about 'natural' propensities towards geographical curiosity and expansion – qualities that have not been central to the values of all other cultures. For Henry Jenkins, in a more culturally and historically specific account, game-worlds provide virtual spaces to be mastered in place of real-world play-spaces that have often been lost as a result of development of the open spaces available to earlier generations, especially in the play-culture of boys.[13] If the appeal of spatial exploration in games is closely connected with a continual search for avenues of fresh stimulation, this might also be strongly resonant with broader processes within capitalist/consumerist culture, which relies on the constant creation of new 'desires' to be satisfied. However it might be understood in social-cultural terms, exploration remains a significant dimension of many games. It is not only the balance of exploratory freedom and restriction that shapes the player's experience of the gamescape, however. It is also important to consider the extent to which, and how, the player occupies or is given a sense of presence within the game-space.

Degrees of Presence

In some games, regardless of the scope for exploration, the player occupies a space clearly distanced and separate from the game-world. In others, the player is given an illusion of presence, of being located inside the gamescape, directly in the thick of the action. Distinctions between degrees of presence are closely correlated with differences in the visual perspective provided on the game-world. The most distanced games tend to be those that use god-like aerial perspectives. The greatest sense of presence, or sensory immersion in the gamescape, is usually provided by games that offer the first-person perspective of a figure located within the fictional world of the game. In between are games that offer a variety of third-person views, located inside the game-world but not directly through the eyes of the player-character. Impressions of presence can also differ within these broad categories, however, depending on a number of other factors.

The most distanced and abstracted view is found in management, strategy and other 'god' games, in which players have a high degree of agency – an ability to affect events in the game-world – but little sense of occupation of the fictional world itself. The player is often positioned as a character in such games – the mayor of a city in *Sim City*, the leader of a people in *Civilization*, the general in charge of an army in *Command and Conquer: Generals* – but one that remains absent from the fictional space of the on-screen world itself. Characterization is nominal, a largely transparent stand-in for the role of players themselves. A marker of the lack of in-world presence created in such games is the frequent use of an isometric perspective, one in which parallel lines remain parallel rather than disappearing to the vanishing point familiar from conventions of linear perspective. Linear perspective, often used in first- and third-person games, is oriented towards a single viewing position, a place occupied by the player that is directly related to the internal architecture of the gamescape. An isometric perspective, which creates an approximation of a 3D view (sometimes known as 2.5D), presents an impossibly 'objective' viewpoint, appropriate to that of a disembodied and god-like abstract player position.

Later versions of classic management or strategy games, such as the *Civilization* and *Sim City* series, offer increasing detailed three-dimensional graphics, including an ability in *Sim City 4* (2003) to look more closely at the cityscape, to detect signs of affluence or decline at the local level. A barrier remains, however, between the overhead view and any sense of presence at street level. The closest the player can move to ground level in *Sim City 4* is in the region of a few hundred feet up in the air. Characters from *The Sims* can be moved in to properties in *Sim City 4*, but not players or player-characters themselves. An even more detailed, close-up view can be obtained in the strategy game *Black and White*, in which players can zoom from on high to gain a point-of-view at the same level as that of the subjects of their world, a move that is functional in making it easier to target individual figures to be assigned tasks such as farming, fishing or coupling. The view is still disembodied, however, rather than creating a sustained sense of presence on the ground.

Third-person games give the player a representative clearly located inside the gamescape, an avatar that acts as the player's agent in the game. A greater sense can be established of what might be termed *being-in-the-game-world*, a phenomenological impression of presence in the gamescape. The sense of presence created by third-person games is least strong in early two-dimensional and isometric examples in which the player's source of representation is somewhat rudimentary: the abstracted chomping mouth of *Pac-Man* or the few pixels that constitute a spaceship in *Defender*. Filmed characters used in some two-dimensional games such as *Phantasmagoria* (1995) provide less abstract and more detailed characters, but a combination of static, stage-like frames and a point-and-click mode of movement creates a fragmented and distancing impression, characteristics also found in games such as the early examples of the *Myst* series and *Baldur's Gate* (1998) (further compounded in the latter case by the use of a 60 degree isometric perspective).

A far stronger sense of presence is established in fully three-dimensional third-person games, in which the player's point-of-view is often anchored directly to the movement of the player-character. A more seamless experience of the game-world is created. Graphical representation is redrawn constantly on the screen, creating an impression of continuous movement through navigable space. A player-character, by definition, acts as the player's on-screen embodiment in the gamescape. The virtual camera of third-person games is usually located behind and often slightly above the character, making the player's experience conditional on the orientation of the character. The player controls and closely follows the movements and actions of the character in the gamescape. The capabilities and limitations of the character are usually shared by the player. If the character has the ability to look around corners, so can the player, as in games such as *The Getaway* in which it is possible to lean out around environmental features to check for the presence of enemies, or to shoot before quickly springing back into cover. If the character cannot perform such manoeuvres, neither in many cases can the player. In *The Thing*, for example, other strategies have to be developed by the player to cope with the various potential threats that might lurk around corners. The first time a substantial threat is encountered the result is often the death of the avatar, the result of a form of attack for which the player is unprepared. On subsequent attempts, the player can take evasive action, knowing what to expect. A shift occurs here between the qualities of surprise (a sudden attack from an unexpected quarter) and suspense (the tension created by the player's awareness that the attack is about to be triggered).

In many cases the player can also move the camera independently of the player-character, swinging it around, past or over the top of the character to gain a different perspective on the game-world. This is often important to the achievement of gameplay activities – getting a better sense of the relative position of Lara Croft in the landscape to perform a precise jumping manoeuvre, for example – but it alters the manner in which the player's presence is established. Character-independent movement ruptures, if momentarily, the alignment of player and player-character. A more disjunctive fracture of player/player-character orientation is found in third-person games such as the *Resident Evil* series and *Dino Crisis* (1999) that use fixed camera angles not connected to the perspective of the character. In this case, the forward movement of the character can require movement of the controller in opposite directions, depending on whether a particular image frames the character from ahead or behind, a disorienting feature likely to reduce the strength of any impression of presence. Lateral movement is also affected by this reversal: when the character moves back towards the player, the controller has to be moved to the right to make the character move to the left, and vice-versa. It is possible for the camera to move between positions behind, in front or to the side of the player-character without creating this confusion, as in *Grand Theft Auto: Vice City*. If the camera starts behind the character in this case, the character can also be turned around and moved back towards the camera. To do this involves a movement forward of the control stick and a subsequent movement backwards. The point of orientation remains that of the player, rather than shifting to follow that of the character. The directional movement of the character remains wedded to a fixed forward-backward axis on the controller, as opposed to the system used in *Resident Evil* and *Dino Crisis*, in which controller-direction maps onto the movement of the character even when the character's viewpoint changes direction independently of the player.

The fact that the player's sense of being-in-the-game-world is mediated is made explicit in third-person games because the player-character can be *seen*, as an entity clearly separate from the player. The character is designed to-be-looked-at, as well as to-be-played-with, which raises a number of issues involving the manner in which characters are represented, an issue to which we return in Chapter 4. One of the pleasures of third-person games is that of watching the player-character in action, performing its moves, a process that entails a combination of distance from character (watching) and proximity (making the character perform, within its established repertoire). The act of stringing together a series of diverse movements into a smooth acrobatic sequence when playing any of the *Tomb Raider* games or *Prince of Persia: Sands of Time* (2003) provides gratifying visual proof of a player's competence.

In some cases, often temporarily, a character acts independently of the player, a loss of control that acts as a reminder of the distance between the two. This can result from the use of the navigational device considered above in which the central character looks in a particular direction according to a preordained cue designed to guide the attention of the player. A similar sense of proceedings being taken out of the hands of the player can be created when the player-character engages in conversation with a non-player character and, most obviously, when the game shifts into a pre-rendered cut scene. At times, players might experience a strong sense of being invested in, bound to or in synch with the character, but they never step fully into the character's shoes, entirely present in the gamescape. The player is not positioned as the direct agent in the game-world, a key factor in distinguishing the degree to which an impression of presence is created in third- and first-person games.

Linear perspective conventions are used in many third-person games to create the impression of a world that is centred on, and revolves around, the position of the player and/or the player-character. Perspective lines that recede to a vanishing point inside the image imply a viewing position in front of the screen. The question in third-person games is whether linear perspective is oriented towards the player or the character, or a combination of the two. Where the player's viewpoint is fixed behind (or slightly above and behind) that of the character, the two are likely to be much the same. Linear perspective is sometimes used somewhat loosely and approximately, making it hard to distinguish minor variations between two positions close to one another. In many cases, the rules of perspective are followed quite precisely, lines of convergence shifting in accordance with movement of the player-character – and thus the player's perspective – within the scene. In one sequence in *Tom Clancy's Splinter Cell* (2002), for example, the player-character is invited to cross a surface comprised of a number of planks lying mostly in parallel alongside two metal floor girders. Planks and girders are presented in linear perspective; they stretch away from the player-character, growing narrower as they recede from the viewpoint. The perspective illusion is maintained, dynamically, as the player-character is moved across. In the middle of the planks, from a position looking downwards from above, their edge lines are parallel; on the far side, looking back, they recede to a re-established vanishing point in the opposite direction from the original.

The fact that movement of the character and movement of the angle of view can be controlled separately in games such as *Splinter Cell* creates the possibility of a disjuncture in linear perspective between player and character, however. This can be seen in an immediately preceding scene in *Splinter Cell* in which the player-character, the security agent Sam Fisher, moves through an office. The office is depicted according to the conventions of linear perspective, lines such as those described by walls and the edges of desks converging towards a vanishing point. As the character moves across the room, the perspective lines readjust smoothly, maintaining the perspectival illusion centred on the view of both player and character. If the character is halted, however, and the direction of view is shifted independently – pivoting around the character but not giving his point-of-view – the linear perspective system shifts to favour the position of the player. If the character is crouched behind a desk, for instance, facing the desk, a viewpoint from behind the character will create an image in which the sides of the desk converge as they recede. If the camera is then pivoted through 90 degrees, to a position at either end of the desk, the perspective system is re-drawn to accommodate the new location of the player: the front and back edges now converge, while the sides that were converging diverge as they are traced away from the position of the character.

The third-person perspective is a strange hybrid in many respects, neither completely objective (the character, viewed from a distance, in the game-world) nor entirely subjective (the game-world experienced directly from the viewpoint of the character). Linear perspective creates an impression of orientation towards the position of both player and character, when the two are in alignment, but the position of the player is usually favoured when they are out of synch. What is presented diegetically as the subjective experience of the player-character is also projected onto the entire gamescape in some instances, in which case the player sees as if through the character's eyes, even where the player remains in view. In *American McGee's Alice*, for example, the player's perspective accords with the predetermined size (tiny, normal or large) of the character at any one time: in one level, where Alice is tiny, flowers tower above the player/character and become life-threatening; in other levels, where Alice is her normal size, they present no such hazard. Distortion of the *player's* perspective within the game-world also results when the title character of *Max Payne* is forced to take drugs or when drinking alcohol in *EverQuest*, where the perspective lengthens and bends like the effect of a fish-eye lens. Games that permit both first- and third-person modes can also create oddly mixed perspective states in some circumstances. If *Grand Theft Auto: Vice City* is played in first person, for example, it seems appropriate that droplets form on the screen when it rains, especially when driving (droplets on the screen when on foot might be a loose approximation of rain being experienced by the individual; when in a car, they are more realistically motivated as droplets on a windscreen, even if far fewer drops appear than would equate with the level of rainfall). The same happens in third person, however, which seems disjunctive:

droplets appear on the player's screen even when the player is following the car driven by the player-character. By contrast, when a spell is cast on players-characters of *EverQuest* that alters their size – a 'shrink' spell, for example – it affects the player's perspective when playing in first person mode. In third person, the player-character appears small to the player, and to others, but the perspective in which the surrounding world is drawn remains the same. A clear distinction is maintained in this case between subjective and objective points of view.

A more immediate and unambiguous centring of the gamescape on the position of the player is found in first-person games, in which the impression is given of a more directly subjective player experience *inside* the game-world. First-person games bind the player directly into the gamescape. The game-world is experienced at eye level, a viewpoint experienced as directly consonant with movements made by the player. First-person interfaces create the impression that the player can look right, left, up and down within an on-screen world that appears to envelop the player, creating a stronger illusion of presence. Hands and arms, or a weapon held by the player-character, are often visible at the lower edge of the screen, approximating the position they would occupy if the screen image really was the subjective point-of-view of the player – an innovation widely adopted in first-person shooters since being introduced in one of the first three-dimensional games, *Wolfenstein 3D*. Legs and feet can also enter the screen when kicking functions are used. The effect is to create the illusion that the game space extends beyond the screen to connect with and incorporate the bodies of players or objects in their grasp.

The different impressions of presence created in first- and third-person modes can be identified most readily in games that permit the player to move freely between one or the other, providing the opportunity for close comparison. In *EverQuest* a shift from first to third person and back again can be achieved smoothly, by the use of the mouse-wheel controller: a continuous camera movement that creates a strange impression of moving into or out-of body. A more abrupt shift is created with the use of the keyboard, which offers a wider range of viewpoint options. A simple press of a console button in *Morrowind* played on the Xbox creates a similarly striking sense of jumping more closely into, or out from, the gamescape. In this case, independent control of character movement and

7. The world of *The Elder Scrolls III: Morrowind* (2002) as experienced in
third person, behind and slightly above the player-character.

player/character look creates a number of possible orientations within
the third-person option. The default is a standard behind-and-slightly
above-character camera position. The viewing angle can also be swung
forwards, to a directly overhead view, or backwards, to a perspective
looking up at the character's crotch from a position between its legs. A
range of intermediate perspectives can also be used, including a position
immediately behind the character. From side-to-side, the view offered to
the player can describe a complete 360 degree arc around the character
in either direction. In each of these cases, the world tilts or turns around
the character in keeping with changes of perspective. Varying degrees
of presence can result from different options within the up/down axis.
The sense of presence is at its lowest when the character is viewed from
directly above. It is at its highest, in one respect, in the view upwards
from the ground, although this is so stylized as to be a distraction and
impractical for gameplay (it is impossible to see where the character is
going, its feet and the ground in front being out of view). For practical
purposes, the greatest sense of presence is created when the viewpoint is

anchored directly behind and at the same level as the character, a position from which the player gains the impression of following in the character's footsteps. This also has shortcomings for gameplay, however, as the figure of the character blocks the player's immediate view ahead, which is why a position behind-and-above is usually favoured in third person games.

In first-person mode in *Morrowind*, the impression of presence is unchanged by alterations in the direction of character view: whether up/down or from side-to-side, the perspective remains rooted in that of the character. While a sideways shift of view in third person circles *around* the character, the same movement in first person is experienced as a pivoting around *of* the player-character, rotating on the spot. Looking in any direction is experienced as directing the gaze *of* rather than *at* the character. How these shifts in perspective affect the experience of being-in-the-world-of-the-game can be illustrated more fully by the use of a concrete example. What happens, for example, when the player-character is walked through vegetation, in this case the fronds of a plant about the same height as the character? In the standard third-person behind-and-above mode, the character walks through the plant, the fronds of

8. Attacked from above: fending off an aerial assault in *Morrowind* in first-person.

which pass out of the lower edge of the screen as the virtual camera moves across it from a slightly higher position. In third-person directly behind-the character, the character passes through and the impression is given that the player follows and also passes through, foliage briefly obscuring the view of the character ahead as the player brushes past. The player's experience here is of a position inside the game-world, much the same as but separate from that of the character. In first person, vegetation again fills most of the screen, giving the player the impression of moving through the plant, although this time the experience is not one of following but of *being* the character. A similar third-person move from above-and-behind to more directly behind, and therefore more present on the ground, is available in on-foot mode in *Grand Theft Auto: Vice City*. In this case a full first person option is available only in driving mode. On foot, first person is used in a more disjunctive manner. It is available only in 'free-look' mode, when the camera can be moved sideways or up/down independently of the player-character, a process that involves an awkward sense of jumping in and out of the shoes of the player-character.

The third-person perspective creates a reduced impression of presence in games such as *Morrowind* and *Grand Theft Auto* but, as with other examples, this can be beneficial to gameplay. The first-person perspective in games lacks one important feature of human eyesight: peripheral vision. Peripheral vision, while less detailed in resolution, is highly sensitive to movement, a factor of considerable importance in activities such as hunting or travelling through terrain such as that traversed in many games, in which the player-character is subject to the possibility of unexpected attack from any quarter. In first person mode in a game such as *Morrowind*, lacking peripheral vision, it is easy to be attacked without having caught sight of the approach of the attacker. The first the player often knows of an attack from above by a pterodactyl-like cliff racer, for example, is the sound of its cry mixed with that of the impact its assault has on the player-character's health. The response of the player might be a hasty process of looking around, down and above before the exact nature and location of the assault is identified and defensive action can be taken. Equally, attack can come from creatures at ground level, close to the feet of the player-character, in this case too low and close to be within the looking-forward first-person field of vision.

The same experience can occur in many first-person games, hampering efforts to deal with sudden threats from close quarters. In third person, any such attack will immediately be visible, making this perspective sometimes a safer bet when straying into particularly hazardous territory. In *EverQuest*, for example, where six fixed perspectives are available, a high overhead view is the most secure option when the player-character is sitting to regain mana (needed to cast spells) or health, a perspective from which the player can see any potential source of attack before it is too late. Attack itself is experienced very differently in first- and third-person modes. In first person, attack is experienced, at one remove, as a personal attack on the player, the monster facing directly at the screen. A more distanced impression results in third-person, in which the player watches (as well as responding to) the monster's attack on the player-character.

Diegetic sound in 3D games is also designed to centre on the player's in-game perspective, especially in first-person games and when experienced through surround-sound speaker systems or with the use of headphones that cut out extraneous sound. In one level of *Unreal II*, for example, the player-character is in a group under attack from enemies coming from several different directions. A high level of attention to sound cues is required to judge the proximity of enemies, enabling players to choose the directions in which most effectively to focus their firepower. Spatial organization of the sound field strengthens the impression of being surrounded by the game-world and increases the sense of danger created by the game. Spatially located sound can contribute strongly to the impression of presence, one study in virtual reality environments having shown that subjects thought the quality of graphics was improved when identical images were accompanied by better quality sound.[14] Sound can also be used to create an illusion of physical presence in other ways, such as marking the footfall of player-characters as they move within the gamescape. Many games offer a footstep sound that does not alter from one type of terrain to another (and that is not always very convincing). Changes in the sound of footsteps according to the nature of the surface on which they walk can heighten the impression that the avatar occupies a world of some substance, either as an added extra or a more central aspect of gameplay strategy. The latter applies to stealth games such as *Splinter Cell*, in which the movement of the player-character in the vicinity of enemies has to take into account the level of noise made by different materials, special care having to be taken on noisy surfaces such as metal or wood. In this case, the exploitation of such effects is more likely to occur in third-person than first-person games, the former lending themselves more readily to a perspective in which the nature of surface textures is apparent to the player. In many games diegetic sound is used to provide cues that relate either to the broader environment of the game or the actions performed by players. Environmental sounds range from the context-specific atmospheric sounds of unseen frogs and other beasts in the Emerald Jungle zone at night in *EverQuest* to the ubiquitous sounds of doors opening and closing in almost any action-adventure game. Sounds that relate more closely to the action of the player-character include the noises made by particular weapons: the swooping 'whoosh' of the scythe weapon in *Undying*, the click of reloading arms in *Unreal II* or the slicing sound made by the knife in *American McGee's Alice*. Often layered with other sounds and organized according to various temporal and spatial coordinates that pivot around the place and actions of the player, sounds such as these enhance impressions of presence by adding to the textural richness of the gamescape.

First-person games typically provide some kind of representation of the player-character at the start of a game, and in cut-scenes where these are used. In many cases these are drawn from a standard range of (generally white male) figures: the ubiquitous marine, special forces operative or undercover agent and a few other variations. An exception to the rule on one count, if not others, is the use of a black male figure in *Unreal II*, while some first-person shooters such as *TimeSplitters 2* (2002) offer a choice of gender (representations of gender and race in games are considered in detail in Chapter 4). The sense that the player's experience is mediated through the character is much less evident than in third-person games, however, especially in the thick of the action. Characters tend to be relatively undeveloped, as suggested in the previous chapter, to function as constructs into which the player can step rather than overly determined figures in their own right. The first person experience is generally closer to one of immediacy than the third person, although reminders of mediation can be frequent: direct address by name to the character from non-player-characters, for example, or the abrupt interruption that occurs when the player-character dies and the player is thrown out of the game-world and into the non-diegetic routines of reloading and starting again. That the third-person perspective implies a player position further outside the gamescape is underlined by the fact that the moment of death in first-person games is often accompanied by a shift into a third-person view, a withdrawal that enables players to witness the death throes of their avatar. An unusual variation is found in *Half-Life*, in which the first-person perspective survives lethal encounters, creating the strange impression of being able to look around through the otherwise immobilized player-characters eyes, often seeing his own body parts lying strewn around the scene.

Even at the frenzied height of the action in a first-person shooter, with the emphasis on attack and survival, overt reminders of the mediated nature of the experience exist in the form of screen displays to which the player must remain attentive, as suggested in the previous chapter – crucial health and ammunition gauges, for example, and inventories of available weapons and other supplies. These can be switched off in some cases to create what is offered as a more immersive and less overtly mediated experience. *EverQuest* includes a mode in which all the on-screen information sources can be removed, which reduces the presence of markers of mediation although at the cost of limiting the player's capacity to respond to events in the game-world, itself an important source of any impression of presence. Ammunition and health gauges can also be removed from the screen in *Vietcong* to create what the manual describes as a more authentic impression of jungle warfare. *Silent Hill 2* is a rare example in which no player-related information is carried on-screen; even the state of health is embedded in the inventory system and can only be checked by a shift out of the main game-space. Information sources can also be realistically motivated within the fictional world of the game, as the heads-up display of a helmet worn by the player-character, particularly in science fiction oriented games such as *Halo* or *Metroid Prime* (2002), as suggested in the previous section. In many cases, however, whether they are overlaid directly on the image of the world or occupy a space outside, on the margins, attention to such displays impinges to some extent on any illusion of presence within the game-space.

Qualities of vision and sound are usually the most potent sources of impressions of presence in games, but a contribution can also be made by the use of haptic feedback devices that work on the sense of touch.

An ersatz impression of physical impact is quite common in the form of a shaking of the image at moments of impact on the player-character, a device that contributes to the sense of immersion in first-person games and is also used on occasion from the more distanced perspective of a strategy game, as in the case of large in-game explosions in *Command and Conquer: Generals*. A similar visual simulation of physical impact is found in shooting games in which the recoil of weapons, if not felt, can be registered as a jump of the weapon's image on-screen, with consequent impact on the aim of the next shot. Two main sources of real haptic feedback are usually distinguished: force feedback, which creates the impression of a sensation of force being imparted on muscles and tendons, and tactile feedback that stimulates nerve endings near the surface of the skin.[15] The most common forms of force feedback in games are the use of joystick or steering wheel controllers equipped with electric motors designed to provide resistance to the player's actions. This can be an effective way of increasing an impression of presence, giving some sense of real weight and mass to an experience such as pushing a racing car to its limits on a track.

Tactile feedback can also be provided through a steering wheel interface, or console controllers, in the form of vibrations designed to create the impression of driving over rough ground in a rally game or departing from the tarmac on a racetrack. The most common source of tactile feedback, however, is the vibration created by handsets such as the PlayStation 'dual-shock' controller. In many cases the effect is crude and lacking in discrimination, of only limited potency in creating an impression of presence. The same basic vibrating or pulsing effect is provided for a range of very different experiences: falling from a height, being hit by a bullet or sword, or being attacked by a monster. More effective is the use of vibration in rhythm-based games such as *Rez* and *Space Channel 5* (from 2000), in which the controller pulses in time with the music; in the former, as the player shoots larger numbers of enemies and progresses through the level, rhythm and pulse rates increase, providing a tactile connection with the world created by the game. In some cases, tactile feedback can provide a sensory impression more closely analogous to a particular on-screen activity, although this is not generally the case. In *Splinter Cell* played on the Xbox, for example, the use of a lock-pick to open doors entails a jiggling manipulation of the left stick controller in a manner not dissimilar to what might be imagined to be involved in the on-screen act, vibrations indicating the points at which each part of the lock falls into place. Similarly, to open rift gates (porting devices) and some other locks in *Primal*, players must rotate the relevant console joystick clockwise at some speed to make the two on-screen characters wind the valve that opens the gate.

The term 'presence' is often associated with concepts of virtual reality (VR), of which games are often seen as a variant, if relatively weak in the existing scale of possibilities. If typical characteristics of VR systems are navigation of 3D graphical environments, interaction, presence and immersion, many games qualify up to a point.[16] With the exception of a relatively small number of specialized VR games, in which the player is equipped with a head-mounted display that shuts off external sources of sight and sound, games fall well short of being truly immersive in terms of sensory perceptions. The illusion of presence or immersion created by contemporary game design and technology is clearly less than that provided by VR systems in which occupants experience a sense of being entirely surrounded by computer-generated environments, often able to reach out and manipulate virtual objects with an interface such as a data-glove.

A number of attempts have been made to introduce elements of VR, or quasi-VR, into domestic gaming systems, but none have so far gained more than a marginal position in the industry. The early to mid 1990s witnessed several innovations, prominent failures including Nintendo's Virtual Boy, a 32–bit table-top unit into which the player peered at 3D graphics produced in shades of red against a black background; launched for $179.99 in 1995, it was withdrawn a year later, a victim of factors including its high price, the discomfort caused by play (back and head aches especially) and what was widely judged to have been a poorly handled marketing campaign. As 'VR', the experience on offer was limited, lacking the head-tracking mechanism associated with VR systems in which a real illusion is created of occupying a space and being able to look around *within* – rather than just *into* – the virtual world. The toy company Mattel introduced the PowerGlove in 1989, priced at about $100, much-hyped at the time as a replacement controller for the Nintendo Entertainment System (NES). A small number of games were designed specifically for the PowerGlove, which enabled an image of the player's hand to appear on-screen, including *Super Glove Ball* (1990), a science-fiction themed maze game, the action of which revolved around the manipulation of floating energy balls. *Super Glove Ball* could also be played with a conventional NES controller, but some moves were only possible with the 'more intuitive control' provided by the glove, another innovation that proved short-lived.[17]

One of the main problems for home VR has been providing a sufficient level of quality at a price affordable to a big enough market to justify large-scale corporate investment in the necessary technology. Affordable head-mounted display units have been of limited quality, reducing their appeal and thus restricting the user-base to a level that does not support the investment required to upgrade the manufacturing process.[18] Virtual reality technology has gained a more substantial foothold in arcade and other location-based games. Arcades have proved a more suitable environment for VR-based games for at least two main reasons. The arcade setting is appropriate for the use of more expensive, specialist hardware of the kind that has generally been necessary for the production of VR experiences of sufficient quality to entice players. A match also exists between the economics of the arcade business and one of the chief limitations of VR systems: the fact that they are relatively uncomfortable to wear and can cause a number of physiological problems, including motion sickness and eye-strain, if used for more than short periods of time. The throughput requirements of arcade gaming require the provision of short, intense bursts of play to which VR is well suited.[19] The pleasure of domestic gaming often involves commitment to longer period of play, in which the sensory immersion provided by VR might exact too high a price not just financially but in terms of player comfort. VR also offers more obvious benefits to some types of games than others, primarily to those that offer an 'intense "in-body" experience' in first person.[20] Home VR-type systems have for many years been seen as 'the next big thing' in games technology, a promise that has yet to be realized for reasons not only of cost and/or quality.

Versions of home videogames have been imported into VR systems, most notably the experimental use of parts of *Quake II* in the CAVE virtual reality environment, one of the best-known forms of high-end VR installation, a system in which the player wearing a headset can move around freely in a room in which images are projected onto walls and floor.[21] Cheaper ways to create an impression of something closer to VR than ordinary gaming include the use of glasses that create an illusion of 3D images emerging from a computer screen, a technology that can also be used when watching television. These can be combined with joystick and force-feedback headphones (creating rumbling sensations) to provide what one supplier terms 'the ultimate low-cost Virtual Reality system', with which a number of mainstream games are said to be compatible.[22] Other head-mounted displays enable game-worlds to fill the visual field of the player, but neither of these examples includes any head-tracking component that would enable the player to look round inside the game-world. At the low-quality end of the VR spectrum, a number of free-standing games are produced, such as MGA Entertainment's 'Color FX Virtual Reality 3D Games' range, including such titles as *Space Invaders*, *Spider Man* and *The Hulk*. Each comes with its own joystick and headset, priced in the same range as a PC or console game, although with graphics of very low quality compared with those of its non-VR contemporaries. A different sense of presence within the game-world is created in the mainstream PlayStation 2 game *Eye Toy: Play* (2003), in which a video camera (an inexpensive peripheral that does not increase the cost of the game) is used to project an *image* of the player into the game-world. Players look at their own images, inside the screen, using real bodily motions (primarily of arms and hands) to move aspects of the image in time to perform whatever actions are required by the various sub-games provided in the package. The player is taken inside the game, in one respect, but only in the form of a double controlled from a position clearly located separately outside.

A scale can be suggested that runs from real world experience through a variety of media, according to the degree to which an illusion of presence can be created. High-end VR would lie towards the real-world end of the scale, although a considerable distance from a convincing illusion of anything like presence in a real environment; VR has generally failed to meet many of the high expectations set by enthusiastic predictions of the later 1980s and early 1990s. Contemporary games occupy a position somewhere between virtual reality systems, including those used in higher-end VR games, and non-interactive screen media such as large-format cinema, conventional cinema, widescreen and conventional television. Impressions of presence can also be created imaginatively by more traditional media, including novels and plays, and in the production of immersive image-spaces that date back to antiquity in examples such as Egyptian tombs, Roman fresco rooms, Renaissance and Baroque perspectival-illusion spaces and 19th century panoramas.[23]

The videogame player occupies what Jesper Juul terms 'a twilight zone where he/she is both an empirical subject outside the game *and* undertakes a role inside the game",[24] experiencing what Barry Atkins terms '*half*-life' (after the game of that title).[25] This is a position somewhere between the real external world and the imagined worlds of representational forms such as literature and cinema in which the reader/viewer has no constitutive involvement in the action. How can this position be understood? One approach is to suggest a state of being-in-the-game-world that can be distinguished both from being-in-the-world, as understood by philosophers such as Martin Heidegger and Maurice Merleau-Ponty, and from the acts of projection into the fictional world involved in the consumption of texts such as books and films. Being-in-the-world, for Heidegger, Alec McHoul suggests, involves the treatment of objects *as*; that is to say, an object is treated *as* the particular thing it is.[26] 'Against this actual', McHoul suggests, 'we might pose the virtual. Here, equipment becomes intangible and its characteristic manifestations would be in art, fiction, poetry, and all the technologies of the imaginary whose mode of understanding is understanding "as if".'[27] This division does not quite apply, McHoul suggests, to what he terms 'cyberculture', which includes virtual reality and videogames among other computer-mediated forms: 'Rather the cyber's unique equipmentality flick(er)s or hovers between the actual and the virtual, between the "as" and the "as if".'

McHoul's argument applies more obviously to VR technologies, the main example he uses in illustration, than to conventional games. If he uses a VR headset and glove to play a version of golf, for example, 'my actual arm moves as it would when addressing an actual golfball on an actual course.' In this case, there is no actual ball or course: 'That is, I address the ball *as* a ball but it has its being "as if". The ensemble or gestalt that *is* the game of "virtual" golf actually circulates at rapid speed between the actual and the virtual.'[28] The extent to which the same can be said of playing games would seem to depend on how far gameplay activities are physically analogous to their real-world equivalents. Using a steering wheel interface in a driving game would qualify, for example, as would the use of a joystick in a flying game or a light-gun in a shooting game: the arms steer *as* they would when driving a real car, even if the car and the surface on which it is driven are entirely virtual; the joystick is moved up/down and from side-to-side in the same manner *as* the joystick of a real aircraft; the gun is pointed at a target and the trigger pressed *as* would be the case in reality, even if bullet and target exist only in the world of the game. Much remains missing in these examples, of course, especially in dimensions such as full-body haptic feedback: a steering wheel might provide some force feedback to the arms, but not the g-forces experienced by driving a real car at speed or occupying an expensive professional racing car simulator; the same can be said of a joystick controller used in anything other than a full-scale aircraft simulator.

More standardized controllers such as keyboard/mouse and console pad generally offer increasingly stylized and abstracted actions in which the *as* quotient is reduced. Steering a car with an analogue console joystick is less like the action performed with a wheel, although the device is still moved in the same direction as that created on-screen; using a keyboard and/or mouse even less so (although keyboard controls also contain some directional motivation: the use of arrow keys, or even just the fact that the 'w' key used to move forward is ahead of the 's' used to move backward and that 'a' and 'd' to each side are used to move in the respective direction). An interesting exception is the use of standard PC controls in *UpLink* (2001), a game in which the player takes the role of a computer hacker, an imaginary character who uses interface technology precisely the same as that on which the game itself is played. The control system used by the game is, in this case, entirely motivated by the diegetic context, creating a greater than usual slippage between *as* and *as if*; the player often acts exactly *as* imagined in the fiction – almost *as if* the game were not a fiction, but a subtle disguise for real covert hacking of the kind around which the game revolves.

Game players are required to act *as* their imaginary real-world equivalents in ways other than those involving the nature of the physical activity before the screen, however. If players/characters become lost during exploration, for example, the physical actions involved in trying to find their way around may not map very closely onto those that would be involved in an equivalent real world situation. Moving around with a combination of keyboard and mouse or the dual control sticks of a joypad is only loosely analogous to the activity of wandering around in the world. The activities represented might be of a similar nature, however. Both are likely to involve a search for recognizable landmarks or other sources of orientation. Both might include consulting a map of some kind (physical in both cases, in some instances, in games for which printed maps or atlases are available; or physical in one case and virtual in the other). Both involve the experience of *really* being lost and/or stuck in their own realm, even if one might have potentially more serious consequences than the other. To be lost in the gamescape is not the same as being lost in the real world, but it shares some characteristics of the real-world experience. The same cannot usually be said of watching or reading about a character being lost in a film or a book: viewers of *The Blair Witch Project* (1999) might empathize with the characters, but are not themselves lost, a quality that would result only in the case of a text with a labyrinthine structure of its own.

A similar point can be made about the experience (or threat) of death in the game-world. The death of a player-character is, clearly, not remotely akin to the death of the player. It can have real consequences of its own, however, of a kind that has no equivalent in fictional media such as literature or cinema. There can be a real price to pay, which can amount to hours or days of effort in a single-player action-adventure game in which regular 'save' points are not available. Lengthy sequences of difficult activity might have to be repeated for the player-character to reach the position at which it was previously killed. The degree to which 'save' points are offered – or to which the player can 'quick-save' at will – can be a factor in the degree of pull exerted on the player by the diegetic illusion; the extent to which something is really at stake during sequences of hazardous in-game activity, *as* it would be in the real-world equivalent, even if the nature of what is at stake in the game is of a much lower order of magnitude. Quick-save regimes reduce considerably the consequences of the player-character's actions. In multi-player online role-playing games, the stakes can be considerably higher, involving the potential loss of hard-earned equipment as well as experience points. The issue of 'permanent death' is a contentious one, 'the single most controversial subject in virtual worlds', according to the design consultant Richard Bartle.[29] Where players may have invested hundreds of hours in games, over periods of months or years, the prospect of permanent death is a much more serious one, to the extent that permanent death is a rarity and is, as Bartle suggests, the unusual and marked term, the norm being some form of non-permanent death from which various forms of resurrection are possible.

For McHoul, what is involved in the mixing of *as* and *as if* is a distinct mode of 'cyberbeing'. In the case of games, at least, this seems a rather grand term, implying a qualitatively different kind of existence rather than a playful experience that can be understood as a specific component of the broader category of normal being-in-the-world. How we understand this might depend on how far the experience of virtual worlds is seen as one that has a real transformational power. Bartle claims, for example, that 'the fundamental, critical, absolutely core point' of virtual worlds such as those found in multi-player online games is the development of the player's identity.[30] Such games do provide scope for the exploration of identity: space to try out forms of behaviour that players might be reluctant to risk in the external world, and that might, once experienced in the virtual, lead to changes in their real-world behaviour. To argue that this is the core point of such games is a large assumption, however, for which no evidence is produced. Being-in-the-game-world might equally well be understood as a *confection*, a pleasurable illusion more than a shift into another dimension of being or a catalyst to the development of personal identity. Part of the pleasure in many cases, for example, might be the pleasurable illusion of being-in-the-world-of-another-fictional-space: being-in-the-world of a familiar movie, movie franchise or TV show, for example. One of the appeals of many games is the capacity they offer the player to explore and take on the role of an active agent within such fictional worlds, either those of particular brands or broader generic regimes such as those considered in Chapter 1. In such cases another stage of removal is involved from any notion of activity in a virtual equivalent of the real world. The virtual world of the gamescape is a version of a world that is already fictional-imaginary. If *The Getaway* produces a detailed simulation of real-world London streets, for example, the experience offered by the game is that of inhabiting the fictional milieu of a gangster epic set in the streets of London as much as or more than inhabiting a version of London itself.

The creation of impressions of presence or immersion is not only dependent on factors relating to sensory perception such as those on which the first part of this section has concentrated. If games create a relatively weak sense of virtual embodiment in the gamescape – or if some games create a weaker sense than others – compensation can be found in other dimensions. Terms such as presence and immersion are often used in vague and sometimes interchangeable ways, as Alison McMahan suggests, that fail to discriminate between different dimensions of the overall gameplaying experience.[31] A distinction needs to be made between perceptual immersion – limited by the technological basis of conventional desktop computer or console/television games, and in commercial arcade settings – and psychological immersion in gameplay activities of the kind examined in the previous chapter. One involves immersion in the *game-world*, the other immersion in the *game* itself (the latter might best be described as 'absorption' to make clear the difference between the two). The distinction is an important one, particularly when it comes to understanding the overlapping, multidimensional nature of many gameplay experiences. A move out of first-person perspective such as those described above in *Morrowind* and *EverQuest* might diminish the relative impression of perceptual immersion, but the gameplay motivation is sufficiently strong to keep the player bound into the game at the psychological level. The same goes for the division of attention between images from within the fictional game-world and those imposed in the form of health bars or other gameplay-specific displays that are not given diegetic motivation. Gameplay activities are likely to be as immersive – very often more so – than devices designed to create an impression of sensory immersion or presence. Psychological immersion can be very strong even where no great sense of sensory presence is involved, as is often the case in management and strategy games of the kind discussed at the start of this section. A number of factors other than those related to impressions of sensory presence, including compelling and well-balanced gameplay activities, can contribute to the extent to which players experience a state of being immersively 'wrapped-up' in a game.

Other factors include what Matthew Lombard and Theresa Ditton, in a review of studies of presence across a range of media, term 'content variables' and 'media-user variables'.[32] Content variables in games include gameplay activities and elements such as the degree of surface realism with which the gamescape is rendered, but also, and often more importantly than realism, the degree of consistency with which the game-world is constructed and how the player can act in and act on the virtual environment. Questions of graphical realism are considered in Chapter 3. Inconsistency is one of the greatest threats to the creation of impressions of either immersion or presence. All players are aware, at some level, that the gamescape is an artificially constructed and limited environment. Players are generally very happy, and willing, to 'suspend disbelief', however, to allow themselves to be taken in by the illusion that the worlds in which they play are more than just entirely arbitrary constructs. Inconsistency of design or functionality is one of the quickest ways to shatter the illusion, an issue to which we return in the following chapter. Inconsistency tends to remind players of the constructed nature of the virtual world, although this tendency can be overstated: a gestalt principle, a psychological propensity to fill-in missing details to make things appear whole, might also be at work in visual and cognitive terms, enabling players to gloss over the gaps.

A sense of agency in the game-world – the ability to affect its contents in ways at least to some extent approximate to the equivalent in the real world – can be a major source of impressions of embodied presence, especially as games are played in the present tense, which gives them a temporal sense of immediacy. Expressions of agency may be gameplay/goal-directed – puzzle-solving, shooting/killing, interacting with weapons, equipment, obstacles or gateways – or free-form and *paidea*-oriented, such as the capacity to shoot up the environment of *Half-Life* cited in Chapter 1. Agency can only ever be limited, however, and much of its scope is usually directed towards the performance of particular gameplay tasks. In many examples of interactive media a conflict exists between interactivity and the creation of an impression of presence in the fictional world, a major theme of Marie-Laure Ryan's study *Narrative as Virtual Reality*. In a hypertext fiction or an interactive movie on DVD, for example, the action stops and any immersive spell is broken at points where the reader/viewer is given a menu from which a choice of options is to be selected. In virtual reality, Ryan suggest, interactivity, experienced as being performed inside the virtual world, tends to reinforce the impression of presence.[33] The situation of videogames is somewhere in between the two. Interactivity via the actions of the player-character has the potential to increase the illusion of presence, but also to reduce

it – depending on the extent to which it is or is not constrained by
excessively arbitrary limitations or inconsistencies. Agency is not always
associated with the creation of presence, however, as in simulation games
such as *SimCity*, in which a high degree of agency is combined with a
low degree of presence.

Content variables relevant to the creation of impressions of presence
include the design of interfaces, as was suggested in the previous chapter.
Interfaces disguised as parts of the in-game-world are generally more
effective in this regard. Non-player characters are often little more than
interface conceits, as Bartle suggests, but this can be an effective way of
clothing what would otherwise be abstract gameplay devices in garb
appropriate to the diegetic environment. Examples include non-player
characters in role-playing games from which player-characters buy and
sell items, training or obtain quests. Guard non-player characters, such
as those found in *EverQuest*, are ways of creating motivation for the
enforcement of gameplay rules such as preventing players from attacking
one another within particular parts of the gamescape.[34]

Media-user variables include important factors such as the degree
to which individual players are willing to suspend disbelief, not to be
distracted by elements that might reduce the impression of presence,
and the player's familiarity with the medium.[35] An experienced player,
familiar with the nuances and full scope of a game or a game-genre,
might also be expected to get more 'into', and get more out of, any
particular title. What might appear to be distracting limitations to others
might be more readily accepted as part of the conventional repertoire.
The social dimension of gameplay can also contribute significantly to
its immersive and engaging qualities, especially in multi-player online
games that create what Lisbeth Klastrup terms a virtual social world,
'both something imagined, something "fake" (something pretending to
be real, as we know it from realistic fiction) and something lived in, an
actualized reality we create, inhabit and share with other people …'[36]
EverQuest was designed to encourage players to band together regularly
in small groups – different character-class capacities complementing
one another and group action necessary to the performance of many
activities – a factor that differentiated it from others available at the time
of its launch in 1999. 'Whatever the reasons people had for starting to
play the game', Bartle suggests, 'they continued to play because of the

other people they had met there.'[37] The world may be virtual, but bonds formed between players can become very real; the result, in this case, as Bartle puts it, is not so much a move further 'into' the virtual world as a move in the other direction: 'Immersion puts the real world into the virtual; community puts the virtual world into the real.'[38]

A sense of participation is central to the experience of all fictional representations, according to Kendall Walton, including media such as books, paintings, plays and films. They all entail a process of pretence, a game of make-believe in the reality of the represented objects. Walton's theory of representation is particularly interesting in the context of videogames given the importance he attributes to similarities with the processes involved in the playing of children's games. 'In order to understand paintings, plays, films, and novels', he suggests, 'we must first look at dolls, hobbyhorses, toy trucks, and teddy bears. The activities in which representative works of art are embedded and which give them their point are best seen as continuous with children's games of make-believe.'[39] A minimal condition for participation in a game of make-believe is considering oneself constrained by the rules of the game. If participation in children's games of make-believe is physical, the emphasis in representational forms shifts towards the psychological.[40] Videogames might, again, occupy a space in between, where the participation of the player is physical, but at one or two removes, and also psychological. The experience of participation, for Walton, is one that occurs in the first person, even when participation is psychological rather than physical. The viewer psychologically involved in a horror film 'does not imagine *that* he is afraid; he imagines *being* afraid, and he imagines this *from the inside*.'[41]

A psychological sense of presence can be created, in other words, without the need for sensory immersion (although Walton does not document the precise formal devices used by films to create or reinforce such effects). This underlines the points we have made above about the variety of ways in which impressions of spatial presence or other kinds of immersion can be created in games. It also suggests that the first person/third person opposition might not always be as strong as it first seems. We can imagine ourselves in first or third person modes, Walton suggests; in daydreams, for example, where we might imagine doing something – his example is hitting a home run – or watching ourselves doing something from an exterior position.[42] We can also imagine ourselves occupying the place of the third-person player-character, even if we seem more removed from the character's perspective than is the case in first person, a fact that accounts for the acceptance of devices such as the examples cited earlier in which the perspective of the third-person player-character is projected onto the entire gamescape. A similar conception is found in psychoanalytic conceptions of fantasy. In the essay 'A Child is Being Beaten,' Freud argues that fantasy scenarios have multiple points of entry: we can be either the child being beaten, the beater or we can look on in a kind of blurred amalgamation of the two positions.[43] Cora Kaplan and Elizabeth Cowie apply this notion to more public, textual forms of fantasy such as films and literature.[44] In fantasy, Cowie argues, the subject is 'present or presented through the very form of organization, composition, of the scene.'[45] First-person (present) or third-person (represented) perspective is, in this account, incidental to the degree of involvement experienced in a given scenario: 'we enter the fantasy-structure and identify *as if* it were our own'.[46] The fact that many games offer a range of points-of-view suggests that players are capable of accommodating shifts in perspective with some ease.

Conclusion

Degrees of freedom of exploration and the extent to which an illusion is created of presence in the game-world are significant aspects of games, although they need to be understood in the context of other gameplay activities and attributes. A negative correlation might be expected to exist between the two, other factors being equal, if only because of the resource demands imposed by both extensive scope for exploration and the creation of a stronger sense of embodied presence. This is not necessarily the case, however, given the limited extent to which most games invest in anything more than a relatively minimal degree of sensory immersion. The fact that games such as *EverQuest* and *Morrowind* can be experienced in either first- or third-person modes, while offering large-scale scope for free exploration, suggests that the greater degree of presence created in first person is, in these cases and many others, a neutral factor in terms of data and processing resources. A stronger investment in sensory embodiment – extensive use of more discriminating haptic interfaces, for example – might alter the equation, but this is not generally the case in contemporary games. Freedom of exploration can certainly be a factor in increasing the sense of presence created by a game, reducing at least one form of what can seem like arbitrary restriction. Games that create stronger impressions of presence are not necessarily those in which exploration looms largest, however, although they may make exploration a relatively less abstract-seeming experience.

3

Realism, Spectacle, Sensation

Qualities such as striking imagery and sound are important sources of pleasure in videogames, as are the sensations and intensities of experience offered by engagement in many gameplay tasks. The qualities of graphical reproduction on-screen, combined with sound effects, can play a significant part in the establishment of many of the dimensions of games already examined in this book. Relatively higher-quality graphical resolution and design/reproduction of sound can increase the extent to which narrative, generic or other contextual frameworks are likely to be in play, giving a stronger sense of the location of gameplay within a particular, realized milieu. They can also increase the pleasures of exploration or the extent to which a sense of presence is created. The above effects might be the case where imagery creates an impression of greater 'realism' (a relatively more convincing impression of the surface textures of the world) or more spectacular vistas (whether these are themselves presented as broadly recognizable/'realistic', the product of fantasy, or a combination of the two). Intensities of engagement can have similarly supportive effects, sometimes increasing the impression of occupying a particular gamescape of one variety or another. Qualities such as realism, spectacle and sensation also offer pleasures in their own right, however, which might be equally capable of working against other forms of immersion in the world on-screen.

Audio-visual qualities have been dismissed by some commentators as essentially cosmetic aspects of games. For the designer Chris Crawford, for example, graphics, animation and sound are necessary but *supporting* elements, secondary to the primary dimension of interactivity. We would agree that dimensions such as realism and spectacle are usually less important, ultimately, than compelling and absorbing gameplay – although the same might not be said of intensity of sensation, which can be closely coupled with the performance of core gameplay activities. The appeal of qualities such as realism and spectacle should not be ignored, even if they are considered to be secondary to other aspects of the gameplay experience. To be secondary is not to be of *no* consequence, as we argued in Chapter 1, and secondary factors might also contribute quite significantly to the manner in which primary gameplay activities are experienced. It is also necessary to consider different dimensions of concepts such as realism, when applied to games rather than other media. We consider realism in this chapter in two main senses. First, in the sense suggested above: realism in terms of certain qualities of graphical representation (along with sound design) on-screen; realism according to an *aesthetic* definition. Second, though, we consider realism at the level of *functionality* within games: realism in the sense of on-screen action and interaction; the extent to which the world on-screen acts and responds (rather than visually or aurally resembles) something like its real or imagined equivalent in the world outside.

Realism

The history of videogames is one that has been dominated, on one level, by investments in increasing realism, at the level of graphical representation and allied effects. Successive generations of games and game platforms have been sold on the basis of the creation of on-screen worlds that bear greater resemblance to the textures of the real world – or, in many cases, the textures of other forms of representation that stake claims to the creation of impressions of verisimilitude, a point to which we return below. Quality of graphics, resulting from increases in processing capacity, has been a major factor in the various 'console wars' that have raged since the 1980s, including the competition between console platforms and

PCs. An early breakthrough was the development of Nintendo's 8-bit Famicom (Family Computer), launched in Japan in 1984, followed by the Nintendo Entertainment System (NES), the modified version developed for the American market.[1] Each offered graphics of a quality superior to its predecessors. In a move that was to set the stage for subsequent developments, the NES was leapfrogged by the 16-bit Sega Genesis, which created 'bigger animated characters, better backgrounds, faster play, and higher-quality sound.'[2] The PC then entered the increasingly competitive fray, along with following generations of consoles, each sold to a large extent on their capacity for the provision of improved graphics. Other factors have also played an important part in this process, of course. Greater processing and storage capacity also creates scope for new developments in gameplay, and for innovations such as the capability for console online play introduced by the Xbox.

Advancements in technology alone have never been sufficient to guarantee success, as demonstrated in the 1990s by the failure of the then state-of-the-art consoles, the Atari Jaguar and Trip Hawkins' 3DO. The dominance gained, at various stages, by companies such as Nintendo, Sega and Sony was the product not just of innovations in technology, but also in marketing, cultural positioning and the provision of a sufficient supply of appealing games.[3] That said, it remains true that the promise of improved qualities of sound and visuals – and especially the latter – has been a major component in the engine that has driven forward developments in games platforms; probably the single most important – or, at least, most prominent – factor. As far as the PC is concerned, it is widely accepted that the demands of gaming play a central role in the advance of the technology as a whole, gameplaying being one of the few activities that requires the higher-end capabilities – especially in graphics cards – of most domestic machines. Improvements in gameplay might result from the purchase of new PCs or consoles, but these are generally less immediately obvious and less easy to feature in the marketing of both games and platforms. Improved graphics lend themselves more readily to such processes, creating eye-catching impressions that can easily be translated into promotional artwork.

Much the same goes for many games themselves. A common feature of sequels to popular titles such as *Colin McRae Rally*, *Tomb Raider* and *Resident Evil* is that sound and visual qualities are improved, usually in the direction towards a greater impression of verisimilitude, to a larger extent than basic gameplay is developed. As is often the case with new-generation consoles or PC graphics cards, increased realism tends to be emphasized in marketing. For *Tomb Raider: Angel of Darkness*, for example, a press release boasts that: 'Fans of the world's most famous cyber-babe have something to get really excited about – she can now be seen in 10 times more detail! The new Lara is made up of over 5,000 polygons as opposed to just 500 in previous games.'[4]

For many commentators, the emphasis put on graphics in the marketing process has had a damaging effect on games, distracting from the core business of providing satisfying gameplay. In the case of *Angel of Darkness*, for example, many gamers found the gameplay to be less compelling than that of earlier iterations, however much improved the graphics. As designers Andrew Rollings and Ernest Adams put it: 'A lot of nostalgic gamers have called for a return to the values of the "golden age" of gaming – the 1980s, when hardware limitations forced developers to concentrate on gameplay.'[5] Core gameplay activities are, arguably, relatively more important in games produced with limited resources – whether in the past or today, for hand-held consoles or non-specialist platforms such as mobile phones or PDAs – where there is little to disguise or supplement any gameplay shortcomings. Given its typical prominence in the marketing process, and the proportion of the development budget for which it accounts, there can be a temptation to rely excessively on appearances. This is likely to have increased in the move, since the early 1990s, towards a highly competitive emphasis on resource-heavy 'photorealism' in games, an effort to produce images that aspire to the higher resolution qualities of still photography, film or television.[6] A significant part of this process was the move from the blocky features of early 2D games to the closer-grained, texture-mapped, multi-polygon constituents of 3D graphics. Almost everyone who writes on this subject has examples to cite of updated 3D versions of earlier games in which gameplay suffered, directly, from the transition to a more fully realized, less abstract appearance (cases cited by Rollings and Adams, for example, include *Robotron* and *Centipede* [initial versions, both 1982], although they also point to instances in which updates have been more successful in maintaining the old game mechanic).[7] The creation of more realistic graphical environments remains an issue of central interest to those working at the most technical end of games production, however, even if for specific reasons of their own. Commercial considerations do much to shape the environment in which they work, but an investment in graphical realism for figures such as the game-engine designer John Carmack can be located in the intrinsic satisfaction of finding elegant solutions to technical challenges.

It is not surprising that many gamers and designers are suspicious of the emphasis often put on 'cosmetic' issues such as graphics quality, with its often concomitant emphasis on increased realism, especially given the extent to which this is seen as a marketing-led phenomenon. Such suspicions risk an overstatement of the case, however, a rejection of the importance of graphics that fails to attend to the considerable contribution they can make to the overall gaming experience. Graphics are one of the constitutive elements of the 'videogame' as a distinct entity, whatever relative importance they are accorded; the precise *qualities* of the graphics on offer, generally or in particular examples, have, therefore, to be accorded some significance if a full understanding of the form is to be achieved.[8] Debates on this subject have a shape similar to disputes about the relative merits of gameplay and narrative considered in Chapter 1: an insistence, in some cases, on the 'purity' of core gameplay mechanics, as the essence of games, as opposed to their 'corruption', as it were, by undue emphasis on secondary qualities associated with other media forms. Some designers, such as Crawford, seem concerned primarily with creating games with lasting appeal of the kind found in long-term classics such as Go and Chess, in which case qualities such as level of graphical fidelity are likely to be of secondary importance. The business side of the game industry tends to be committed to a process of constant technological (if not other forms of) innovation, however, founded largely on appeal that is more ephemeral in nature, subject to a constant process of upgrading and reiteration in which improvements at the level of appearances tend to figure largely in the marketing equation. Our argument, as previously established, is that games and the experience of gameplay are complex and multidimensional. Dimensions such as narrative or, in this case, aspirations towards graphical photorealism, or the other qualities considered below, contribute to the total effect offered to players – even if or where they are, ultimately, considered to be secondary. They certainly shape the nature of the games that are available to play, if only for reasons of commercial convenience, a factor that cannot be ignored, even if some commentators believe it should not be the case. They can also significantly shape the experience of the player – again, whether or not that is always regarded as 'desirable'. Our aim in this book is not to be *prescriptive* – arguing what 'should' be the case, or decrying what some might see as shortcomings – but to analyze existing games and trends and the kinds of experiences they offer.

What, then, is offered to the gameplay experience by graphical and other qualities that stake claims towards greater realism? Why should a greater impression of realism be attractive, and how importantly is it likely to figure in the overall gameplay experience? The degree to which games create such impressions certainly seems to figure as a significant factor for many gameplayers, as well as to industry marketers. As Mark Wolf suggests, games graphics 'were, and to a large extent still are, the main criteria by which advancing videogame technology is benchmarked by the buying public'.[9] It is, perhaps, somewhat patronizing to dismiss this dimension of the experience of many consumers of game software and hardware.

Graphics that offer more closely grained or photorealistic impressions of the world on-screen can increase – at least relatively – the resonance of the experience: the sense of acting within a more realized virtual environment, of inhabiting a 'world'. This effect is not easy to pin down, however, and is likely to be highly variable. A range of factors might be suggested that make it more or less likely that such qualities figure importantly or substantially in the overall gameplaying experience, factors broadly similar to those considered in Chapter 1 in relation to the relative importance of background contextual material such as narrative, genre or ideological resonances. The degree of photorealism achieved by graphics is more likely to figure strongly in some types of games than in others. It might be expected, all else being equal, to be more important in games that are less fast and furious, in which more time is available for detailed consideration or exploration of the on-screen world (hence the prominent place of *Myst* and its sequels in the historical record of games celebrated for the realistic and/or spectacular quality of their graphics). It is especially more likely to be a prominent dimension of the experience in the earlier stages of new games, or initial titles supplied for a new platform. Improvements in qualities such as realistic visual textures and sounds offer a novelty effect that can be appealing in its own right, but that is also likely to wane over time. We quite quickly become accustomed to a new level of textural detail, taking it for granted and becoming habituated to what it offers – at which point it is, generally, more likely to recede relatively into the background. As in the case of narrative, genre and other contextual material, the admiration of the qualities of graphics is also less likely to figure during the most frenetic periods of gameplay, in which insufficient cognitive resources might be left for the appreciation of the aesthetic dimension. The orientation of the individual player is another important factor. So-called 'hard-core' gamers, extremely familiar with a particular genre, are probably less likely to be seduced by improvements in graphics and more concerned with getting to the 'stripped-down' basics of core gameplay mechanisms or innovations at this level. More casual players are, on balance, more likely to be impressed by new generations of graphical realism and texture fidelity. This association with the mass-market gamer, rather than the core enthusiast, is one of the factors that has contributed to the dismissal, by some, of the importance of the 'graphics quality' component of games, a potentially somewhat elitist approach.

The question remains, though: what, exactly, is the basis of the appeal of graphics and other effects sold and experienced as 'more realistic'? This might be divided into two parts. First, pleasures might result from the sheer quality of graphical resolution alone, in its own right, an issue that overlaps into the subject of the second section of this chapter, where we consider the spectacular qualities offered by some games. Second, improved graphics quality can contribute directly to gameplay itself, rather than remaining an essentially secondary phenomenon, a point that is often overlooked.

A noticeable improvement in degrees of resolution – as, for example, in direct comparison between one iteration of a game and its successor – can create a sense of greater visual plenitude, of richer sensory experience, that is inherently pleasurable. Pleasure, here, lies largely in the quality of difference; a supplement measured in relative rather than absolute terms, what one iteration or addition to a genre adds to its predecessors rather than how close it comes to the qualities of an external point of reference. This pleasure includes a celebration of the capacity of the technology itself, a significant factor in games as in other media such as special-effects oriented cinema.[10] This can be the case regardless of whether the on-screen world in question is intended to be a work of fantasy or one that has an identifiable real-world referent, although an additional impact might be created in the latter. *The Getaway* is a good example. Part of the pleasure of the game results from a combination of graphical-realist detail in itself and the fact that this is used to recreate aspects of the real-world geography and landmarks of central London as an environment within which gameplay tasks are set. For the player familiar with this landscape, an extra degree of *frisson* is created, potentially, the result of a process in which photographs of real buildings, objects and surface textures are mapped onto wire-frames to create a 3D environment recognizable in real geographical terms (albeit with some game-task-specific geographical licence). The same could be said of the more spatially limited arenas used in many sports-related games: models of real, identifiable stadia or real-world golf courses, for example (for which licences usually have to be obtained). There is a significant difference between playing a game set in a relatively identifiable or convincing simulation of an actual real-world environment and one in which a more generic equivalent is used (or in which the referent is from the real world but the quality of resolution makes it less recognizable as such). The experience of driving at high speed around the simulated London of *The Getaway*, chasing enemies or seeking to escape from the police, adds an extra dimension to the equivalent experience in the generic 'New York' and 'Miami' clones (Liberty City and Vice City) found in *Grand Theft Auto III* and *Vice City*. A similar difference of experience is found in playing a fantasy golf course and a simulacrum of a widely recognizable course such as St. Andrews – provided that the graphics reach a certain quality threshold, the precise location of which remains relative rather than absolute. To play 'St Andrews' in *World Class Leaderboard* (1986) on the Commodore, for example, or subsequent versions on platforms such as the Sega Genesis, is to engage with a graphics simulation restricted, by today's standards, to broad and blocky fields of colour. The resulting experience is more abstract than that offered by a recent title such as *Links 2004* (2003), in which the famous course is simulated at a much greater and more concrete level of detail. Aspirations towards greater realism at the level of image resolution alone can apply equally to real and imagined courses, however, just as it can also to the rendering of the environments of many

9. Golf simulation in broad and blocky fields of colour: *World Class Leaderboard* (1986) on the Commodore 64.

games set in worlds associated with science fiction and/or fantasy. Even if an environment or character bears little relation to what we might encounter in the real world – a scaly bipedal lizard wearing armour and wielding a sword, for instance – a high level of detail in appearance and movement can increase the degree to which it seems believable, in its own context, no matter how fantastical its nature.

Greater degrees of image resolution, creating more realistic textures, can also add significantly to the impression of sensory immersion in the game-world. Environments constructed with cel-shading graphics, for example, might be three dimensional, but the impression created by the use of discrete blocks of saturated colour tends to be rather flatter than that created by games that use texture mapping and other means to build surface variation. An increased impression of space that can be occupied by the player-character is created by the use of texture mapping and a variety of other techniques employed to increase the subtlety with which such images are constructed: anti-aliasing (to smooth blocky edges), bump-mapping (to create random deviations in a plane), vertex and pixel shading (dynamic lighting), depth fogging (to create a greater sense of perspective), raytracing (to create shadows and reflections), particle effects (to create clouds, mist, smoke, fire effects), keyframe interpolation (for complex facial movement and speech) and the DirectX pipeline (to create better real-time delivery of graphics/data).[11] To stand the player-character on the tee of some earlier generation golf games, for example, is to be given the impression of facing what appears to be a largely two-dimensional flattened picture of a hole. Later games such as *Links 2004* create a much stronger sense of looking into a substantial three-dimensional space into which the virtual ball can be hit.

Higher standards of resolution are measured to a large extent by the degree to which they remove the more obvious reminders of the status of the game as a construct. Increased realism is largely a matter of the reduction or disappearance of obviously pixelated or flat-plane surfaces in favour of more subtle and closer-grained textures, the constituents of which are less clearly drawn to the attention of the player. The world of *Actua Golf 2* (1997), for example, on the PlayStation, is one in which the building blocks of vegetation in the landscape are clearly on view and in which trees appear to shuffle around on-screen in any sequences involving movement of the in-game camera. In *Links 2004*, detail is much more

10. The much more 'photorealistic' simulation of golf offered by *Links 2004* (2003).

textured and discriminating, down to the level of individual leaves and the stems of smaller plants. Trees, bushes and other forms of undergrowth retain their positions and a sense of solidity when the camera moves (the result of the use of more sophisticated and rapid delivery of data to the screen). A slight agitation effect is noticeable among leaves and plants, although this is motivated at least partly as an impression of wind motion, noticeable as such when the camera comes to a rest. In some cases the issue is one of consistency. *Max Payne* was widely lauded on release for the 'realistic' quality of the graphics of its gritty, urban noir landscape, although it is far from visually consistent. Certain parts of the gameplay screen are more visually detailed than others, creating a patchwork effect likely to draw attention to the issue of variable degrees of realism. Even when the game is run at recommended PC specifications, a marked visual distinction exists between some environmental objects and others. Posters appear on the walls of the Roscoe Street subway station, for example. Many are photos simply pasted into the game environment, as are a number of pictures and paintings that appear in domestic interiors. These flat two-dimensional objects have a smoothly detailed quality that contrasts quite strongly with the rest of the gamescape. When Payne stands in front of one of them, the rather harsh 'blockiness' of the character is drawn to attention. Particle effects used for representations of fire and explosions also produce a more than usually realistic effect, with a visual complexity not matched by the surfaces used for larger segments of the environment. The game benefits generally from the use of texture mapping, based on the use of photographic sources, creating greater differentiation of tone in individual surfaces; but this, too, is not applied uniformly. One of the principal advances of the sequel, *Max Payne 2: The Fall of Max Payne*, is the creation of a more seamless and consistent aesthetic. Many of the planes from which 3D objects are comprised are less distinct than in the original. Objects are generally more rounded, their planes more smoothly integrated. This is most obvious in a comparison between the shape of Payne's head in the two versions. The Max Payne of the sequel is less 'squared-headed', the planes of his face far less noticeable as distinct features when seen in profile. Complexity of detail is more evenly distributed across the whole visual field, including Max himself, rather than restricted to the more localized zones of greater photorealism characteristic of the original.

If graphical realism is, essentially, a relative quality, degrees of difference can be located between games or between versions of games, or, as in the case of *Max Payne*, within an individual title itself. One of the most obvious instances within games is the gap that often exists between pre-rendered cut-scenes and in-game graphics limited by the demands of real-time delivery. In *The Lord of the Rings: The Return of the King*, for example, cut-scenes are often comprised of material lifted directly from the film series, creating a very noticeable difference in graphical quality even though the transition into gameplay is otherwise relatively smooth. In the *Final Fantasy* series (from 1989) – among many others – cut-scenes are of higher resolution and exhibit more mobile characters and camera effects than the playable parts of the game. A similar effect in *Enter the Matrix* is given motivation by the narrative context: cut-scenes are presented as located in the 'real world' of the game while gameplay occurs after transition into the computer matrix of the title, although this is a rationalization that contradicts a key point of the film series – the fact that the world inside the matrix is realized at a level of detail that makes it indistinguishable from everyday reality. In each of these cases, the relatively low-level graphical resolution of the playable parts of the game is likely to be drawn to attention by juxtaposition with more photorealistic or cinematic cut-scenes. Other games, such as *Halo*, have sought to avoid this problem by using the same engine to generate both cut-scenes and gameplay, leaving little distinction between the two. This might mean having lower-grade cut-scenes but has the benefit of creating a more uniform aesthetic in which the relative limitations of gameplay graphics are less likely to be drawn to attention. The *Max Payne* titles demonstrate a rather different approach. Here, the role of cut-scenes is performed by comic-book style static panes that employ a painterly, almost impressionist style in which brush strokes are clearly visible and the bleeding of colour and blurring of lines creates a somewhat dream-like quality. In this case, the effect of comparison between these and playable sequences is to make the latter seem the more solidly 'realistic'. A similar phenomenon is created in *Manhunt*, although more ambiguously: low-grade CCTV-style footage used for cut-scenes increases the comparatively photorealistic impression created by higher-resolution gameplay sequences – although the low-fi CCTV effect has itself become a cultural signifier of access to the real.

To what exactly is being aspired in the search for greater realism is not a simple matter, however. It is not just a question of seeking to mimic an unmediated impression of the real, exterior world. Two points of orientation often come into play. One, looking backwards, is the standard of previous entries in the field, as suggested above. Games make claims to realism on the basis of comparison with what has gone before. But looking towards the ideal against which existing qualities are measured, the benchmark is as often set by other forms of mediation as it is by the ultimate real-world referent. In golf games, for example, and most other sports simulations, the primary point of reference is television coverage of the sport, rather than the experience of the sport itself. Perspectives provided on the action are, generally, closely correlated with those typical of such coverage: shots from behind the golfer during the swing, for example, aerial footage of the ball in flight, fly-by previews of holes, and the wry musings of commentators, often voiced by real-world broadcasters. It is in the moving-camera fly-by sequence in *Actua Golf 2*, for example, that trees appear to shift around in their most distracting and cartoonish manner; what *Links 2004* simulates so much more convincingly, in audio-visual terms, is the impression of a helicopter-mounted TV camera flying over a real hole, as much as the immediate experience of play itself. Devices such as simulated lens flare, created when shooting with a real camera towards the sun, are used in many games to signify the impression of action being witnessed in already-mediated form. Relatively few sports games, in fact, offer the player a first-person perspective, as if inside the experience. 'Replay' sequences available in many also mimic television coverage, in this case creating an objectified impression of the action completed by the player: the effect here is to create a sense of the player having participated in something akin to the 'real thing', in its mediated form, especially where the player's performance is sufficiently good to stand visual comparison with the professional equivalent or the computer-controlled competitors (*Links 2004*, for example, offers a 'highlights reel', recording the best moments of a completed round). For many action and action–adventure type games, the benchmark, as far as audio-visual qualities are concerned, is cinema or television. Games often create their impressions of realism or immediacy precisely through their use of devices familiar from other media – as, in their own realm, signifiers of verisimilitude or immediacy

– as is suggested by the use of the term 'photorealism', implying as it does a second-order realism, an impression created through reference to another form of mediation.[12]

Improvements in graphical resolution are not just a question of aesthetics separated from gameplay, however. The two often work together. Graphics establish the setting in which gameplay occurs, thus creating many of the parameters within which gameplay has to operate. Leaps in the quality of graphics can, in their own right, contribute directly to the quality of gameplay: creating the impression of a real golf or driving simulation, for example, in comparison with sketchier earlier standards, in which a sense of taking part in a version of the real-world equivalent seems more notional and abstract. According to Jason Rubin, co-founder of the Sony subsidiary Naughty Dog, improvements in graphics have driven sales to date by making games both look *and play* better. This has been the case, Rubin argues, during 30 years of technical improvements, a series of leaps forward having been experienced in each successive move from early games to eight bit, 16-bit, 32-bit, early 3D and the state of the art in the early 2000s.[13] Particular gameplay effects can also be dependent on quite specific thresholds of visual resolution. In the stealth game *Thief* (1998), for example, as Katie Salen and Eric Zimmerman suggest, it is essential that the standard of visual representation is such that the player can distinguish between areas that are well lit and those in shadow, because the distinction is a key aspect of gameplay: the ability of the player-character to use shadows to avoid detection.[14] The stealth feature of the game would not function in a graphical environment in which this distinction could not clearly be maintained. The same goes for many other titles in which stealth is an important factor. In some cases, higher-resolution graphics provide a level of detail required more locally, in examples such as the solution of visual puzzles. In *Prince of Persia: Sands of Time*, for example, the player-character is required to manipulate a series of visually complex gears in order to align particular symbols and gain access to a new area. Puzzles of this kind appeared in many previous games, but in this case a greater degree of complexity is made possible by a high level of close environmental detail.

Greater levels of graphical realism can make it much less arbitrary-seeming to locate mechanisms such as the ubiquitous switches, levers and other objects that need to be manipulated as part of the core gameplay of many games, especially in the action/adventure formats. If such devices cannot be represented in something akin to their real textural detail, they have to be made to stand out in other ways, which makes them more arbitrary and less well-integrated in the game-world. With higher qualities of graphical realism, they can be identified in terms closer to what might be experienced in the real world. Need a stake to dispatch marauding vampires in one of the *Buffy* games, for example? Find a wooden bench or crate and break it up to create a suitable weapon. Without the use of reasonably convincing texture maps it might prove difficult to distinguish between objects supposed to be made from different materials. Have to jump across a yawning abyss, requiring close attention to where exactly the edge lies? Greater graphical realism might help the player to be more precise in determining exactly how far it is safe to go. None of these actions are impossible in games in which graphical detail is more limited; but they can be made more satisfying, as part of a relatively more immersive experience, once certain thresholds of recognizability are reached.

With greater processing power, game designers can construct more complex environments, containing wider ranges of interactive objects. This may open up the environment to support different ways of achieving central gameplay tasks. In earlier action/adventure games, the 'crumb-trail' laid down to enable players to work their way through the gamescape is often quite clearly visible as a result of anomalies in the level of graphical reproduction. In the early *Tomb Raider* games, for example, a section of wall that stands out because it is coloured slightly differently from the rest is likely to be a visual clue that it (alone) will respond to a particular action. This might be helpful to the player, on one level, as part of the exploratory infrastructure examined in the previous chapter. An entirely uniform quality of representation might, in this sense, make gameplay harder. The fact that this is still seen as a useful device is demonstrated by its continued use in later games such as *Buffy the Vampire Slayer: Chaos Bleeds*. In the Sunnydale Zoo level, the player-character is required to smash a sheet of plate glass in the reptile house to reach a wall panel that leads to the next area. That this particular pane, among others, needs to be broken is indicated by the presence of a frame outline on the rear wall of the exhibit, the area inside the frame being coloured slightly differently from the rest. Visual clues such as these are convenient devices, saving players from what might be the more tedious task of investigating aspects of the game-world at greater length. A trade-off exists here between the demands of navigational aids and the relative seamlessness with which the game-world is presented, although it would be possible to create forms of signposting that did not rely on either hierarchical degrees of graphical realism or obvious highlighting of certain items (or to give players the option of settings in which highlighting could be turned on or off). Greater uniformity of detail can make the task of locating required objects both more realistic and more difficult. In *Max Payne 2*, for example, visual complexity can make it quite hard to distinguish useful objects, such as ammunition, from their background environments, especially when gameplay demands leave little time available. This can be seen as a handicap to the immediate demands of gameplay, but can also encourage the situation of such objects in locations that seem less arbitrary and more integrated into the game-world: power-ups in the form of pills, for example, found in appropriate locations such as bathroom cabinets.

To offer high levels of detail in some areas is to create a similar expectation in others that might not be fulfilled; the result can be to attract attention to shortcomings that might not otherwise become an issue, as in the first *Max Payne* game. The increased level of visual character detail that comes with upgrades to *EverQuest* tends to make the rest of the world look relatively sparse, for example; to improve detail throughout might be desirable, but would cause problems of processing lag, although some attempt to make the world and its inhabitants equal in terms of graphical detail is promised in the sequel, *EverQuest 2*. An example in which consistency of detail is maintained is the single-player *Unreal II*, in which higher levels of rendering are not reserved for characters or for elements that stand out as of particular importance to gameplay. An interior science fiction gamescape is created, full of video screens with moving images, 3D wire-frame terrain maps and detailed console panels with arrays of blinking lights, dials and buttons. Outdoor spaces are also heavily populated, in some regions, with organic rather than cubic-looking plant life. As with the more graphically consistent *Max Payne 2*, the effect is to create a stronger impression of the game-world as a seamless virtual place rather than a functional construct built around a few key gameplay options.

Increased levels of graphical realism can also open up other areas of expression in games, including a greater dimension of emotional engagement, a quality often seen as lacking in many games. Characters can be made more expressive. The use of motion capture techniques and appropriate sound effects can heighten qualities of anthropomorphism and enhance the capacity of characters to be made to express emotion. This has been one effect of incremental upgrades to *EverQuest*, increasing the visual detail provided in the case of both player and non-player characters. In first-person mode, player-characters cannot see themselves, but they can observe the reactions of others, both visual and audible. In a world reliant on text-based communication between players, touches such as this – yelps synchronized to mouth movements or animated 'social-emotes' such as doing a dance of joy to celebrate the accomplishment of a task or doubling up in laughter – compensate for a lack of emotionally rich speech, helping to animate and vitalize the inhabitants of the game-world in a richer and more responsive manner.[15]

A combination of detailed graphics and expressive qualities also breathes an added sense of life into the central character of the fantasy-based action-adventure, *Prince of Persia: Sands of Time*. In this case, a third-person game, the central character is visible to the player: a highly acrobatic and mobile figure with a movement profile built from a large library of motion-captured elements. In terms of graphical representation, action and verbal reactions, the prince creates an impression of rounded, emotionally rich character rare in the world of games at the time of its appearance, with attributes designed to be relatively closer to those of figures more normal-seeming than the super-tough characters typical of most action-adventure titles. Balanced precariously on one of the game's many vertigo-inducing ledges or tightropes, for example, he often struggles to maintain balance, flailing his arms and emitting cries that express human fragility and a recognizable reaction to environment – responses that, in contrast with the cool and silent manner of a figure such as Lara Croft, are designed to solicit the concern of the player to ensure the character does not come to harm. Graphics capable of making characters more expressive can, in the process, make a significant contribution to the narrative dimension of games, helping to communicate both story-related material and emotional resonance. As Drew Sikora puts it: 'graphics in games today are no longer used merely for "eye candy", but as visual effects to help tell a story that the player can internalize and enjoy.'[16]

Greater degrees of realism, in aesthetic terms, can also raise the stakes involved in a number of more contentious issues related to games. The whole question of violence in games, a subject of frequent moral panic, is likely to be heightened by every increase in the verisimilitude of in-game representation (an issue to which we return in Chapter 4). One of the principal defences used by the games industry, in the face of threats of more stringent regulation, has been the fact that game violence is usually comic-book style rather than realistic, and as a result more clearly marked off as essentially non-serious and unthreatening. If higher standards of resolution have the potential generally to make gameplay activity more rich and meaningful, as seems likely to be the case, the same applies to what many see as the potentially disturbing aspects of some games. A significant difference of experience might result from the blasting of a fuzzy bunch of pixels – whether representing a fantasy monster or a human figure – and the shooting in finer-grained detail of something more closely resembling a fully realized being. In gameplay terms, of course, this might have the benefit of enabling players to target enemies more precisely, where shots at heads or chests result in cleaner kills and resultant savings in ammunition.

How far increased levels of graphical realism will continue to contribute to gameplay remains subject to debate. Jason Rubin argues that graphics will keep improving, but that the return in terms of gameplay is rapidly diminishing.[17] Recent leaps in graphical quality have been smaller than those of the past, he suggests, the pay-off at the level of gameplay being incommensurate with the level of technical advance and the costs incurred by developers. Beyond a certain threshold of high-resolution 3D, he suggests, mass-market gamers will cease to be attracted by increased graphical quality alone because there is no scope for a future shift that has an impact equivalent to the move from early abstraction to more realized 2D, or from 2D to early 3D or early 3D to a more fully realized 3D: 'there is no 4D'.[18] If graphical realism has been substantially more than just icing on the cake in the past, this will cease to be the case, forcing developers to look elsewhere to attract consumers. At this point, Maic Masuch and Niklas Röber argue, gameplayers might be attracted by a range of more artistic, non-photorealistic graphical styles.[19]

Sound can also play a strong part in the creation of impressions of realistic texture. If sound effects often serve to increase the effect of sensory presence created by games, as suggested in the previous chapter, they can also be deployed in a manner that is more or less realistically layered or modulated. In earlier games, sounds often exist as separate and discrete events, appearing one at a time. The function of sound in some such cases is to provide aural signification of activities, such as the picking up and putting down of objects, that could not be presented graphically because of very limited resources. *Doom* marked a significant step forward, producing a range of different sounds simultaneously, closer to the manner in which sound is experienced in the real world. Sounds are often abruptly cut short in *Doom* when new events are triggered, however, resulting in a jarringly disjointed soundscape. A more seamless impression is created in subsequent titles such as *Max Payne 2*, in which sound-bridges are often used to smooth breaks between one part of the game and another (from cut-scene to gameplay sequence, for example). More generally, naturalistic sound effects often contribute to the extent to which the game-world provides a realistic sensory impression of its real-world equivalent: the sounds of objects in use, from keys turning in locks to the sound of swords clashing in battle; the sounds of the footsteps of player and non-player characters, or aural responses to changes in environmental conditions such as the use of echo effects in large underground chambers or the reverberation of engine noise when a racing car enters a tunnel.

Recordings of 'real' sounds can provide compensation for relatively lower levels of graphical fidelity, contributing to the overall impression of verisimilitude. *Max Payne 2* uses a large number of recorded sounds to construct a complex and multi-layered soundscape. Ambient sound provides a sense of increased dimensionality in interiors, examples including the opening of doors, muffled voices behind closed doors and variable footfalls. The sounds of a thunderstorm are orchestrated in one level to increase the sensory depth of the playing experience. The sound of rainfall is triggered as the player-character steps closer to an open window, the volume increasing as he moves outside. The effect is to sketch the impression of a wider outside environment within which the game is situated, the background of thunder and rain also contributing to the melancholic tenor of the piece. Enemies are often heard before they are seen, a device that provides an aid to the player – providing danger cues – but that also contributes to the realistic effect through the creation of aural depth, texture and perspective. The effect of depth of aural dimension is reinforced by other devices, including the gap between the voice of Max – close to the player – and that of his accomplice, Mona, 'tinny' and distant, directing his movements via a telephone headset. The intimate presence of Max's voice is also a vehicle for nuances of character emotion.

Digital processing techniques, known as psycho-acoustic processing, are used to heighten the spatial and textural sound effects in *Max Payne 2*, created by the use of the proprietary sound manipulation software EAX and enhanced by the use of high-quality audio recording to provide high-frequency content that makes subtle effects more audible (helped, for the player, by the use of 5.1 speaker systems or headphones). Tiny delays between left and right sound channels are used to fool the player's perception into believing that sounds are coming from sources wider apart than the speakers. Changing the length of the delay makes a sound appear to move, creating a heightened sense of spatial location when combined with conventional sideways panning from one speaker to another. These kinds of effects are used most strikingly in the sound that accompanies the transition to 'bullet-time', the voices of distant non-player characters and the sound of rainfall. Reverberation is also employed to increase the effect of distance between sound-source and player-character. Used in combination, these effects create a more than usually realistic-seeming and dramatic three-dimensional quality to the soundscape.[20]

'Realism' is a complex term, suggesting the extent to which representations accord not just with the real world, or imagined versions of reality, but also their relationship with other representational forms. Realism in games also needs to be considered at the level of functionality, however, of actions rather than qualities of sound and image, a dimension that very clearly impacts on the core mechanics of gameplay. A greater degree of realism can be created by aspects of gameplay that function consistently, for example, just as it can result from consistency at the level of graphical detail. Objects that fail to act consistently tend to remind the player of the arbitrary character of gameplay, as an abstracted activity, rather than contributing to the broad – however partial – impression of immersion in the world of the game. In *Primal*, for example, one player-character can scale walls, but only some walls, not others, for no reason motivated logically from within the game; similarly, in *Red Faction* (2001) some walls can blasted to rubble, but not all. An example cited by Steven Poole is the fact that a rocket launcher available in *Tomb Raider III* (1998) can blow up enemies but does no damage to a simple wooden door. A specific gameplay requirement – the demand that the player finds a rusty key with which to open the door – undermines any greater degree of approximation to the more real-world logical capabilities of the item. As an example of much greater consistency of functionality, Poole cites *Legends of Zelda: Ocarina of Time* (1998), in which many objects can be put to multiple uses appropriate to what would be expected to be their nature in something relatively more analogous to the real world.[21]

In general, a richer and more responsive game environment increases the potential for immersion in the game-world. As with graphical photorealism, the issue is often framed negatively, limitations tending to be more prominent than strengths. Fundamental aspects of the game-world that most closely resemble their real-world equivalents are less likely to be drawn to the attention of the player. As Richard Bartle puts it: 'The more that players don't have to think about interacting with their environment, the less they *will* think about it, and therefore the more immersive their time in the world will be.'[22] If gravity pulls people downwards in the game-world, as in the real world, as Bartle suggests, players will simply take it for granted. If gravity does not work consistently – unless specifically motivated by the use of a device such as a levitation spell in a fantasy/magical context – it will be likely to stand out and intrude on the gameplay experience.

All game-worlds *are* arbitrary and limited constructs. They have nothing remotely like the complex functionality of the real world. But a greater depth of functional detail can contribute to the relative degree of immersive illusion that is created, although it can also be a novelty that draws attention to itself. The environment of *Max Payne* is responsive in more detail than most of its contemporaries, for example. Many background items have a degree of functionality beyond that required for central gameplay tasks, as mentioned in Chapter 1. Television sets can be switched on and off and toilets can be flushed. Functional details such as these create the sense of a game-world comprising more than just a series of graphically rendered backdrops. The player's sense of the arbitrariness of activities required for the completion of levels – or just for survival – is reduced a few notches by the fact that it is not only objects designed for a specific purpose that have any degree of functionality within the diegetic universe. If the sequel increased the level of graphical realism, a similar upgrading is found in the dimension of functional depth: more objects with which the player-character can interact, a further reduction in the extent to which non-mission-critical material is merely inert background. This indicates a situation in which surplus resources are available to the designers, perhaps suggesting that the scope for additional graphical detail has been exhausted on a particular console or graphics card.

Degrees of functional realism are also important for objects more crucial to core gameplay activities. Military games often invest quite considerably in the creation of functionally (relatively) realistic weaponry, set out in sometimes near-fetishistic detail in the manual. A game such as *Medal of Honor: Allied Assault* seeks to replicate some of the key characteristics of different weapons, as suggested in Chapter 1: their relative values in particular situations of close or more distant combat, or specific details such as the difficulty of reloading the M1 Garand semi-automatic rifle when its clip is partially used – framed as both historical fact and a factor to be considered during gameplay. Weapons create a fairly realistic impression of recoil that makes targets harder to hit. When using a rifle with a telescopic sight to pick off more distant enemies, the barrel jumps sharply upwards after each shot, throwing off the aim and putting a premium on one-shot success (missed shots tend to draw the fire of the enemy, the impact of which creates jolts that make aiming increasingly difficult); when using a sub-machine gun, the player has a choice between the greater firepower of lengthy bursts, in which the muzzle shakes and accuracy is lost, or more carefully controlled single shots or shorter bursts of fire. Details such as these appear to be modelled, if only approximately, on the real-world equivalents; such an *impression* is given, at least, for the benefit of those for whom this is an important issue, even in instances where it might be greatly simplified. A clear distinction is apparent between this approach and shooting sequences in games such as *The Getaway* and many others in which devices are available to target enemies automatically, making gameplay easier but several degrees further removed from any kind of functional realism. A particularly controversial example of functional realism in this domain is the use of 'realistic' body hit zones in *Soldier of Fortune* (2000): 26 different 'hit locations' are structured into the bodies of non-player characters, which respond differently – 'appropriately' – depending on the aim of the player: characters shot in the lower body scream and writhe with pain, for example, rather than dying instantly.

A broad sense of some reality-equivalence of functionality is also implied in real-time strategy games such as the *Command and Conquer* and *Age of Empires* series. Details of the relative capacities of different military units are provided, many of which seem to have some grounding in real-world equivalents (obvious examples being the fact that archers in *Age of Empires* are more effective from relative distance while swordsmen can only perform in up-close engagement). Details such as these are partly driven by the game-specific need for the balancing of the range of different forces and resources provided to each of the various sides that can be played with and against. The result sought by many real-time strategy titles is a relationship between the different sides equivalent to that found in the game 'Scissors, Paper, Stone', in which each side has its own various potential strengths and weaknesses, none of which ensures either overwhelming superiority or inferiority.[23] Variation in detailed, specific capacities also creates an impression of relatively fine-grained distinctions that contributes to a sense of greater reality of function. This might be based to a significant extent on real-world equivalents, as in *Medal of Honor* and *Age of Empires*, but it can also – like quality of graphical rendering – lend a sense of reality to the more imaginary creations of science fiction or fantasy games, or to reality/fantasy hybrids such as the extrapolations from existing technologies found in many games.

Modes of transport can also be provided in this kind of functional detail, from the military vehicles of *Medal of Honor* to the various cars available in many racing games. Some of the latter clearly invest more in notions of realism of behaviour within the game-world than others. Environmental factors can also be modelled with varying degrees of functional realism. If snow appears on the road surface, its contribution to impressions of realism comes partly in its graphical rendering – not the most difficult of challenges, in this case – but also in the extent to which it adversely affects the handling of a vehicle in a manner at least analogous to its equivalent in the real world: that is, the car skids and loses control if driven, cornered or braked too hard (more or less forgivingly, depending on factors such as difficulty settings or the design of particular games).

The issue of realism-of-function is especially prominent in sports-related games, including many driving-related titles, because, as Rollings and Adams suggest, they take place in environments about which the player is more than usually well-informed from experience, even if this may be the mediated experience of watching on television as much as actually taking part.[24] Golf games, for example, offer a number of different types and degrees of realism in terms of their functionality.

Two basic mechanisms have generally been used to simulate the golf swing. The original variety involves a three-click operation, using either a mouse or console buttons. An abstracted graphical representation of the path of the swing is provided on-screen, as an out-of-game-world part of the interface. The player clicks once to start the swing, a second time when the gauge reaches the top of the backswing and again in an area marked as the 'hitting zone'. The swing constructed in this way is then acted out, automatically and separately, by the player-character figure of the golfer on-screen (*Links 2003* [2002] offered a development in which the mouse-click swing was performed in real-time, the on-screen figure beginning its backswing at the same time as the player). The aim is to time mouse or button pressing to achieve the required length of backswing and to hit the ball at the ideal sweet spot at the end of the downswing. Getting the former wrong affects distance; the latter affects quality of contact and/or direction (typically, 'hitting' too early produces a slice off-target to the right, too late a hook to the left). This mechanism replicates one important aspect of a real golf swing – timing – but little else; and the way timing is achieved (or not) is via a device used generically in other sports games rather than having any particular 'golf-ness' (the player has to press a button at the right moment to stop the surging line of a power-meter within pre-set limits, either exactly, for a perfect shot, or approximately, for one that is acceptable; exactly the same is used for ambitious shots in the tennis game, *Topspin* [2003], among many other examples).

Later golf games adopted a mechanism that maps significantly more closely onto the real-world experience: the use of a console analogue-stick controller to produce a real-time version of the swing. The left stick on the PlayStation 2 or Xbox is used to enact a miniature swing: pulled back for the backswing and pushed forward for the downswing. The result is something that feels much more like swinging a golf club – not as much as the VR equivalent imagined by McHoul in the previous chapter, but an interface mechanism distinctly analogous, in its own thumb-scaled realm, to the real-world action. This also creates the opportunity for further realism at the level of functionality. If the stick is moved jerkily, a poor shot results, as is the case usually with a jerky golf swing. If the stick is moved forward and back other than in a straight line, slices or hooks are likely; this, again, is relatively close to the real-world equivalent, if somewhat simplified. Other aspects of functional realism also feature in some golf games: the fact that the ball is likely to be hit to the left if lying on an up-slope or to the right on a down-slope; that the quality of the lie affects how well the ball can be hit; that various kinds of spin can be imparted to control the behaviour of the ball in flight or on landing. Realism-of-functionality can also extend to the level of the emotional reactions of the player: the creation of very golf-like frustration and anxiety in relation to shot-making. On its beginners setting, for example, *Links 2004* often seems rather easy, giving the novice player the capability of a tournament professional: booming long drives off the tee into the fairway and sending iron shots close to the pin. Bad shots tend to infect the level of play, however, much as they do on the real golf course. While playing well, the swing of the analogue stick seems simple and easy. Once a player becomes self-conscious about the motion, however, usually after a mis-hit, more errors are likely and confidence can easily be lost (and annoyed frustration result!).

The emotional dimension is explicitly built into the mechanics of *Outlaw Golf* (2003), a title that in other respects invests less than major franchises such as *Links* and *Tiger Woods* (from 1998) in qualities such as sober graphical realism and the replication of recognizable real-world courses. *Outlaw Golf* is peopled by unlikely players – thugs and scantily clad women-with-attitude – and favours imagined courses such as a New Jersey links crossed by resolutely un-scenic features such as an elevated highway and a pipeline. The general level of graphical detail is less than that found in *Links 2004*, but an extra functional feature is found in the shape of a 'composure meter'. Bad shots make the composure meter fall – which tends to make more bad shots likely to follow – while good shots have the opposite effect (true to the 'tough/attitude' tenor of the game as a whole, the most effective way of improving composure is beating up your player-character's caddie, although certain feats of gameplay are required to earn the 'beating token' that allows this to be achieved).

Functional realism at a relatively high level of detail often marks the difference between simple abstraction and more substantial simulation: the difference, for example, between the classic *Pong* and a tennis game such as *Topspin* on the Xbox. Relatively simple abstraction has an appeal of its own, reducing more complex activities to a few clean and satisfying lines, as in the case of *Pong*. As a simulation of table-tennis or tennis, it reduces the game to a very limited number of parameters: basically, a dot to be hit backwards and forwards across a line representing the net. The only real variation available to the player is exactly where on the paddle to catch the 'ball'; either centrally, to hit it back directly, or towards the extremities, in which case shots can be directed at an angle. Compare this with the more literal transcription of tennis found in *Topspin*. The game is, obviously, more 'realistic' at the level of graphical representation, providing a three-dimensional figuration of recognizable tennis players, stadium and court, and a regime of 'cut-away' shots and other transitional devices closely modelled on television coverage of the real thing. It is also much more 'like' tennis in functional terms, enabling player-characters to produce versions of specific tennis shots, using topspin, backspin, lobs and drop-shots, and to develop strategies during rallies – placement of the ball, playing safer or more risky shots – that also mirror, quite effectively, the real-world equivalent.

There are, of course, limits to functional realism, in these and other cases. This is partly a matter of finite resource capacity and the restrictions imposed by game controllers and gameplaying environments, few of which are ever likely to constitute anything close to a full virtual reality version of games such as golf or tennis. Some games, such as the music or rhythm oriented rail shooters *Rez* and *Amplitude* (2003), bear very little in the way of functional realism; they remain abstract in functional and visual terms, making little reference to the function of real-world objects. Limited functional realism is also a positive requirement of games more generally, however – if they are to remain, precisely, *games*. Too much realism of function would make sports and other games simply too difficult, and would diffuse the definition of core gameplay features. A perfect simulation could only be played really well by the very small number capable of performing to the same standard on a real golf course, tennis court, race-track or other sporting arena. Generally, the whole point of games is to be easier and, for most players, more fun as a result of the fact that they can achieve things they would find impossible in the outside world. There is a clear difference between what is usually expected from a game and a more substantially realized training simulator (a golf device, for example, in which a real club is used to hit a captive ball, from which a graphically displayed model is produced of the shot likely to have resulted from the actual dynamics of contact; or a highly expensive cockpit simulator used in the training of real pilots). What might often be desired in games is sufficient functional realism to create an impression of 'something like' the real thing – necessary, in games with that aspiration, for the creation of a feeling of achievement, rather than a sense of a game being made too easy, abstract or over-simplified, without this being taken too far, to the point at which the dominant experience might become one of frustration. Where this point might lie for one player or another is far from easy to judge, which is one reason why degrees of functional realism – like other difficulty-related aspects of gameplay – tend to vary, both from one game to another and within the settings available in a single title. *Links 2004*, for example, can be played on three different difficulty settings. The more difficult the setting, the relatively more functionally realistic are the parameters of the thumb-stick swing. On easier settings, the game is more forgiving of swings that shift slightly off-centre. On the hardest setting, errors are punished more severely, and other elements such as wind direction have a greater impact on shots – although it is still much easier to hit top quality shots than would be possible for most players in the real world.

The market for driving games is sharply divided, Rollings and Adams suggest, between those who are happy with an enjoyable if very approximate simulation of something like the real driving experience and those who demand a much closer modelling of the real physics of vehicle-handling at speed.[25] Most racing games provide some simulation of aspects of real forces that shape performance, 'career' type modes of play usually allowing for the improvement of various dimensions of performance through the purchase of upgraded vehicles or components. The inclusion of multiple factors determining relative degrees of performance helps to increase the impression of functional realism, while also supplying the constituents of greater depth of gameplay in its own right; ideally, the two can work in mutual reinforcement. The 'fun' element of games for many players, however, is dependent upon considerable departure from realism of function: the pleasure of belting a virtual golf-ball 300 yards down the fairway quite consistently or whizzing around a race-track, bouncing off crash-barriers and other cars without any substantial damage. A higher quotient of pleasure might result when more work has been required for more difficult success to be achieved – as in the periodic breakthroughs that act as motivational carrots in difficult stretches of a wide range of games – but quicker pay-offs are also desired on many occasions. To cater for both, as Rollings and Adams suggest, many sports games offer a combination of more exacting 'simulation' and more immediately accessible 'arcade' modes, the latter including a greater fudging of key aspects of functional behaviour.[26]

Other aspects of functional realism are often downplayed very strongly. In war-based games, for example, whether first/third-person shooters or strategy games, particular weapons and units might be simulated with a degree of authenticity – but the extent to which they are put into action is not. The number of actual instances of direct combat is enormously exaggerated in most if not all such games. The real experience of warfare is, generally, governed by very long periods of tedium and discomfort, only occasionally punctured by moments of combat action, in which the act of directly killing an enemy in close combat is a rarity. To mirror the American military experience in Vietnam, for example, would be to factor such features strongly into the gameplay – which might make for an interesting and original title, but not one likely to appear on the game-shop shelves. What games offer is a variable blend of elements that aspire or make claims to different kinds and degrees of realism – and that simplify, stylize, reduce or exaggerate as a result of, on the one hand, capacity and other limitations and, on the other, the positive requirements of enjoyable play. This is a balance central to gaming both today and back to the origins of the form, as David Myers suggests in the case of *Spacewar* (1962), the design and subsequent modification of which was shaped by two sometimes conflicting sets of rules: those of simulation and those of play.[27] As the game was modified, in successive versions, physical realism – in the modelling of movement and forces such as gravity – was reduced, precisely in order to increase the specific quality of play.

Are there any games that offer complete functional realism? There may be one exception: the format that calls upon the player to perform computer-related activities identical in form to those required in the fictional world of the game. Examples include *Uplink*, considered in the previous chapter, and the puzzle game *In Memoriam* (2003). In the latter, the conceit is that the game-disk has been sent to the player, among many others individuals, as part of an attempt to solve a kidnapping case involving a serial killer. The actions then required are precisely the same as their real-world equivalent would be, once the premise – however unlikely it seems – is accepted. The player has to engage in activities such as the use of internet search engines to explore both planted and pre-existing real-world information resources. The villain is framed as a crazed genius, fond of setting puzzles and mini-games designed to exasperate the player/detective, a device that produces perfect motivation for the most arbitrary of tasks imposed on the player: the whole point, in the diegetic universe, is that they *are* arbitrary games, the gameplaying arch-fiend being a narrative prototype familiar from other serial-killer fictions. The impression of overlap between real and fictional world activity is increased by the use of the player's email account as another source of information. 'Mixed reality' or location-based games go further in blurring the line between game and real world spaces and activities, . examples including *Botfighters* (2001), produced in Sweden, in which mobile phone text-messaging is the principal medium for locate-and-destroy contests between players in real urban environments. Physical movement and the locating dimension of the game are, functionally, fully realistic – although not the destroying, of course, reduced to the sending of a 'shoot' message when the target is within range, or the being-destroyed, which entails a web-based 'recharging of batteries' before the player can rejoin the game.[28]

Spectacle and Sensation

Realism at the level of graphical representation can reduce the extent to which the attention of the player is drawn to the issue of image-quality itself, especially when enacted in a consistent manner on-screen. It often declares its status *as* realism, however, especially in the context of the heavy emphasis sometimes put on such qualities in marketing and other discourses surrounding the playing experience. Realism might, in one sense, be intended to create a relatively transparent effect, based on not drawing attention to deficits in the level of representation achievable in the playable parts of games, or reducing somewhat the gap between visual resolution in games and audio-visual media such as film and television. But it also offers what can often be termed a 'spectacle' of realism: degrees of graphical realism that are flaunted and designed to be admired as striking or impressive images in their own right. As a form of spectacle of this kind, as in other respects, realism can be a source of appeal in the realms of either real-world reference or more outright fantasy. The *Max Payne* games, for example, offer environments that tend to be somewhat dingy and functional − office spaces, warehouses, apartments and the like − rather than being inherently spectacular. Spectacle is offered at the relative (in game terms) level of detail or consistency with which such environments are reproduced, especially for players equipped with the most up-to-date graphics cards or consoles. Other games offer environments that lend themselves more obviously to the production of spectacular vistas: the various exotic locations of *EverQuest* or the *Tomb Raider* series, the swirling voids and strange other-worldly landscapes of *American McGee's Alice*, the planet-scapes of *Halo* or the multicoloured pulsating-neon computer interiors of *Rez*.

Spectacle is found in games in a number of different forms, including spectacular audio-visual effects realized by the actions of the player. One possible starting point is to consider two different modes of spectacle also found in recent/contemporary Hollywood action or special-effects oriented cinema − as a source of both comparison and contrast with the way spectacle is located in games.[29] Some forms of game and cinematic spectacle invite the player to (in effect) sit back in a state of admiration, contemplating the scale, detail, convincing texture or other 'impressive' attributes of the image. Others seek to create a more aggressive, explosive and 'in your face' variety of spectacular impact (although the distinction is not always entirely clear-cut). In cinema, the more contemplative variety tends to offer longer and more lingering spectacular vistas while the latter is more reliant on rapid montage-style editing and/or camera movement to create its visual impact.

The more contemplative variety invites the *look* of the viewer or player while the 'impact aesthetic' offers something closer to an assault on the sensations, a vicarious impression of participation in spectacular action/destruction on-screen. These map onto games to some extent, but with some crucial differences. Spectacle of the contemplative variety is offered by some videogames, although it is more likely to figure prominently in some than others, particularly in slower-paced games (or slower moments within particular titles), as suggested above in relation to the appeals of graphical realism more generally. New or unfolding spectacular vistas – including those supplied in the form of cut-scenes – are frequently offered as reward and incentive for the completion of particular tasks, sub-sections, levels or entire games. Spectacular vistas can offer compensation for periods in which players become stuck or are forced into repeated attempts at a task, although the opposite might also be the case: pleasures created by even the most spectacular and impressively realized environments are likely to wane as a level or section is failed and restarted for the umpteenth time. Sources of spectacle range from large-scale aspects of the game environment – spectacular imagined landscapes – to closer detail, including the qualities of design and motion of player- and non-player characters.

Many games include large-scale 'vista' shots in their expositional cut-scenes, partly to establish a sense of space in the player's mind, but also often as an enticement to explore the game-world. A panorama of global scale is found at the start of *Age of Mythologies*, for example: the camera pulls out from a localized scene to show a complete world on which various landmarks are viewed along with figures of people going about their various tasks. *Spellforce: Order of the Dawn* (2004) offers a pre-rendered opening cut-scene that leans heavily on the type of fantasy-oriented cinematic spectacle provided by the *Lord of the Rings* films. Swooping camera movements arc between violent subterranean volcanic activity, a vast battlefield through which it explodes and the conflict between two arch-foes that takes place in a tower high above the main battleground. The visuals, rendered in high quality animation, create an impression of dynamism and exhilaration, although the in-game imagery is not of a comparable standard.

Quieter varieties of spectacle are also found, as in the glowing and airbrushed, dreamlike quality of *Prince of Persia: Sands of Time*, suited to its Arabian Nights fantasy setting. At certain moments in the game, the usual pattern of jumping and fighting activities is halted to allow the player-character to admire strange new spaces, clearly marked as magical dimensions existing outside the normal diegetic environmental fabric. In a section titled 'Did I really see her?', a dark, enclosed passage is

11. Spectacular vista: the bridge-crossed void in *Prince of Persia: Sands of Time* (2003).

entered, to the accompaniment of non-diegetic, low-key tinkling-bell sounds of the kind often used to figure the presence of magic in fantasy games. The screen goes entirely black, disorienting the player. Out of the darkness, a spectacular vista appears, framed by an elaborate golden arch in which the player-character stands. The virtual camera is located at a distance, behind and above the character, to maximize the depth, scope and impact of this new and 'othered' space. Stretching out below is a bottomless smoky-blue void, criss-crossed by rope-and-wooden-slatted bridges strewn with torches emanating an unearthly blue glow. 'What the...?', asks the character, as he takes in the spectacle, cueing the player to join him in regarding the space with contemplative awe. In this case, the fantasy-world-within-fantasy-world also serves a functional purpose, as the player-character crosses a bridge to find a health-increasing magical fountain. Magically transported back to the confined hallway of the palace, we hear that he now feels 'wonderful', a term that captures both the 'wonder' of the world he has visited and the increased ability gained as a result.

Many games draw on the rhetorics of visual spectacle associated with established genre territories, especially science fiction, horror and high-fantasy. Early games with limited graphical resources, such as *Space Invaders*, used the black void of outer-space as merely the backdrop for gameplay, the emphasis being on intensive gameplay rather than space as a source of spectacle. Later games provided space and planetary vistas closer to the equivalents found in film and television science fiction. Despite being rather blocky in its graphical qualities, the slow-paced puzzle game *Dig* (1994) presents images such as Earth as seen from space, asteroids and glowing celestial bodies, as well as depicting the landscape of a desolate planet. Similar environments are realized in greater detail in later science-fiction oriented titles, from the fine detail of the spaces of *Unreal II* to the spectacle of a pair of alien moons rising against a purple sky in *Halo*. In horror games, the dominant source of spectacle lies in the visceral and the monstrous, in assorted weird and wonderful forms. Spectacle serves here not just to solicit the gaze of the player but also to unsettle.

Environmental spectacle that evokes myth, magic and mystery is particularly important to games set in high-fantasy locations, which often create extensive worlds composed of various differently styled landscapes designed to engage the look of the player journeying towards the achievement of particular quests. High-fantasy offers much that lends itself to spectacular visuals, its imagined medievalist past providing imagery such as highly decorated guildhalls, temples, castles and fortresses, and landscape features ranging from the volcanic to deserts and sea-scapes. The gaze of the player is often the first thing to be engaged by a dark forest that habours ancient ruins and fabulous beasts, or impressive cityscapes such as Vah Shir, home of the cat people in *EverQuest* – before the striking impression gives way to renewed emphasis on performance of the game-tasks in hand. Many players of *EverQuest* and other such games spend a great deal of time travelling to see the different spaces of the game-world, acting like tourists of the virtual landscape (maybe even snapping photos with the game's screen-shot facility). Such activity is promoted in some cases by the fact that certain spaces are only available for short periods of time.

Spectacle can also be found more locally, sometimes used to mark out significant and sought-after objects. In Warren Robinett's early action-adventure title, *Adventure* (1978), the object of the quest is an 'Enchanted Chalice', presented with a shimmering effect to express its importance and magical qualities, an impression created by an image that cycles rapidly through the spectrum of available colours. In *Buffy the Vampire Slayer: Chaos Bleeds*, the final boss can only be defeated by the use of a special weapon, Hope's Dagger, an object that is hard-won by collecting the pieces of the character Hope's body throughout the rest of the game. The dagger is presented as a glittering jewelled object that stands out from more utilitarian weapons such as wooden stakes and gardening tools used during the game. Light effects are a frequent source of the more localized variety of visual spectacle, ranging from the neon-glowing body-suits of *Tron 2.0* (2003) to the cloudy masses of glowing colour used synaesthetically to represent different types of collectable smell in *A Dog's Life* (2003). Games that feature the use of magic often use particle-based lighting effects, combined with animation, to indicate the use of spells. A range of different visual effects are produced, for example, by spells cast by key-pad combinations when playing the witch, Willow, in *Chaos Bleeds*. The numerous spells available in *EverQuest* have their own individual spectacular qualities, examples including grasping hands summoned from the earth to claw at a targeted enemy and a spell that produces a large glowing yellow shield around the targeted player. Other spells transform player images into various forms: bears, wolves, or the 'boon' spell that strikingly turns a player-character into a scarecrow with a pumpkin head and light shining from the eyes. The main player-character, Jen, is subjected to spectacular magical transformations into various demon forms in *Primal*: at the player's command, a cut-scene ensues in which she lifts into the air, bends backwards and is surrounded by a glowing starburst (a rather orgasmic image), before changing into monstrous new form and gaining increased powers. Players of *EverQuest* can also buy diversions such as fireworks that have little purpose related to gameplay and can be used to produce spectacle for its own sake – often advertised for the enjoyment of other players.

Lizard-like alien creatures, muscle-bound barbarians, well-stacked warrior women, cute little dragons and hulking monsters: characters and non-playing characters are also potential sources of spectacle in games. Some allow considerable scope for players to map their own 'skin' designs into the game. Player-characters range from the excessive

Press U and E together to execute a finishing move.

12. Spectacular transformation: cut-scene in which the principal player-character of *Primal* (2003) is about to shift into new and more powerful demonic form.

in appearance (the likes of Lara Croft and Duke Nukem, the gender-political dimensions of which are considered in the next chapter) to more 'ordinary' figures such as the protagonists of *Max Payne, The Getaway* and *Silent Hill*. Spectacular foes range from the skinless zombies, cloven-footed demons and blood-thirsty vampires of horror games to the assorted alien forms found in science fiction. High-fantasy offers its own array of fabulous beasts, from the obligatory unicorns and dragons to more inventive creations or combinations.

Where they are found, the potential pleasures of spectacle designed to attract the 'look' of the player are often interrupted, however, by the immediate requirements of gameplay. Too much idle enjoyment of spectacular environments or other features can be bad for the health of the avatar, who is liable to be shot, eaten or to face some other unpleasant fate in many games if attention is directed solely or excessively to the quality of the surroundings – whether those of landscapes or antagonists. The very notion of 'sitting back' and merely contemplating aesthetic qualities is anathema to most forms of gameplay, the demands of which require, in many games, a more or less constant level of response from the player. The urgency of the need to focus on pressing gameplay requirements can be a powerful distraction from any close consideration of qualities such as graphical realism or spectacle – a blessing, probably, for games lower in such resources, but also a reminder of the fact that, in the last resort, the demands of core gameplay are paramount. That said, it is notable that even the most frenetic first-person shooters figure among games highly rated for the quality of their visuals: Gamespot's ten 'best-looking' games poll of 2001, for example, included *Unreal* (1998), *Half-Life*, *Unreal Tournament* (1999) and *Quake III Arena* (2000) as well as perhaps more obvious contenders such as *Myst* and *American McGee's Alice*.[30] Audio-visual qualities of realism and/or spectacle are likely to be appreciated somewhat subliminally in many cases, contributing to the overall impression created by games but in a manner that is far from always at the forefront of attention.

If the demands of gameplay are often a bar to more leisurely or contemplative enjoyment of spectacle, they clearly offer much potential for the extension of the kind of impact-aesthetic provided by some films. Techniques such as hyper-rapid editing, unstable 'subjective' camerawork and the propelling of objects at high speed out towards the screen are often used in Hollywood action sequences to create a heightened impression of viewer proximity to, or participation in, the action. Some of these are directly mimicked in games, including the impression created of a shaking or unsteady 'camera' at moments of impact on the player-character, as suggested in the previous chapter. Games can go much further, though, in the translation from spectacular action to the creation of intensive *sensations*. Impact that remains entirely vicarious in the cinema can become more literally and physically transmitted to the gameplayer, if in highly stylized forms. The shaking of the camera when the player is under dangerous assault can have effects that are not just aesthetic but functional, affecting the ability of the player to engage in the task at hand (when a player-character in *EverQuest* is subjected to a strong blow, for example, the camera spins, creating disorientation on the part of the player). Impact can also be translated through the various kinds of haptic interface devices considered in the previous chapter.

Combat sequences in many games create a sense of assaultive impact and sensation that can send the pulse racing. Limited scale and relatively low fidelity of graphics reduces the audio-visual impact of such sequences to a level far below that achieved in the cinema, although the 'in-your-face' variety of impact is increased in a literal sense through the close proximity in which the player is often located to the screen (especially in the case of PC games). Entire new dimensions of impact and sensation result, however, from the central fact that the player has to *respond*. Explosive spectacle in action films impacts *on* the viewer. For action-movie fans, part of the pleasure is one of being 'done to', as it is put by Martin Barker and Kate Brooks.[31] Action-oriented games offer a similar pleasure of sensational impact, of things happening forcefully *to* the player, via the avatar, but one founded on the requirement for a substantial reciprocal response from the player: a 'doing to' as well as being 'done to', an opportunity to engage with the source of sensational impact: to fight back, to attempt to negotiate difficult and potentially hazardous terrain, and so on. This can entail a frenzied response on the part of the player, as, for instance, in *Max Payne*, in which a difficult shoot-out might be re-attempted rapidly many times in succession in an extremely compressed burst of intense interactivity. If flames and fireball effects come out at the avatar and at the screen in one punishing sequence, in which Max has to be negotiated through a restaurant wracked by a series of explosions, the player has also to plunge him (repeatedly) *into* the inferno – in an active attempt to negotiate the threat – rather than just being assaulted by cinematic dimensions such as jarring and camera-shaking impact.

Pleasures resulting from spectacle and from a physical intensity of engagement are often combined in individual game sequences. In one mission in *The Getaway*, for example, the player–character is called upon to break a villain from a police van near a virtual equivalent of the Old Bailey courthouse. As the player–character arrives close to the scene, a non-player character member of the criminal gang involved in the operation comments 'wait 'til you see this', cueing the player to anticipate something spectacular. A police car escorting the van is then torched as part of the escape plan, a fairly small-scale outbreak of spectacle – after which the player–character is required to chase the van, as it makes off at speed, and eventually crash into it repeatedly to force it to a halt. The player–character has to steer around the blazing police car and then go *full pelt* after the van as it careers off into traffic. The experience is one of great intensity, encouraging considerable peripheral exertion from the player: pressing much harder than functionally necessary on the accelerator button on the console controller, leaning forward and/or from side to side while dodging other vehicles, *shouting* (fruitlessly, of course) at other vehicles to get out of the way – all of which can be taken as indicators of a heightened degree of imaginary presence in the game-world, as well as being signifiers of immersion in the game *as* game.[32] Gameplay of this kind is exciting, and can also be highly frustrating, especially on repeated attempts and in relatively lengthy missions that – in this case – cannot usually be retried only in part. Failure means starting again, which raises the stakes once part of a mission has been accomplished, thus increasing the intensity of investment likely to result in the remainder. A similar kind of intensity is offered by many other games, especially in sequences in which the player is put under increased pressure by factors such as particularly heavy assault, tight deadlines or direct competition with others (human or computer-generated). Examples include the frantic button-mashing characteristic of many beat-'em-up games or the intensity created in racing games when straining 'desperately' to overtake or avoid being overtaken by another vehicle. This kind of pressure can be increased in multi-player games by the sense that the player's actions are being monitored by others, particularly when the fate of other player-characters might also be at stake.

The experience offered by this kind of intensity of gameplay has something in common with one of the four basic qualities outlined in Roger Caillois' typology: games that produce what he terms *ilinx*, from the Greek term for 'whirlpool', the source also of the Greek expression for 'vertigo'. Games which produce a vertiginous experience 'consist of an attempt to momentarily destroy the stability of perception and inflict a kind of voluptuous panic upon an otherwise lucid mind.'[33] In its most literal sense, this involves games that entail a physical whirling or spinning of the human body. Impressions of something like vertigo – nausea, at least – can be created by some videogames, especially when played in the first person and when rapidly navigating tortuous spaces, a gaming tradition established by the vertiginous high-speed play of the pioneering first-person-shooter titles *Wolfenstein 3D* and *Doom*. An impression of giddiness can also be created in third-person games such as *Prince of Persia: Sands of Time* by combinations such as the use of high-angled camera positions, camera movement and player-character activities such as balancing on precipitous ledges and swinging across yawning voids. A more displaced sense of *ilinx* is also created by sequences such as the one from *The Getaway* described above, and many other high-intensity gameplay activities, an impression verging on frenetic paroxysm including elements described by Caillois such as 'a question of surrendering to a kind of spasm, seizure, or shock'.[34] High-intensity sequences can certainly generate, in some circumstances, feelings of frenzy and panic that can override more rational and effective activity (wild shooting in all directions rather than more measured response, for example), just as intensive assault in the real world tends to result in a momentary by-passing of the more rational parts of the brain. Games that contain this kind of material tend also to provide quieter interludes to modulate what might otherwise be an overwhelming and less pleasurable experience; the police-van-break mission from *The Getaway* is followed by a stealth-based sequence that creates intensity of its own, but in a very different, un-frenetic register.

One of the reasons for the prevalence of violence in many games is, almost certainly, the extent to which violent action (and the effort to preserve the life of the player-character) lends itself readily to the production of this kind of intensity, in the same way that it produces a clear sense of action/feedback cause-and-effect in gameplay. Conflict, for Chris Crawford, is one of the defining characteristics of games, and as Crawford suggests, violence is the most extreme form of conflict: 'gorily physical, utterly direct, and maximally intense.'[35] For many, including Crawford, the degree to which games rely on these qualities is questionable, on aesthetic as well as moral grounds, demonstrating a lack of subtlety and variation in game design; an emphasis on what Crawford considers to be essentially child-like direct, intense and physical engagement, a niche into which he suggests much of mainstream gaming has become stuck.[36] Many games also offer intensity of experience of a less crude variety, however, including the multi-tasking required by real-time strategy games. In the most intensively heightened games, the focus tends to be relatively narrow, as in the heat of the action in a first-person shooter, in which concentration is focused on the immediate tasks of navigation, shooting, survival and the inventory-management required to support these core aspects of gameplay. Strategy games usually offer a broader and more diffuse range of tasks to which simultaneous or alternating attention is required.

Different types of game offer different kinds and degrees of intensity, not all of which are appealing to all actual or potential players or in all playing circumstances. How the basis of the appeal of the most intensified gameplay sensation might be understood is not an easy question to answer with any certainty. It might be associated primarily with particular demographics, as Crawford suggests, especially relatively young males, given the consonance between direct, intense and (mostly virtual) physical engagement and prevailing constructions of masculinity. The intense, sensational experience might also have wider appeal, however, as one ready source of the 'flow' state examined in Chapter 1; or, more generally, as an experience defined by intensity and clear-cut action that contrasts pleasurably with the more mundane, routine and complexly ramified nature of daily life for most people.[37] It is sometimes argued that contemporary media have a particular leaning towards the production of such experiences, an emphasis on 'surface' intensity ascribed to a 'postmodern' era and often contrasted with 'deeper' experiences such as those associated with literature or less mainstream cinema. If the intensity of experience offered by some media, including games, has increased over time this can also be explained more locally, however, without the evocation of large-scale social-cultural change. Certain tendencies towards 'upping the ante' are built into media such as these if a broadly equivalent impact is to be maintained over time, given the extent to which viewers or players are likely to become habituated to particular effects, once established as part of a familiar repertoire. Impactful sensation also has a longer tradition in popular culture, however, in events such as festivals and carnivals and, closer to the world of games, location-based entertainments such as those provided by rides in amusement and theme parks.

Music and other sound effects can also be used to crank up the intensity of gameplaying experiences. The soundscape of *Silent Hill 2* is designed to discomfort, to jar and to set the player on edge, as befits a horror game. Scratchy, sharp, metallic sounds are combined with a piano-frame being hit at the bass end, heavy echo creating a diffused skein of dissonant sound that appears to come from some hellish depths. The disordered crackle of radio-static adds to the cacophony, alerting players to the proximity of monsters veiled in the mist that cloaks much of the gamescape and often inducing a panic-stricken reaction in which the player-character is spun around in search of the source of threat. A similar level of intensity is promoted in different form by the fabric of sound created in *Unreal*

II. An onslaught of noise fills the air when the player-character is caught up in a dog-fight between aliens and soldiers in the dark. Soldiers shout directives and scream for help when attacked; weapon-fire is heard from what appears to be a 360 degree perspective around the player-character (and it is raining heavily). Cued by pleas for help from other soldiers, the player-character runs around in the darkened space, attempting to locate and contain the threat. The intensity of the sequence comes to a head when a spacecraft hovers overhead, assaulting the ears as its volume drowns out everything else. The weight and density of the soundscape creates a real sense of disorientation and panic, clouding the ability of the player to think more rationally about what action to take. Much the same effect is achieved in the Normandy beach landing sequence of *Medal of Honor: Allied Assault*, closely replicating the aural assault created in the scenes from the film *Saving Private Ryan* (1998) on which it is based.

Quieter sensations of unease and uncertainty can also be created, as in many horror games, including vicarious feelings of claustrophobia in dark, enclosed spaces. Strong impressions of suspense and anticipation are also generated more widely in games, especially in the moments preceding the more frantic or furious engagements in gameplay: when about to lean around a corner not sure what to expect (the first time), or when knowing what to expect but not *exactly* when or how well the player will fare (on subsequent attempts at the same stretch of gameplay).[38] Tension can also be created when playing against the clock, another situation in which intensity can have a deleterious panic-inducing impact on the quality of play. The achievement of goals offers a relaxing of intensity, a sense of relief often coupled with an impression of mastery – until, that is, the next task/level/game is attempted.

Games can also create sensations based on particular impressions of movement through the gamescape. One of the pleasures of *Descent* (1995), an early first-person PC game in which the player-character occupies a small mobile spacecraft, is the sensation of flying effortlessly through space, unhindered by gravity and arcing smoothly and swiftly through the subterranean tunnels of an alien planet. A more enhanced sensation of this kind is provided by *Rez*, the on-rails motion of which creates an impression of lightness and of inexorable movement towards an ever-receding vanishing point, a feeling that carries with it something of the sublime: a sense of the player-character being overwhelmed but also liberated within an infinite space. A smooth-gliding sensation is also created in travel by mini-hovercraft in *Beyond Good and Evil* (2003), which can be experienced in both first- and third-person modes, and which is enjoyable for its own sensual appeal in addition to its functionality as a mode of transport and for in-game racing competitions and exploration. Levitation spells such as 'Dead Man Floating' in *EverQuest* create a similar sensation (as well as keeping the player/character out of the reach of earth-bound enemies), distinct from the usual slightly jerky running motion used in the game.

An important dimension of the spectacular and sensational qualities offered by games is the extent to which these can actively be created by the actions of the player/player-character – a dimension specific to games, in comparison with spectacular/sensational media such as Hollywood cinema. In many cases, this is a spectacle rooted in destruction, although players might also gain pleasure from contemplation of structures they have created in construction-based games such as the *Sim City* series (from 1991), the spectacular and/or realistic qualities of which usually increase with each new iteration. The pleasure of blowing up buildings or shooting enemies spectacularly into pieces is clearly factored into many titles, some of which have become notorious as a result. The fact that gameplayers are actively involved in such processes – rather than just watching them on a screen – is usually seen as having significant implications for the social-cultural dimension of such material in games, an issue to which we return in the following chapter. Spectacular destruction of bodies tends to be found most commonly in game-worlds in which the bodies involved are either fantastic or exaggerated, rather than in those with the greatest aspirations towards representational and/or functional realism. Exceptions to this tendency, such as *Soldier of Fortune* and *Manhunt*, are usually sources of particular controversy. This is largely a matter of moral sensitivities. War games based on real, historical conflicts tend to produce relatively unspectacular enemy deaths, as is the case in titles such as *Medal of Honor* and *Call of Duty* (2003). The more fantastic the opposition, the freer developers generally feel to allow indulgence in player-created gore-fests. Examples include the protracted fights with various hybrid part-human/animal/plant monsters in *The Thing*, where several weapons – bullets, flamethrowers, grenades and the like – are often required to dispose of resistant threats, or the relentless shooting needed to dispatch the seemingly endless zombie hordes of *House of the Dead III* (2002). Where gory effects related to human rather than fantastical bodies have been treated as the stuff of spectacular exultation, controversy has usually resulted, the most notorious example probably being victory sequences in *Mortal Kombat* in which the player-character performs moves such as ripping out the opponent's heart or pulling out their skull and spine.

Games produced by id software and Rockstar have particularly excelled in the spectacle of death. The reduction of foes to cartoonish messes is clearly marked as 'unrealistic' in the likes of *Doom* and *Quake*, and to a large extent in Rockstar's less fantasy-oriented *Grand Theft Auto III* and *Vice City*. A gratuitous spectacle of violence is available to the player as an optional extra in *Grand Theft Auto III*, in which non-player characters can be killed and then excessively beaten after death, with resulting splurges of blood on the floor. *Manhunt* opts for a more realistic and disturbingly intense aesthetic, including up-close methods of killing such as suffocating a victim with a plastic bag over the head or using a shard of glass as a knife, the effects of which are more than usually realistic at the level of both graphics resolution and in the absence of the buffer created by a more obviously fantastic framework. The deaths of player-characters can also offer servings of spectacle, which might be considered as compensation for moments of failure. Max Payne often performs a pleasing pirouette at the moment of death while the player of *Half-Life* is given the strange perspective cited in the previous chapter of a first-person view of the dismembered remains of the player-character's own body.

Spectacular destruction can also be wreaked on inorganic matter. Parts of the in-game environment can often be destroyed, as part of the requirements of gameplay objectives and/or for the specific pleasure of the spectacle that results. In *Max Payne*, for example, objects such as televisions explode in a pleasing manner – entirely gratuitous – when shot. In driving games such as *Colin McRae Rally 4* (2004) that register damage on the image of the vehicle (when played in third-person perspectives), enjoyment closer to the *paidea* than the *ludus* end of the scale can result from experiments in the extent to which a car can be wrecked before becoming inoperable. War and other combat-oriented games often require or permit the player to use explosives to destroy enemy vehicles or structures, although this is another case in which the enjoyment of the spectacular results is often leavened by more pressing gameplay requirements such as escaping the blast radius or avoiding some other form of ongoing attack.

The creation of spectacular action is specifically rewarded by some games, forming the basis for gameplay in many stunt-based games, including the *Cool Boarders* series (from 1996) and *Tony Hawk's Pro Skater* series (from 1999). The creation of more destructive spectacle is rewarded in examples such as *Burnout 2: Point of Impact* (2003), which has a 'crash mode' in which points are earned for creating spectacular vehicular pile-ups. The spectacular results of gameplay can also be available for more leisurely contemplation, in the form of replay sequences or 'cinematic' cuts away from the immediate action, as provided in *Need for Speed: Hot Pursuit 2* (2002), in which 'zone' and 'jump' cams provide instant slow-motion shots of exploits such as slamming into road blocks or making vehicles fly through the air.

The pleasure of player-generated spectacle may be two-fold: the pleasure of the spectacle in itself, as in other cases, but also the very game-specific pleasure of these forms of spectacle as a vivid example of feedback, one of the key qualities of gameplay considered in Chapter 1. To witness, in striking form, the destruction of buildings or enemies brought about by the player is to receive strong evidence of cause-and-effect, specifically of the *effect* of player/player-character agency, a quality that can contribute to the wider impression of immersion in the game-world (as suggested in Chapter 2). A dimension such as the spectacular, then, which might from one perspective appear to be somewhat secondary in games, can contribute to very central aspects of the broader gameplay experience. The same can be said of the various forms and degrees of realism offered by games. They all contribute to the overall experience, their level of significance varying from one game – and from one player, or one playing circumstance – to another.

4

Social, Cultural and Political Dimensions

Games have their own dimensions, distinct from those of other media forms, as we have argued in the previous chapters. But games are also social-cultural products, involved in the broad processes through which meanings are circulated in the societies in which they are produced and consumed. Games do not exist in a vacuum, as we suggested in Chapter 1. They often draw upon or produce material that has social, cultural or ideological resonances, whether these are explicit or implicit and whether they can be understood as reinforcing, negotiating or challenging meanings or assumptions generated elsewhere in society.[1] Obvious examples include the kinds of characters given dominant representation in games, as well as the social implications of the narrative, generic and other associational frameworks on which games draw – issues to which we return below. Core gameplay itself can also be freighted with a range of social-cultural-ideological meanings, numerous examples of which will be considered in this chapter. If associational meanings might often occupy a space in the background, as suggested in Chapter 1, social-cultural dimensions embedded in gameplay are given potentially increased potency through the active nature of play. The activity of the player is essential to the realization of much of what unfolds in the playing of games, even where the parameters are clearly established in advance. As a consequence, the player can seem more directly implicated than traditional media consumers in the meanings that result. This is one reason for the degree of controversy often stirred up around games, especially in areas such as on-screen violence and representations of gender, two issues addressed in more detail in this chapter.

In most cases, the social-cultural or political-ideological dimensions of games are implicit rather than the outcome of conscious or deliberate design. Gameplay and other features that have such implications are usually designed to be appealing in their own right, in many of the ways already considered in this book. One way to demonstrate how much potential games have for the construction of particular social-cultural meanings is to start by considering some examples in which this dimension is made highly explicit: games designed with specific ideological agendas in mind. These range from brief, rhetorical interventions to more fully elaborated versions of familiar genres. An example of the first variety is *September 12*, designed by Gonzalo Frasca, the aim of which is to make a simple point about the so-called 'war on terror' announced by president George W. Bush in the wake of the attacks on America on 11 September 2001.[2] The player is presented with a screen depicting an animated version of a Middle Eastern urban scene: a marketplace surrounded by flat-roofed buildings, populated by figures characterized as civilians, in blue, and weapon-carrying 'terrorists', in green. The player is given control of a targeting reticule that can be used to launch missiles at terrorists. They are not easy to hit, however, and the missiles tend, as in the real world, to cause 'collateral damage' to civilians and buildings. Each time a terrorist or civilian is killed, a few civilian figures gather on the scene and kneel down to go into 'mourning' animations, accompanied by the sound of sobbing: they then transform into terrorists. The more death and destruction is wreaked, the more terrorists are created, and the game is structured to prevent the possibility of victory (a time delay built into the targeting reticule ensures that all terrorists or buildings cannot be wiped out before the former multiply and the latter are rebuilt). If the player stops firing, the number of terrorists gradually reduces, but they do not disappear. The message built into gameplay has clear real-world reference: to try to destroy 'terrorism' through direct military assault is counter-productive, only increasing the kinds of grievances that usually lead to the creation of the phenomenon in the first place. Taking no action is not offered as a panacea, merely as something that does not make the situation worse, but anyone encountering the game is expected to do something and is forced to confront the no-win scenario.

More fully realized games have also been designed as interventions into this geo-political territory, including two Arabic first-person shooters. *UnderAsh* (2001, developed by the Syrian publisher Dar al-Fikr) is based on the Palestinian intifada. The player takes on the role of a young Palestinian, Ahmed, following his development from stone-throwing protestor to armed resister, fighting against Israeli soldiers and settlers in the occupied territories. A mission downloadable as a demo sets the player/Ahmed the task of rescuing the people taken captive in a village and preventing it from being demolished to make way for a new Israeli settlement.[3] Another mission situates Ahmed in the environs of a virtual equivalent of the Dome of the Rock, close to the Al-Aqsa mosque in Jerusalem, a key flashpoint in the real-world conflict. *Special Force* (2003) was developed by the guerrilla group Hizbollah to simulate

13. First-person freedom-fighter: Palestinian resistance figured in-game in the precincts of the Dome of the Rock in *UnderAsh* (2001).

its military operations against the Israeli occupation of southern Lebanon. Military posts to be attacked by the player are described as 'exact replicas' of positions used by Israel during the occupation, which ended with the withdrawal of Israel in 2000. The game also includes pictures of real-life 'martyrs' killed in the conflict.[4] Both games were designed specifically to offer Arabic players – especially youths – an alternative to American-dominated games in which Arabs and Muslims are often portrayed as terrorists or other kinds of enemies.

Others have also seized on the potential of games as bearers of particular messages. If the first-person shooter format has been used as a way of figuring Arab resistance to Israeli occupation, it has also been employed, perhaps less obviously, in Christian-oriented games such as *Eternal Wars: Shadow of Light* (2002) and *Catechumen* (2000). The former, built on the *Quake* engine, situates the player as Mike, an angel dispatched by God to do battle with demons in a struggle over the soul of a troubled teenager.[5] *Catechumen*, set in the Rome of AD171, has the player-character fighting demons and possessed Romans in order to rescue captured Christians who face execution for refusing to renounce their religion. The game offers a number of context-specific twists on the usual first-person shooter format, including a 'faith meter' on the heads-up display and the screening of Biblical verses when the game is in pause mode. Foes are not killed by the player-character's weapons, a variety of beam-projecting 'Swords of the Spirit': demons, when hit, are sent back to the underworld, while Romans are converted to Christianity; they kneel down and pray.

Games such as these aim to achieve a balance between getting across a message and offering generic gameplay pleasures; the latter is seen as important if they are to attract the target audience, primarily consisting of young people likely to be drawn to such games more generally. Games are understood here, as in other circles, as having educational potential. In less controversial territory, the pedagogical uses of games have been explored by initiatives such as the 'Games-to-Teach' project at MIT, in which games were designed to aid in the teaching of maths, science and engineering at advanced secondary and early undergraduate level.[6] In the 3D action/racing game *Supercharged!* (undated), for example, the player was taught principles of electromagnetism by learning how to navigate a miniature space pod through a scenario in which it had been sucked inside the circuitry of a film projector. The qualities of gameplay more generally can also be seen as embodying useful pedagogical principles such as active problem solving and learning through practice.[7] Most games do not have overtly expressed educational or ideological dimensions, however. The primary aim is usually to provide entertainment, of one variety or another, rather than to convey a message of any kind. All games can be said to be carriers of social-cultural meanings, however, sometimes with more acute political-ideological implications. The moment any choices are made about what material to include, how to treat it and what kinds of activities are required of players in order to succeed, particular meanings – or the potential for such meanings – are created. Play is always shaped by, and appears within, particular cultural contexts, even if these are often largely implicit and kept in the background. These contexts are often quite broadly framed, particularly in games designed for something close to a global marketplace, although particular types of games and game content are sometimes favoured in one place more than another (in Japan, for example, one of the major poles of the games business, role-playing games are generally more popular than in the US or European markets).[8] It is with material that exists at the level of background settings and scenarios that we begin to explore these dimensions in more detail. Subsequent sections of this chapter will consider meanings created within the processes of core gameplay mechanics. The two will be separated out here, initially at least, although significant overlaps are often found between them.

Background settings and scenarios

It is in the dimension of background settings, scenarios and the qualities ascribed to player- and non-player characters that the social-cultural implications of games have most in common with those of other media products such as film and television. The broad contexts within which gameplay occurs – as opposed to gameplay activities themselves – are repositories for a range of social-cultural or political-ideological resonances, and for some widely repeated scenarios. If many shooter and action/adventure type games draw on the quest format or the hero's journey archetype, for example, this has social implications of its own, suggesting a substantial cultural investment in the notion of the individual as a source of heroic agency. The value of formats such as these for games is their very familiarity, as we suggested in Chapter 1:

the extent to which they can readily be drawn upon without needing a great deal of explicit elaboration. The same goes for their social or political-ideological resonances. Assumptions of individual freedom and agency are deeply ideological, especially given the extent to which they are celebrated in capitalist/western societies the nature of which ensures that such freedom is denied to many, both close to home and elsewhere in the world. Such assumptions have achieved wide levels of acceptance, however, as one of the key ideological underpinnings of the societies in which they are promoted. Many games buy into this ideology, as do many other products of popular culture, a factor that may be related to the absence of real agency in many areas of life. The figure of the individual hero, the player-character, faced with some kind of upheaval that leads to a quest against powerful forces is common to many games – from science fiction, adventure and fantasy oriented titles to crime-thrillers such as *Max Payne* and *The Getaway* – even if the requirements of gameplay are such that success is often not easily achieved. The hero is, typically, presented as a figure hyperbolically reduced to the status of lone individual assaulted from all sides, with the exception of the occasional ally, at war with both police and criminal gangs in *Max Payne* and *The Getaway* or with alien invaders, denizens of evil and fellow humans (chiefly, marines) in the *Doom*, *Quake* and *Half-Life* varieties.

The particular circumstances in which individual human agency is celebrated also draw, in many cases, on material with broader social-cultural resonance. The individual hero is pitted in some games against a conspiracy of one kind or another. In *Half-Life* a combination of external and internal threats are proposed: externally, the threat of alien invasion unleashed by scientific experiments; internally, the machinations of sinister government forces.[9] In both cases, the game draws on material that has real-world social/political reference. In the concern it implies about the unwise dabbling of scientists, the game plays into broader cultural discourses about the possible dangers of scientific interventions into and manipulations of the world. In its government-conspiracy dimension, the game evokes both long-standing and contemporary suspicions of government – especially, in the United States, distrust of federal institutions. In bringing the two together, the game has much in common – at the level of contextual background – with many other cultural products, including science fiction films and *The X-Files* television series. The dominant tenor of such material tends to be politically conservative, playing on fantasies shared by American right-wing fringe groups (and, arguably, distracting attention from more real and significant unaccountable government actions under guises such as 'security' and the pursuit of foreign policy). Other, more complex networks of conspiracy are found in the *Deux Ex* games.

If the individual heroic action of *Half-Life* is framed as being in opposition to alien attack and government conspiracy, that of the *Tomb Raider* games is situated in a context equally freighted with (reactionary) ideological resonances. The 'alien' in this case is largely equated with the 'foreign', sources of danger to be exploited by the aristocratically situated Lara Croft in the name of high adventure. The scenario of the earlier games in the cycle can be read, as Barry Atkins suggests, 'as providing a remarkably consistent metaphor for a kind of (British) imperialism that is, understandably, only rarely celebrated in contemporary culture, and only rarely offered up at all without accompanying critique.'[10] Foreign space 'is full of traps and snares, and the threat that it represents is only defused through violence and (often) through the application of superior technology.'[11] Representatives of indigenous populations are often depicted stereotypically, significant only as mute aides or objects to be dealt with violently, or are present only tangentially through the material remnants of their culture. The value given to indigenous cultures, as Atkins and many other have suggested, is as sources of exotic spectacle and artefacts to be stolen for their value to others, rather than any real engagement with their own qualities.

The broad contours of fantasy worlds, including those found in massively multi-player role-playing games, can also be read at the level of their social-cultural implications. A similar range of historical and cultural influences are found in many such worlds, including *EverQuest*, *Ultima Online* and *Asheron's Call*, as Eddo Stern suggests, including 'a wild amalgam of Celtic, Gothic, Medieval and Renaissance combined with a deep commitment to a Wagnerian, Tolkienesque, Camelotian and *D&D*'ish verisimilitude.'[12] What, Stern asks, is the contemporary basis of the appeal of the neo-medievalist character of such games, as a form of pleasurable escape from daily reality? One answer, for American players, is the offering of a sense of historical lineage more befitting the globally dominant superpower than the literal account of a history that leads through colonialist adventures to 'a disconnected and un-inscribed Native American past.'[13] More general conclusions could also be drawn about the potential appeal of the neo-medieval, which can be divided into two categories that carry rather different ideological resonances.[14]

The first is the medieval as *romantic*. Characteristics such as nobility, honour, grandeur and magic prevail, attributes perhaps less easily imagined in a contemporary setting. This elevated rendition of medievalism is best illustrated by *The Lord of the Rings: The Two Towers*. The game's epic battles are framed by contextualizing backstory: the agrarian idyll of Middle Earth is threatened by dark tyrannical forces that will kill or enslave its people and exploit natural resources. Rather than the struggles between various religious factions and cults that characterized the real medieval period in Europe, the game's romantic take on the medieval enables heterogeneous races and factions to band together under the aegis of fellowship and a battle against tyranny: universal good pitched against universal evil. This framework helps to justify violent action. The solidity with which good and evil are presented accords with an idealistic mythic-romantic sensibility and locates the characters in clearly morally grounded ways. But what are the implications of this moral order for a putative ideal social structure, as implicitly rendered in the game? The concepts of fellowship and honour are married to the preservation of a hierarchical feudal social order, in which the strong protect the weak and must resist the temptation to pursue material gain. This provides the grounds for a unification of the social and moral order. The romantic view of the medieval provides a patchwork of conservative and liberal values that can be understood as speaking of the present through an imaginary past.

The second category is the medieval as *barbaric*. Civilized behaviours have little or no place; social cohesion is minimal. Brute force, amorality, self-interest and chaos prevail. In many respects this version of the medieval is filtered through the visceral macho aesthetics of 'heavy metal' and the vagabond adventuring of Robert E. Howard's *Conan* cycle, as reflected in the mise-en-scene and colour palettes of games that lean in this direction. *Enclave* (2003), for example, is composed mainly of dungeons, forests and fortresses; overcast skies and the predominance of grey stone lend a sense of foreboding gloom. While the demonic is defined as an evil that must be dispatched in the more romantically inclined games, here players are often invited to partake of the pleasures of being aligned with the dark side; cast in the role of amoral vampire in *Blood Omen 2* or choosing to play a dark elf necromancer in *EverQuest*. The long-ago, far-away fantasy context and the provision of an environment marked as potently 'uncivilized' provide players with a licence for indulging – playfully – in what might otherwise be considered unconscionable acts. Games that deploy this barbaric context offer a fantasy escape from mundane existence, behavioural restraint or alienation. Rhetorics of 'liberation' of this kind are often used by players describing the pleasures of such games.[15]

The clearly defined Manichean – good-versus-evil – structure that characterizes most of the games that fall into the romantic medieval category helps to locate them within the regulatory system as suitable for a younger audience, thereby maximizing their potential market (*Lord of the Rings: The Two Towers* for example is rated in Britain as 12+, while *Blood Omen 2* is rated 15). The romantic rendition of the medieval might offer players a relief from the moral, religious and political complexities of contemporary existence. Games that fall into the barbaric category are often morally more complex, although at times it is a simple case of being on the 'other' side. The popularity of the neo-medieval in games might, therefore, lie in providing either compensation for a lack of moral certainty or the pleasures of aligning with the 'transgressive' (albeit versions of transgression that take conventionalized forms). Many games combine the romantic and barbaric modes of neo-medievalism, drawing on the appeals of each, particularly those which offer choices in moral alignment or that allow a certain licence to do 'bad' in the service of 'good'. A Manichean moral structure is used by the majority of fighting-based games, not just those using neo-medievalist settings, suggesting a general industry consciousness of the need to contextualize violence, often within fantasy frames, to avoid possible censure or restriction to niche markets.

The fascination with the medieval as romantic and/or barbaric is not a recent phenomenon or, of course, restricted to games. Eighteenth-century gothic novelists, Victorian artists and cultural commentators and 'new age' culture have all looked to the medieval as an era of lost values or as a lucrative source of supernatural and visceral horror. Seeking a broader cultural-historical explanation for its popularity, Umberto Eco suggests that 'every time Europe feels a sense of crisis, of uncertainty about its aims and scopes, it goes back to its own roots – and the roots of European society are, without question, in the Middle Ages'.[16] The appeal of the medieval might be understood today, beyond Europe, in the context of various concerns about 'postmodern' relativism or the loss of 'traditional' values. For media such as videogames, it also has more immediate sources of attraction, providing thematic structures and design rhetorics well suited to games. It offers a repertoire of mythically styled heroes and anti-heroes to be played.

Player- and non-player-characters are repositories of social-cultural values to which attention has often been drawn, especially in terms of representations of gender. The typical hero of the first-person shooter, and many other shooting and/or action-adventure games, was originally a very obvious macho template: large, thickly muscled, gruff and craggy-featured – ideally suited, in fact, to the limitations of blocky graphics. This figure has since been supplemented by a wider range of types, although it is still very much in evidence.[17] In many role-playing games, for example, a choice of body types is often on offer. These are often aligned with race, class and occupation, warriors and melee class characters often appearing more muscled than clerics or magic-casters (such as wizards). Across the range of game types, the tough macho image fits closely with the kinds of actions usually required of many characters, combining individualist with patriarchal resonances. The world of games ranging from *Doom* to *Max Payne* is not suited to 'wimps', even if a slightly greater variety of emotional expression has been permitted in some titles. Max Payne, for example, is not a muscle-bound hero/anti-hero, nor does he have the cyborg-enhanced attributes of characters such as *Halo*'s Master Chief. As his name suggests, Max Payne suffers. Unlike the Master Chief's mechanical attitude to mowing down alien hordes, Payne's engagement with his enemies is emotional. With his wife and child dead, Payne is out for revenge. In combination with being subjected to mind-games and a variety of drugs, he comes over as a feverish, highly expressive character of the type associated with film noir, in the grip of a floridly melodramatic psychosis. The expression of Payne's emotions is framed in masculinist terms, however. Rather than being frozen by grief, he is compelled into a frenzied and active mode of shoot-first-ask-questions-later violence. Action equates here with traditional concepts of masculinity found in a wide range of popular media. The figure of the Prince in *Prince of Persia: Sands of Time* is neither mechanical, psychotic, muscle-bound nor gruff, offering an alternative version of the male action hero. With his rather warm and encouraging direct speech to players ('no, no, no, that didn't happen. May I start again?' when he dies, for example), his floppy-hair, a slender body and harem pants, he is presented in more feminized guise than the traditional macho equivalent. Strength and agency are provided, but in the form of quick sword-play and light-footed acrobatics rather than brute force and muscles-as-body-armour. Physical power might also be tempered with other attributes: the playable characters of *Lord of the Rings: The Two Towers* might be good in battle, but they are also heroes with quite humble attitudes and regularly express concern for their fellows; this configuration is cued by the game's romantic neo-medievalism but also makes for more rounded and human-seeming characters.

Hyper-masculine images in popular culture have been read by critics such as Susan Jeffords as attempts to recuperate traditional gender roles that have been thrown into question elsewhere.[18] Images of militaristic or barbarian heroes might be seen as offering virtual compensation for what is experienced as a lack or loss of agency and bodily power in the real world. These bodies are also designed specifically for their spectacular qualities, however, to be visually arresting, as suggested in the previous chapter. The constructs of 'raw' masculinity offered by fight-oriented games are not always meant to be taken seriously, exaggeration sometimes tipping towards parody, as in the case of the unreconstructed cigar-chewing protagonist of *Duke Nukem* ('The Man – The Mission – The Babes'). In *Land of the Babes* (2000), the Duke is transported to a world in which all the men have been killed and the women are enslaved by an alien race. He is given many of the characteristics of Arnold Schwarzenegger's Terminator: the pumped-up muscles, the military flat-top (peroxide blonde), the bike and the one-liners. The Duke's clichéd speech is delivered in a staccato, gravely-voiced drawl: 'no-one messes with my babes', 'chew on this' and, when he dies, 'I'll be baaack'. Compared with the female head of the 'Unified Babe Resistance', he is inarticulate and capable of only very basic motivation. She explains the situation and gives him commands, which he translates into his own monosyllabic terms: he may have the muscles, but is not too bright. Rather than saving humanity or family – the stock situation for many action-adventure heroes – his task is to save 'his babes' (who regularly call for his help and dive into his arms during or after danger). Instead of an ideal masculine hero, the Duke is presented as a figure of fun, highlighting explicitly the absurd nature of the hyper-macho figure found in many popular texts.

The representation of women in videogames has promoted much controversy, especially given the influence of feminist thought on the analysis of popular culture in recent decades. The aim of much of this work has been to demonstrate the existence of masculine and patriarchal agendas in games. The earliest representations of the player-position in games were gender-neutral (*Pong* paddles, spaceships, firing devices). The first explicitly gender-marked avatar was female, in the shape of *Ms. Pac-Man* (1980), signified by the addition of a pink bow and a mouth lined with red. The dominant form in which female characters were found in many games until the 1980s was in the shape of the stereotypical 'damsel-in-distress', in examples such as *Donkey Kong* (1984; player-character's girlfriend to be rescued from clutches of a huge gorilla) and *Dragon's Lair* (1984; princess kidnapped by evil wizard).[19] This format was challenged in some 1980s titles, in which female characters were presented as either stronger antagonists (the crafty art-thief of *Where in the World is Carmen San Diego* [1985]) or player-character protagonists (the princess seeking a magical cure for her dying father in *King's Quest IV: Rosella's Peril* [1988]).[20] It did not disappear, however, the rescue of women–in–danger featuring in later games including *Duke Nukem: Land of the Babes*, if in more tongue-in-cheek fashion. Even in the critically lauded *Ico* (2001), a similar dynamic is found: a male avatar whose mission is to rescue a delicate-looking girl from trouble. In games based on the damsel-in-distress formula the rescue scenario is configured on conventionally gendered lines. Masculinity is defined as active, resourceful, powerful; femininity as weak and in need of strong male protection.

Many games have also featured female non–player characters as sexualized objects of the male gaze. The opening cut-scene of *BMX XXX* (2002), for example, intercuts filmed footage of teenage male bike riders performing tricks with images of half-naked 'exotic' dancers. Both are designed for the gaze, but with two very different economies at work: physical skill on display in the former, sexualized bodies in the latter (it is important to note, however, that in the game itself players can choose to perform BMX tricks as either male or female). Gameplay itself is

14. Sexist imagery, combined with action-stunts, in *BMX XXX* (2002).

laced with misogynistic 'street-speak' in which player-characters of either
gender are called 'ho's' and threatened with being 'cut', and a male non-
player character repeatedly states 'I've got a hot salty nut sack here' while
another comments on the status of his 'wiener'. Contempt for women
also seems to underlie the fact that prostitute non–player characters can
be beaten up and robbed in *Grand Theft Auto III* (the same can be said of
all non-player characters in the game, but an additional edge seems to be
in play when this happens after a virtual encounter for paid sex). If these
examples are particularly blatant, more subtle forms of patriarchal bias
can be found elsewhere.

The sexualized appeal of women characters is a tool used by many
games to attract attention in a competitive marketplace: from explicitly
pornographic and sleazy representations in the likes of *Virtual Valerie* (1990)
and *Erotica Island* (2000) to the women warrior figures of games such as
Primal and *Buffy*. At one end of the spectrum are characters designed
purely as objects of desire; at the other are female characters who are
afforded significant degrees of subjectivity. Many hover somewhere in

between, as is the case with *Dead or Alive: Xtreme Beach Volleyball*. The game is clearly informed by a soft-core 'cheese-cake' agenda. It begins with a montage of high resolution pin-up clichés: a parade of slender, long-legged, busty women perform various coquettish acts, flirting with the camera, dancing, feeding each other strawberries and undressing. One of the key attractions of the game, featured strongly in reviews at the time of release, is the way the characters' breasts jiggle in coordination with their movements, emphasized by the fact that they are clad in skimpy bikinis. Rather than the blatant sexual movements of the dancers at the start of *BMX XXX*, the inhabitants of *Xtreme Beach Volleyball* are more demure and playfully flirtatious (and therefore, perhaps, less sexually threatening to a teenage male audience). The players are given individual personalities – particular likes and dislikes, playing strengths and weaknesses – which suggests that they are accorded some degree of subjectivity at the same time as being blatant objects of the male gaze.

The game that has probably attracted most attention in gender terms is *Tomb Raider*, which offers Lara Croft as a combination of both object and wilful subject of her own action-adventure franchise. With her monumental breasts, waspish waist and long legs, Lara is clearly designed to arrest the gaze (the heterosexual male gaze in terms of lust, but perhaps soliciting more complex reactions from others). As Helen Kennedy notes, Lara offers a 'bimodal' form of address, in which different attributes are used in combination, sometimes sitting uncomfortably together, in an attempt to appeal to both male and female players.[21] In 1996, when the first in the *Tomb Raider* series was released, most games were still dominated by male avatars. It was refreshing for many gamers to play as a feisty and resourceful woman. While some women gamers welcomed the addition of Lara to the repertoire of action/fight-based games, others found her hyper-feminine figure troubling. Diane Carr, for example, suggests that Lara's activity, resourcefulness and aggression are compromised by 'exaggerated dream girl proportions ... inflated by a reactionary imagination'.[22]

The women warriors in *Primal, Xena: Warrior Princess* (1999) and the *Buffy the Vampire Slayer* games might not have the exaggerated 'sex-doll' proportions of Lara,[23] but they are still conventionally coded as 'attractive' in appearance, even if they are tactically smart and lethal in combat. The games industry appears to believe that 'girl-power' is combined to best commercial effect with physical attractiveness along rather narrow lines. This is essentially a trade-off based on making a notion of 'girl-power' sexually appealing to heterosexually-identified male players, a strategy at work more generally across a range of media to broaden the gender appeal of action-adventure formats. The inclusion of 'good-looking' powerful women in the products of popular culture can be regarded as a 'post-feminist' gesture; certain feminist ideas are included to speak more directly to female players, but at the cost of excising their overt political basis. Unlike the rather distant and cold Lara, who rarely lets the player know what she is thinking, *Primal's* Jen and *Buffy* are sharp and witty. They often comment with irony and sometimes sarcasm on the way their gender is perceived by male NPCs as a sign of weakness. The inclusion of more speech in games, a factor that might be related to the availability of increased resources for large sound files, gives these characters greater levels of subjectivity than game-Lara (although it could be argued that her outings in other media and the presence of more speech in *Angel of Darkness* than in previous games has boosted to some extent her complexity as a character). *Primal* and the *Buffy* games

15. Ordinary girl with extra-ordinary powers: Buffy as 'kick-ass' woman warrior in *Buffy the Vampire Slayer* (2002).

also reverse the gendering of the background rescue scenario: Jen's primary motivation, in most of the game, is to save her boyfriend from the clutches of an agent of chaos; *Buffy* saves various male and female characters from marauding vampires and demons. It is significant that the power of both *Buffy* and Jen is derived from supernatural sources. They are ordinary girls with extra-ordinary slaying powers, in contrast to male figures whose power is often derived from their own masculine form. The implication is that such power is less 'natural' for female figures, even though the powers of some male characters (such as *Halo*'s Master Chief) are also presented as the result of artificial supplementation. This device also permits the reconciliation of physical prowess with the use of figures who remain otherwise implausibly 'pretty' and petite. While some feminist critics argue that the recent flourishing of 'post-feminist' action-heroines plays entirely to the male-gaze and objectifies or fetishizes women, others have embraced representations of women heroines as a relief from the traditional male hero that has dominated western mythology and fiction.

Body shapes that accord with dominant/conventional notions of beauty also dominate the character types chosen, from a range of pre-set features, by players of online role-playing games such as *EverQuest*. There are many more slender blonde high elves played by women than there are female ogres or trolls. This might result from the importance to the game of cooperation with other players: the more visually appealing a character, it might be thought, the more likely they are to receive help from others. There is scope to build characters that do not accord with convention, however, including the possibility of creating a bearded female dwarf. Many role-playing games give players a choice of physical features, although choice of build is less commonly available. An exception is *Uru: Ages Beyond Myst* (2003), in which characters can range from the very slender to the moderately rounded. Plump is not on offer, however, suggesting that this game, like most others, buys into limited notions of beauty/appeal. If media such as film and television offer the pleasures of viewing figures of idealized beauty, to which most spectators cannot realistically aspire, games go a step further, in offering players the chance to occupy an alternative 'skin'. The fact that many games are designed for a teenage male market probably goes some way to explaining the predominance of stereotypical and sometimes demeaning representations of women. That does not mean, however, that all players 'read' or use the signifiers of gender and appearance in the same ways. Merely switching to more 'positive' representations has shortcomings of its own, itself having limited effect on the realities of gender equality, and potentially excising the ability of game character representations to speak to the real and contradictory conditions prevailing in daily life.

Racial/ethnic stereotyping is also to the fore in many macho action/ shooter heroes, the majority of which are white. In general, analysis of the representation or construction of race in popular culture is focused on non-white characters. As Richard Dyer argues, whiteness as a racial construct is frequently ignored because it operates in discourse as a 'naturalized' norm against which others are defined.[24] It is as important to consider meanings that circulate around 'white' characters in games, therefore, as it is to look at the characterizations of representatives of other groups. Games offer the potential to 'build' or inhabit, virtually, bodies of a fantastical and idealized nature. What ideologies of race underlie the pleasures of playing in the skin of such bodies? The muscled male body connotes physical power and control, but the meanings of these shift depending on skin colour. Dyer argues that images of white muscled heroes signify aspects of white masculinist supremacy. Black muscularity signifies differently. Within a racist paradigm that has its roots in Victorian uses of theories of evolution to shore up ideologies of white power, black muscles come to be regarded as 'natural' rather than acquired, indicators of primitivism rather than ultra-civilization. This equation is complicated, however, by the fact that in many games the presence of *white* barbarian figures also suggests a kind of liberating and powerful primitivism (the Nietzschean tagline 'what does not destroy one, makes me stronger' being used to advertise the *Conan* game [2004], for example). Commentators such as Donald Bogle and Frantz Fanon have argued that the implied potency of black muscular figures has the potential to provoke anxiety for white men.[25] Such ideologies might not always be activated in gameplay, as in other acts of media consumption, but they form an underlying structure of meanings that appear to be coded into many texts at some level, if only implicitly. Binary oppositions of this kind seem more explicit in games in which conflict occurs between groups defined in terms that include a more obviously racial/ethnic component, including war-games with real historical referents such as *Vietcong* or *Black Hawk Down*, in which a sense is sometimes created, as suggested in Chapter 1, of killing large numbers of 'faceless' enemy 'aliens'. A racial dimension can also be read into examples in which the alien is taken more literally, in forms such as extraterrestrials or zombies, although this operates at a level of metaphor in which the otherness of enemies can be open to a wider range of interpretations.

The player-characters of first-person games are often kept relatively undefined, leaving plenty of space to be occupied by the player. A white (male) player-character is often implied, however, the absence of much location-specific material having much in common with Dyer's formulation of a form of whiteness that gains its dominance partly through a lack of articulation of its own qualities. The first-person format is sufficiently open to accommodate players of any race or gender, but the white male is usually privileged by whatever markers of identity are supplied. What happens, then, when the player-character is explicitly characterized differently, as in *Unreal II*, in which ex-marine John Dalton is presented as African American? The setting, an intergalactic future, is one in which such ethnic/national identity seems to have no bearing. Dalton's skin is black, when seen in cut-scenes, and his voice a racially coded deep velvet. None of these characteristics have any bearing on his behaviour or gameplay, however. The same applies to other black characters, such as the black American female scientist in *Dig*. A more sexualized and fetishistic approach to non-white characters is evident in some games, including *DOA: Xtreme Beach Volleyball*. The women have different racial characteristics, including white, black and Asian, indicated by skin tone and facial features. Their bodies are similarly proportioned, however, and their characteristics broadly similar, suggesting that racial/ethnic features are cosmetic rather than grounded in any real cultural difference. As is the case with many pornographic texts, race here becomes just a matter of erotic novelty, like the choice of different types of chocolates offered by a selection box.

Some games are less restrictive in these dimensions, permitting choices about the racial and gender figurations of player-characters. *Deus Ex: Invisible War* (2004), for example, allows the player-character to be male or female and permits the player to select from a range of skin tones.[26] A similar facility is permitted in many other titles, including sports games such as *Links 2004*, in which skin-tone and gender are among many details of physical appearance that can be selected. In these cases also such choices are largely cosmetic, rather than affecting gameplay capabilities. If you choose to play as a female golfer you do not, as a result, hit the ball shorter distances, as would usually be the case in reality. The overall gameplaying experience can be affected by changes of this kind, however, particular at the level of the relative degree of identification created between player and player-character. For a woman playing *Half-Life* in first person to be hailed as 'Gordon', for example, can be jarring.[27] Such an effect is likely to be increased in games played in the third-person, in which the player is constantly reminded of gender, racial or other characteristics projected onto the avatar. *Deus Ex: Invisible War* follows the example of the original *Deus Ex* in providing a gender-neutral name, Alex (J.C. Denton in the first iteration), thus avoiding the problem at the level of verbal address from others within the game. As a first-person game, its visual field is more neutral, creating a space to be filled by any kind of player, although this is not the case in the relatively frequent cut-scenes. Cut-scenes, in an example such as this, provide a reminder of the particular characterization that has been provided or chosen. Cut-scenes are moments in which immediate identification is reduced, structurally, in first-person games, which might reduce the extent to which gender or racial colouring really 'matters' to the player; but it might still be a significant factor for many players. Studies of gender and racial/ethnic issues more generally suggest that media consumers tend to prefer texts in which they feel that their own particular identities are represented, centrally rather than in the margins. Games are different, in that what matters is not just *representation* but also the active process of gameplay, as will be argued in more detail below; but that is not to say that representation is of no consequence. It remains part of, if far from the whole, experience.

Decisions about details of player-character constitution are of more immediate significance in some games, most obviously role-playing games in which the particular capabilities of the player are determined to a significant extent in the process of choosing 'race' and other aspects of character type. Race, as well as class and gender, is an important attribute when choosing the make-up of a character in *EverQuest*. The creature races apart (bi-pedal tigers, lizards, frogs), there is a range of human-like characters (gnomes, dwarves, elves, ogres, barbarians, erudites and humans). Sets of facial and hair types are on offer for each race, some offering different skin tones (dark elves come in various shades of blue). Human characters can have hair colour ranging from blond and redhead to brunette, the latter having a slightly 'oriental' cast, but there is no variation here in skin colour. The human race as represented in this game is uniformly, universally, white. There is another race, however, that has black skin and a range of African/Arab facial characteristics, the erudite, which originate from the city of Paineel. While a choice is offered between classes that lean towards good (healing clerics) or bad (necromancers, best suited to solo play), the ambience of Paineel is coded towards the latter. With many living dead wandering its hallways, it is a dark city – compared with the wholesome qualities associated with human home cities or the spectacular baroque cities of the high elves – leading out into a dangerous forest full of toxic ooze. A number of black players have stated their approval of the existence of well-rendered black characters, with differential facial characteristics, but the erudite city and its inhabitants also carry resonances of the 'dark continent' from racist/colonialist literature. Erudites are spell 'casters' rather than being figured as muscled warriors, an absence that might suggest the operation of the kind of anxiety about black muscled figures suggested above; they are extremely powerful figures in the game, however, often sought out as a resource by other players (along with enchanter and wizard figures of other skin colours) because of their capacity to inflict a great deal of damage. Strategy games can also provide options for playing as various racially or ethnically coded social groups: Britons, Celts, Vikings, Japanese and Mongols among others available in *Age of Empires*, for example. Each has its own unique class of unit, along with particular strengths and weaknesses and more superficial ways of coding difference (the accenting of the faux-language responses of characters to directions have resonances with the real-world equivalents in some but far from all cases, for example). In general, however, the broad basis of gameplay varies less on this basis in strategy titles than tends to be the case in role-playing games.

Meanings created in gameplay

What, then, about meanings created in the core process of gameplay itself? These can vary from the widest parameters to much closer detail. Starting with the former, it is important to note that even such 'fundamental' qualities such as contest and competition have social-cultural and, indeed, political-ideological dimensions. Contest and competition – Caillois' *agon* – are widely viewed as among the most defining features of games in general. Within particular social or economic/political contexts, the foregrounding or celebration of such qualities is not a neutral process – even if they are so prevalent as to seem ubiquitous. That life is, largely, competitive, enacted on a playing field in which the rewards go to the best, and in which all start off with a relatively equal chance, is a core assumption of capitalist ideology, if modified in some cases by varying degrees of recognition of inequalities and provision of support to the disadvantaged. This does not mean that all competitive games are nothing more than expressions of, or participants in, the propagation of this ideology; merely that those which exist within this broader context cannot entirely be separated from it. That competition might be seen as close to universal, as a taken-for-granted aspect of social experience – including games – rather than as a particular value, celebrated in particular contexts, is itself a strong indicator of its ideological colouring. The most potent ideologies achieve precisely this status, being taken for granted as part of the 'commonsense' understanding of particular regimes, rather than recognized *as* ideology.

In many games, contest and competition, with their ideological resonances, are closely combined with the focus on the heroic individual. Cooperation also exists as an important dimension in some games, however, and might be seen to some extent as offering a pole rival to that of individually centred competition. In some action-adventure games, for example, the player-character is required to cooperate with non-player characters in order to proceed. This often takes the form of the player-character being supported by members of a squad team, largely in games with a military leaning. The actions of team members are sometimes automatic, helping out in fire-fights and other exploits without the need for any intervention by the player. In many cases more active support is required on the part of the player/player-character. In *The Thing*, for example, it is up to the player to ensure that squad members are sufficiently supplied with materials such as weapons and armour, often being required to give up resources from the player-character. A dimension of emotional support is also incorporated in this case, if somewhat crudely, the player having to monitor and respond to the 'fear' levels of non-player characters. Something more than just rampant individual *agon* is structured into gameplay, in other words, even if this remains a relatively superficial gloss on the overall experience offered by the game.

In *The Thing*, the bottom line remains focused around individual-centred violent engagement, even if the help of other characters is required and their status has to be monitored as a result. Some games have received critical praise for offering more options to the player within broadly similar generic and individual-centred confines. *Deus Ex* is particularly innovative in this regard, permitting a number of different modes of play, a choice particularly between direct-violent and more indirect-stealthy means of progression. The game and sequel also employ dialogue/action choice structures familiar from the history of role-playing games. In particular gameplay situations, the player is often given the choice of one from a list of dialogue responses, ranging from being meek and cooperative with interlocutors to being curt and offensive, and some points in between. The nature of the response has both immediate and longer-term implications for the action that follows, giving the player a significant if bounded degree of control over the attitude of the player-character and the exact shape in which the game unfolds. Conflict-based strategy games also provide opportunities for cooperation as well as contest, usually featuring 'diplomacy' interface options in which, for a price, alliances can be established with neighbours. Cooperation is built much more extensively and centrally into massively multi-player role-playing games such as *EverQuest*, in which collaboration with other players is a major dimension of gameplay, essential if the player wishes to progress more than a relatively short distance through the level hierarchy of the game. Even here, cooperation with other players is tied up with contestation – against non-player creatures to be despatched in return for level points and other commodities; or, for those so inclined, in direct player-v-player conflict in areas or servers where this is permitted (or more generally where the consent of both combatants is granted).

If conflict and competition have ideological resonances in a very general sense, some forms have more particular social-cultural dimensions. An imperialist/colonialist dynamic is built into the gameplay structure of the *Civilization* series, for example, as many commentators have noted. In order to succeed, players have to build and expand their own civilizations, a process based on a number of implicit but far from neutral assumptions about what constitutes 'civilization' in the morally loaded sense of the term: scientific-technological and/or military advancement, for example, as opposed to any alternative such as a sustainable and non-expansionist state of equilibrium. A key source of understanding the social-cultural leanings of games is to examine the conditions for victory structured into gameplay, the kinds of activities in which the player has to engage in order to succeed. *Civilization* offers a range of 'win-condition' options, as suggested in Chapter 1, but the parameters are limited and all based on a fundamental notion of competition-leading-to-dominance, of one form or another. At the start, a colonialist/expansionist approach is essential, the spread of the player's settlements and forces into territory figured as 'empty' – occupied only by occasional 'barbarian' groups, the function of which is to be displaced and to act as periodic sources of annoyance. *Civilization* can be won through diplomacy, by becoming elected head of the United Nations, but this is another form of dominance, based on diplomatic wheeler-dealing rather than enlightenment or notions of viable mutual co-existence. The number of victory conditions has expanded with subsequent iterations. They remain limited, inevitably, by practical considerations, but also restricted in kind to conditions that embody particular (and contested) ways of understanding the world. As Janet Murray asks: 'Why should global domination rather than, say, universal housing and education define the civilization that wins the game? Why not make an end to world hunger the winning condition?'[28]

To ask such questions need not be to seek to impose another agenda on game designers (although that might also be a legitimate aim), but to call attention to the particular nature of the meanings structured into the activities required for success in the game. Game design issues often involve value-judgements, most if not all of which have social-cultural dimensions, some more overtly political-ideological than others. Chris Crawford recalls, for example, the number of thorny problems that had to be addressed in the design of his environmental-issues game *Balance of the Planet* (1990), in which the relative weighting of a number of different factors had to be determined. The decision, in the end, was to leave the exact weighting up to the player, within pre-set upper and lower limits, the result of which is to make the player take some responsibility for determining the relative importance accorded to variables such as energy production, the creation of pollution, disease or the loss of human life – drawing attention, in the process, to the contested nature of such judgements.[29]

For William Stephenson, *Civilization* can be read as 'a classic demonstration of the logic of imperialism outlined by Marx.'[30] Stephenson also suggests a Marxist reading of other aspects of the game, including its modelling of internal conflict. Progress can be interrupted by outbreaks of 'civil disorder' within the player's chosen civilization. To deal with this, the player has a number of options. Distractions can be provided by turning some citizens into entertainers or by shifting part of the manufacturing process into the production of luxuries; alternatively, military units can be stationed to impose martial law. 'Thus the class struggle is regulated from above by means of the carrot and stick principle.'[31] A similar principle can be read into the entertainment of the player, Stephenson suggests, in an example of the kind of localized spectacle-as-reward considered in the previous chapter. In *Civilization II*, one of the sources of reward is the completion of 'Wonders of the World,' each of which not only provides a new advantage to the player's culture but also triggers a brief cut-scene of higher visual quality than the usual game screen: a distraction, Stephenson suggests, from the work required by the more routine playing of the game.

The basis of the gameplay of *Civilization* lies in three activities seen by Andrew Rollings and Ernest Adams as central to many strategy games, often in combination: conquest, exploration and trade.[32] Taken together, the three are close to providing a definition of imperialism/colonialism. If conquest is a function of the broader quality of contest/competition, exploration, a dimension of gameplay highlighted in Chapter 2, often takes on connotations of colonialist adventure. Many games, including *Tomb Raider*, involve the exploration of spaces characterized as exotic and/or alien; territories into which the player or player-character moves in order to defeat enemy inhabitants and in pursuit of material rewards, the latter translated into game-world currencies and resources. From the perspective of American culture, it is possible to read many of these as displaced versions of the frontier experience, the mythology of which remains an important feature in the ideological landscape of the United States.[33] The dimension of trade, and allied economic processes, is another respect in which many gameplay processes can be seen as to some extent replicating real-world equivalents of a particular social-political slant. Cycles of production and consumption are built into many strategy and role-playing games, which often encourage their own version of the capitalist work ethic, a striking characteristic given that games are usually assumed to offer pleasurable escape from such real-world demands. In a real-time strategy game such as *Age of Empires*, for example, regular attention has to be paid to the supply of food and raw materials such as wood, stone and gold, resources required for the development of all other quantities. In the multi-player context of *EverQuest* a highly complex economic system is in play that has implications for the social dimension of the game.

Players of *EverQuest* are encouraged to group together to kill monsters to gain experience points. These are needed to gain more levels and increase basic skills. Killing monsters also yields in-game objects that can be sold to player- or non-player characters, the proceeds being used to buy enhancements that make players more effective. Player-characters can also work at various trades to manufacture artefacts to sell to other players. 'Caster' characters often sell 'buffs' (enhancements that aid in fighting). Trading is central to the structural and geographical organization of the game. Most towns and villages have shops in which players can buy or sell goods. The Bazaar is a designated place in which goods can be sold, with a range of features built-in to aid the process. A strong work ethic is intrinsic to successful and rewarding gameplay, with creative entrepreneurialism yielding significant rewards. The game is founded on processes of acquisition and exchange similar to those of capitalist economics; as in the external world, economics does much to shape social structure. A variety of social networks are provided in the game to support players in their effort to build more powerful characters, including player-created guilds and websites that provide support and knowledge helpful to the process of advancement. Pressure to adhere to the work ethic is bound tacitly into the social dynamics of the game: if player-characters are to keep pace with those with whom they have built relationships, they must put in the hours to ensure that their levels are comparable (if too great a difference in player-level is permitted, the lower level player-characters will not get experience points from group activities). The economic dimension of the game also extends into the real world, with items such as artefacts, maps, modifications to the game interface and *EverQuest* accounts (with characters that have been levelled-up) regularly sold on e-bay and other internet sites, an extra-gamic economy that operates outside the jurisdiction of Sony, the operator of the game.

Subscription-based games such *EverQuest* require players to invest a great deal of time and money if they are to become competent and well equipped. This might narrow the possible market for the game, but long-term commitment is rewarded by devices such as titles given to characters that reach certain levels (surnames can be given to characters that have reached level 20 and the titles 'Venerable' or 'Baron' after level 55). Such titles denote status and constitute a significant part of the game's extremely hierarchal social structure. Players often comment in-game on the compulsive nature of the work ethic built into the processes of advancement. At the same time, attention is often brought to the fact that family and friends consider sustained play to be a form of time-wasting, an activity regarded as having no real benefits (unlike, for example, learning a musical instrument, a language or any skill that has practical use in the real world). If playing *EverQuest* requires labour, it is usually seen from the outside as essentially unproductive labour, like that consumed in many other leisure activities or hobbies. From the inside, however, it is labour that can have a real output, at the level of a particular kind of social experience. It can also be seen as reinforcing real-world capitalist dynamics. Why, then, should players find the experience a relief from real-world labour? Long-term players generally regard *EverQuest* play as quite different from real-life work, despite the existence of structural similarities between the two. The answer might lie in a number of factors resulting from the different context of in-game labour, including the fact that it brings very clear-cut benefits to the player-character (a far greater and more immediate sense of progression-through-labour than is usually found in real-world employment) and the fact that it occurs in a pleasurably sociable fantasy context as an activity freely chosen by the player.

The more specific qualities of contemporary western consumerism are a prominent feature of *The Sims*, which perhaps rivals *Civilization* in the extent to which it has drawn ideological readings of its core gameplay activities. *The Sims* offers a consumer-capitalist version of utopia: a home-owning middle-class world in which every Sim is created equal. Each character starts out with the same amount of money and there is no discrimination on lines such as gender or sexual orientation. Female characters earn the same salaries and have the same opportunities for career success as male characters. Gay or lesbian couples can be constructed, and can adopt children, even if they cannot actually marry; they face no other forms of discrimination, in a game in which the building of social networks is an important feature.[34] The chief aim of *The Sims* is to make your Sim people happy and successful, which is defined in particular, value-laden terms. The development of personal skills is important, but for instrumentalist purposes, for the building of personal networks and for career advancement. The latter brings increased income, the principal purpose of which is to permit the purchase of more and better consumer items. If the game seems broadly inclusive in some dimensions, these are limited. As Miguel Sicart suggests, the game has little tolerance for 'misfit' characters that refuse to play by the rules. His attempt to create a Sim version of the deceased rock star Kurt Cobain – comprised of a deliberately unbalanced guitar-playing character complete with a Cobain skin downloaded from the internet, a dissolute lifestyle, a superficial marriage and no social life – was resisted by the game, which took control of the character against the player's will, making him want to have friends, a job and to be nice to his wife.[35]

Most games produced for the western market are, implicitly, based on some version of dominant western/capitalist values, although there is room for some variation. Dominant values are likely to be structured into gameplay and representational frameworks, in games as elsewhere, simply because they are dominant, and thus familiar and often taken for granted, capable of providing what appears (ideologically) to be a relatively neutral background for in-game tasks. *Balance of the Planet* is one example that goes against the dominant grain, a factor probably not unrelated to its failure in the commercial market (although, Crawford suggests, it proved a hit with educators and environmentalists, those most likely to be interested in the 'message' in its own right).[36] Compared with the implicit politics of many games, *SimCity* (from 1989) is in many respects a distinctly liberal entry, with its acknowledgement of the importance of 'social' factors such as the provision of public transport and other services. There is no single 'win condition' in *SimCity*, but values such as these are structured into the game as necessary conditions

– among others – for the creation of a thriving metropolis, motivated at least in part by the game's aspiration to the establishment of a degree of functional realism in the simulation of the various pressures faced by the leaders of a contemporary urban environment. The game includes elements that have more reactionary connotations, however, including its attitude towards crime. To tackle crime, the game suggests, it is necessary simply to build more prisons and police stations. As Shawn Miklaucic puts it: 'To play *SimCity* uncritically is not just to be told this is so, but to learn it experimentally. Prisons and police stations must be the answer to crime, one can come to believe, because look! – when I build more prisons my crime rate drops.'[37] There is also, Miklaucic notes, no dimension of race, gender or social class involved in the way crime and punishment are modelled. Other 'god games' leave a wider range of moral choices open to the player, more or less overtly political in nature. In *Black and White*, the choice is between options framed in the Manichean terms of 'Good' vs. 'Evil'. A more overtly 'political' scenario is found in *Tropico* (2001), in which the player is El Presidenté of an imaginary Caribbean island that can be run on capitalist or socialist lines. The player is far from entirely free to determine policy in *Tropico*, however, and can face interventions from the game that mirror real-world constraints; the player who runs up too great a budget deficit, for example, faces intervention from the game's version of the World Bank, an enforced capping of the wages of the workforce.

Choices such as whether to align with good or evil, or to be morally neutral, also have implications for gameplay in games of a neo-medieval/ barbaric character, examples such as *War of the Ring*, *EverQuest* and *Baldur's Gate*. They can affect how non-player characters react to player-characters (a player-character aligned with good in *EverQuest*, for example, will be killed on sight in some cities aligned with evil, and vice-versa; for neutral characters, the reaction is often more arbitrary). The opportunity to choose to be 'evil' or morally neutral can allow players space to reject traditional hero roles that seem outmoded, dull or that carry objectionable ideological baggage. Players aligned in this way can indulge, vicariously, in the transgressive social behaviours consonant with the role of thief, ogre, barbarian berserker or evil wizard. Competition between players in online games often results in aggression and self-interest overruling in-game values such as nobility and heroic status, even where cooperation is required for particular tasks. *EverQuest* accommodates ignoble behaviour, including the killing without consent of player-characters who stray inadvertently into Player-Versus-Player areas or deliberately providing misinformation to other players. The emphasis on personal progression and self-interest contributes to the frontier world status of the gamescape, a source of particular appeal in the mythic landscape of the United States.

An 'alternative' patina is given to some games, at the level of background context/scenario, which might offer relatively little difference from more dominant convention at the level of gameplay. *State of Emergency*, for example, is usually viewed in the light of anti-globalization protests such as those surrounding the Seattle meeting of the World Trade Organization in 1999. The game situates the player as a civilian caught up in a riot organized by resistance against the near-future dominance of a powerful global corporation and won over to the side of the opposition. The framing devices seem to have leftist and anarchistic adversarial resonance, even if set within an exaggerated background scenario in which any vestige of democratic government or politics has been displaced (thus implicitly coding an oppositional stance as more 'normal'). Gameplay is mostly more conventional, but not entirely devoid of radical connotations. The player can adopt 'Revolution' mode, a mission-based form of gameplay more familiar than the name suggests. But the alternative quick-play 'Chaos' mode does create something of the frenzied glee of assaulting the material fabric of consumer culture, the opportunity to run riot in environments such as a shopping mall in which bins and other objects can be used to smash shop windows and aggressive police (and assorted gang members) can be attacked. The radical dimension of gameplay such as this might be rather limited and superficial, heavily qualified by generic fighting/action game features, but it is a potential element in the mix. Opposition to capitalist consumerism, and specifically to an equivalent of the World Trade Organization, is one dynamic structured into the variety of different factions competing for influence over the player-character of *Deus Ex: Invisible War*. The game's own WTO is oriented towards the values of multinational capitalist 'free trade' and consumerism. Directly opposed to the WTO is The Order, an anti-materialist sect. The player is given a choice of allegiance between these and other groups, shaping the manner in which the game unfolds. Basic gameplay revolves either way, however, around the same central process of progression and resource-acquisition/consumption, regardless of affiliation or the choice of whether to play in more or less aggressive modes.

Which brings us to a consideration of violence, an ingredient of gameplay that we have visited before in this book. Violent action is well suited to some of the demands of gameplay, as suggested in Chapters 1 and 3: it offers an easily available source of both action/feedback and of the intensity of sensation offered by many games. Gameplay based on the violent activity of the player-character can also be considered in social-cultural terms. This is a useful point at which to step back and look more closely into the question of how or to what extent games might 'position' players, as active participants in, rather than just observers of, the on-screen action. Games can be understood, up to a point, as particularly potent sources of 'interpellation', in the sense in which the term is used in the theory of ideology developed by Louis Althusser. One of the strongest effects of ideology, for Althusser, is its tendency to 'hail' the observer or participant, to create what is in effect a 'call and response' relationship in which the subject answers the call and, in the very act of acknowledgement, is thus situated in a particular position – in the case of capitalist ideology, that of the individualized subject.[38] A work of art using the principles of linear perspective, for example, creates a position for the viewer in front of the frame. This approach has been widely used in film theory, especially in conjunction with the psychoanalytical theories of Jacques Lacan, to suggest how mainstream films might 'position' the viewer in a similar (and similarly restrictive) manner.[39] Games seem to lend themselves even more readily to this approach, for the simple reason that the player is explicitly required to take on a particular role, to some extent, rather than just to identify from a more detached perspective that has no influence on the unfolding of the action on-screen. The player is rather more literally interpellated, at the different degrees of relative proximity or distance involved in games played in the first or third person or at greater remove (as examined in Chapter 2).

How this process might work in games can be considered at two levels. First, there is the general sense of the game hailing the player as an individual subject – offering itself up as an experience that requires a response from a being already constituted as individual (*always-already* constituted, as Althusser would put it). In this sense, games can be seen as among many other sources that function effectively to confirm – if not to constitute – the status of the player as individual; creating a space that can be occupied only from this position. Multi-player as well as single-player games can be understood as having this implicit premise. This form of interpellation exists at the level of player *as player*, self-consciously aware of the act of playing – including all the out-of-game-world operations that involves – as well as any potential to function in terms of player identifications with roles or figures existing within the game. The latter dimension is more complex and controversial. Are players, really, interpellated to any significant extent into the *particular kinds* of subjectivities offered by the in-game diegetic universe? As the question is often framed: is the player of a game such as a first-person shooter interpellated into that particular violence-oriented mode of being? If so, does this apply only while playing – or does it have any impact beyond the bounds of the game itself?

What does it mean, then, to be 'interpellated' into the world of a first-person shooter? To what extent might it involve the player taking on some of the characteristics of the behavioural model required for progress within the game? It is easy to overstate parallels and exchanges between the game-world and that of the world outside, as we suggested in a similar context in Chapter 1, when considering the distinctive modality in which such activities are pursued in games. Plenty of markers exist that clearly announce the large gulf that exists between playing a game such as a first-person shooter and engaging in anything like the equivalent action in the real world. But there are, also, certain homologies. How far these come into play depends on a number of factors, including the two forms of realism considered in the previous chapter, which can shape the extent to which the game experience approximates that of the real world. Functional realism might seem particularly important here, in the sense of calling upon the player to perform actions of a kind more or less analogous to those of real-world equivalents. The activities required of the successful player of a first-person shooter are crude and limited, in comparison with those of the real world, as we suggested in Chapter 1. In some cases, however, they seek to offer a more detailed modelling of real-world activity. In *Black Hawk Down*, for example, the manual includes what is presented as factual background detail about weapons and tactics used by the US forces in Somalia. One section describes the team strategy used for the clearing of rooms during urban conflict: the four-man team lines up outside, one throws a 'flashbang' grenade into the room and the team rushes in, executing a predetermined set of moves to ensure that they act in unison. The gameplay section of the manual includes the version built into the game, with specific instructions to the player on what moves to make ('move to the far corner to stay out of your team's line of fire').[40]

There is, clearly, potential for gameplay such as this to be used to 'train' the player, up to a point, to provide knowledge about the employment of particular military tactics that might also be used in the real world, as evidenced by the use of this kind of simulation in some cases by the military. The classic example is the *Marine Doom* mode, but many other games have also been used, from *Military Battlezone,* a more functionally realistic adaptation of Atari's tank warfare arcade title *Battlezone* (1980), to *Battlefield 1942* (2002).[41] An example of a cross-over in the opposite direction is *Full Spectrum Warrior* (2004), a commercial/entertainment product based on an infantry training simulator designed for the US army. *America's Army* (2002), the free online multi-player shooter run by the military, looks in both directions: used for training purposes by the army and as a PR and recruiting device for players outside the service. Games such as *America's Army* and *Full Spectrum Warrior* make particularly strong claims, unsurprisingly, to the status of functional realism. The former requires the player to pass training courses that include real-world educational content before being able to take on particular in-game roles. Gamers who wish to play as medics, for example, 'need to pass four separate training courses: airway management, controlling bleeding, treating shock and a field test', followed by a classroom-style lecture and a multiple-choice test.[42]

Computer simulations of combat have been used by the military in recent decades in response to both the cost of live-action simulation and the increasingly computer-mediated character of some forms of real-world conflict. The experience of the player of a first-person shooter is relatively closer today to that of some real soldiers than would have been the case in historical conflicts such as the Second World War or Vietnam. Devices such as head-mounted displays can be worn by troops, projecting onto their field of vision data not dissimilar to some of that provided in games, including information presented in real-time from over-flying aircraft. The US army, following the experiences of the navy and air force, is described by James Der Derian as 'leaping into a realm of hyperreality, where the enemy disappeared as flesh and blood and reappeared pixelated and digitized on computer screens in killing zones, as icons of opportunity.'[43] In this environment, both training and actual combat might have relatively more in common with video gameplay than would usually be the case, the military having looked to Hollywood and videogames in the late 1990s after realizing that it was being outstripped by entertainment media in the field of simulation technology.[44] The distinction between reality and simulation might occasionally appear to blur, like something out of the pages of Jean Baudrillard, as Der Derian suggests in the case of the events leading to the Gulf War of 1991.[45] The notion of a broader slippage between the two can be seductive, especially to those well armed with quotations from Jean Baudrillard and other theorists of the postmodern, but it is easily overstated.[46] The contexts of real and gameplay activities generally remain worlds apart, not least in the obvious difference in what is potentially at stake in real and virtual instances of combat.

An argument for a stronger connection has been made by some, notably the much-quoted military psychologist Dave Grossman, on the basis of the fact that simulations are used by the military as part of the process of *conditioning* recruits to be able to kill.[47] Repeated simulation is used to create a conditioned response, to enable troops to kill reflexively, without conscious thought. Reluctance to shoot at other human figures is conditioned out, according to this argument, through repeated experience of simulations in which the victims are given relatively realistic representation, as opposed to the use of abstract targets. If this works for the military, the logic goes, it also applies to shooter games used for entertainment, effectively conditioning players to become potential killers; not just by teaching particular strategies and tactics, but by creating the capacity to kill automatically, to overcome normal restraints. Games might be capable of such an effect in exceptional cases, in which many other factors are always likely to be involved (and likely to be more decisive),[48] but this argument fails to account for the very different contexts involved in military-training simulation and gameplay. Military use of videogame-like simulations occurs in a context in which it is clearly understood to be part of training in the ability to kill, and in which this is reinforced by other factors such as the broader military environment and the use of live-action simulation and real weapons. Players of videogames understand themselves quite clearly to be *playing*, not training. If Grossman were right, vastly more instances of mass shooting prompted by violent gameplay would be in evidence, given the numbers who play such games (even if they remain a minority of games overall). Grossman himself argues that the ability of soldiers to kill on the battlefield depends on a range of other factors – such as the existence of a context of authority/leadership, in which troops act under strict orders – which he ignores when making the assumption that videogame 'training' is likely to have the same impact as its military equivalent.[49]

The notion of 'media effects' in general, in the sense of media consumption directly leading to specific, identifiable behaviour, is fraught with difficulty.[50] Our concern in this chapter is not with a notion of 'effects' of this kind, the evidential basis for which is hotly contested, but with more diffuse ways in which the meaning-creating potential of games might be at play in the culture at large – a dimension equally resistant, however, to any hard certainties of knowledge. If playing a first-person shooter is far from being the same as undergoing or training for the equivalent experience in the real world, it might be argued that it is not *entirely* different. The difficulty lies in assessing where, exactly, the experience might lie – in one situation or another – in the considerable space between these two extremes. To play a first-person shooter is not to be *shaped into* the role of a shooter. It is to *play at* that role, which is very different. But to 'play at' does suggest *some* potential level of investment in at least some of the resonances that might be associated with the real equivalent. One way to understand this is in rather more general terms than those often used in this territory. Playing a military/ shooter type game might be understood as one part of a broader cultural investment in the kind of mind-set or cultural attitude associated with the terrain. The prevalence of games of this variety might, therefore, be taken, among other examples, as evidence of a cultural investment in that kind of mode of behaviour. It might also make a contribution to that investment, although not one that can be measured at the level of immediate impact on particular, identifiable behaviour (because it is not possible satisfactorily to isolate one variable from all of the other factors involved). Investments of this kind can be understood as the product of particular social-historical contexts. An excessive investment in direct military action in the recent and contemporary United States might be understood, for example, in the context of a period in which this has been an arena in which the US has enjoyed superiority and on which its foreign policy has tended to place an emphasis, playing to its strengths (as opposed, say, to its relative weakness in a global diplomatic forum such as the General Assembly of the United Nations). In Britain, a similar investment might be understood in the context of a valorization of past military 'glory' such as the role of the nation during the Second World War. Other cases may be less straightforward, however, and play-fantasies based on the ability to take direct action of a violent or otherwise destructive kind may be more culturally and historically widespread.[51]

The level of concern about games expressed from (primarily if not exclusively) politically and culturally conservative sources is somewhat ironic, given the extent to which the violence foregrounded in games tends very often to be framed contextually as violence in the form of the maintenance of existing forms of order. As Clive Thompson suggests, only a relatively small number of games, such as *Kingpin: Life of Crime* (1999), *Grand Theft Auto* and *Postal* (1997) 'ever dare to have you act as criminals or psychopaths.' Far larger numbers present violence in more reactionary form, as a means of 'quelling social disturbances'.[52] The extent to which game violence is taken seriously is also subject to sharp swings of attitude, as Mia Consalvo suggests in an analysis of the use of games as a point of reference during news coverage of the American-led invasion of Iraq in 2003.[53] In this context, rather than being seen as 'dangerous', videogame violence tends to be viewed as 'fake and trivial', from various perspectives, when compared with the realities of war. Contradictions such as this, as Consalvo suggests, underline the extent to which media discourses around games tend to be in the service of a number of other agendas rather than attending to the specific nature of games in their own right.

The important point here is not to overlook the specific qualities of play, fantasy and the imagination. Investments in particular kinds of behaviour found in games, violent or otherwise, can largely be understood at this level. The kind of behaviour familiar to individual players from particular types of games might be expected to contribute to the repertoire-stock of their imaginations. In particular situations, a game-type response to a situation might be fantasized: an angry employee might, for instance, imagine letting loose in the office with a BFG.[54] Some would argue that this is dangerously close to creating the potential for real-world violence, but that is to underestimate the gulf between imagined and actual behaviour (how many of us have imagined behaviour we would never remotely consider in real life?). The fantastic or imaginary have points of contact with the real world, and can be read in terms of their real-world resonances or implications, as we have done above in cases such as the neo-medieval. But fantasy and imagination also function as negative points of reference, as experiences that can be pleasurable precisely because they are *not* available in the real world. The pleasure of violent activity in a videogame might lie in the degree to which it is clearly understood to be forbidden in reality. One of the functions of play, as Gerard Jones suggests, 'is to enable children to pretend to be just what they know they'll *never* be. Exploring, in a safe and controlled context, what is impossible or too dangerous or forbidden to them is a crucial tool in accepting the limits of reality.'[55] Rather than causing confusions between the two, the experience of fantasy and play, according to this argument, is important to the development of an understanding of the distinctions between the real and the unreal.[56] As part of the process of socialization, children (as well as adults) need to gain an understanding of what is and is not permissible in a given context. Many fictions communicate a sense of such boundaries. Games in particular might offer a heightened experience of the permissible limits of agency, because limits have a profound impact on gameplay through regimes of progress and 'punishment'. Rather than simply occurring at the level of imagination, as in purely representational media, choices made in a game context are experienced more concretely, in terms of cause-and-effect outcomes. In focusing excessively on the literal, Jones suggests, critics of violence in games and other media overlook their emotional meanings, the impressions of power and control they offer as counters to the anxieties of life, an argument that might apply to the experience of many adults as well as the children who are the focus of his work. Violence that is often raw, loud and angry appeals to children, Jones argues, because it has the strength sufficient 'to match and master their own anxiety and anger.'[57] [Game violence] considered offensive by many adults[can provide a safely exaggerated forum in which children are able to deal with real-world fears] its 'shocking' nature also offers older children a way of marking-off their sphere from that of parental values.[58] Violence in games can be positively beneficial to children in this manner, Jones suggests, although not necessarily in all cases.

For something to have an impact primarily at the level of fantasy, imaginary or compensatory repertoires is not for it to be of no social-cultural or ideological significance. Imaginations, like enacted realities, are both culturally shaped and active parts of the cultural environments in which we live. Game activities with less basis in existing real-world complexes might be rather less likely to become subject to imaginary investments, however. It is rarely suggested that a player might become 'positioned' or interpellated by an experience such as playing as the alien in *Alien vs. Predator 2* (2001), for example – investing in or being 'shaped by' activities such as seeking out a human victim in the 'face-hugger' stage of the development of the species. Counter-examples such as this underline the likelihood that gameplay – along with other acts of media usage – has more potential to re-confirm (or respond to) existing cultural tendencies with which it resonates one way or another than to create something distinctly new of its own.

We could return here to broader implications of gameplay of the kind considered earlier in this chapter. Particular assumptions are structured into gameplay, both generally and more specifically. These can be understood as taking their place in the wider context in which such assumptions are generated (or challenged, an issue to which we return below) in a particular cultural-historical conjuncture. Broad notions such as 'progress' and the assumption that individual action is likely to be effective and that mastery can be achieved are implicit in very many games, for example. The experience of these qualities in games can be seen as a contribution to the wider propagation of such concepts – concepts that have ideological implications when applied to understandings of the world more generally (the notion of 'progress' is structured deeply into western/capitalist ideologies, as is the notion of individual agency, as suggested above). One of the pleasures of gameplay is the impression of effective action that is created within the game-world; or, at least, an impression of always receiving clear feedback on actions, even when they are unsuccessful (as they are often likely to be in many games). The external world is rarely so receptive to action or as clear-cut in its provision of feedback. Playing games that offer such qualities could be understood, then, as playing a part in the wider process in which such assumptions are confirmed and reconfirmed. This, for Andrew Kurtz, is the most potent level of interpellation in games.[59] Interpellation at the level of the specific representational material of a particular game is reduced, Kurtz suggests, by the limitations of the virtual reality effect achieved by games, principally by the player's constant awareness of essential out-of-game sources of information (health bars, etc.), as we discuss in Chapter 2. The relationship is not just that between player and game-world, but a three-way exchange between 'representation, individual, and technology.'[60] The point at which the player is most strongly interpellated, Kurtz argues, is not one of 'disappearance' into the game but that at which he or she manipulates the computer hardware to respond to representational information from the game-world: 'At this point, the player articulates the very heart of liberal humanist ideology, the impulse to counter the irrational and the unforeseen with individual free will.'[61] In more specific relation to the technology involved, Brian Sutton-Smith suggests, the cultural context of videogames is one in which they offer a forum for demonstrating mastery of computer/ computerized technology. If games in general can be seen, from an anthropological perspective, as adaptive responses to social problems (as suggested in passing in Chapter 1), videogames are a response to fears of the computer and related technologies, creating an arena in which such fears can be conquered.[62]

Others have argued that what is involved here is interpellation into the form of activity or subjectivity encouraged or required by an information-processing centred economy; that, as forms of socialization or familiarization, games perform a role more closely related to their own economic, technological and cultural domain. For Patrick Crogan, the player of a first-person shooter is engaged in a ludic variety of a more widely establishment model of real-time information processing.[63] For Ted Friedman, 'the way computer games teach structures of thought – the way they reorganize perception – is by getting you to internalize the logic of the program', which is what he sees as a source of the flow-state in games: 'The pleasure of computer games is in entering into a computer-like mental state: in responding as automatically as the computer, processing information as effortlessly, replacing sentient cognition with the blank hum of computation.'[64] Along similar lines, and in the context of a reading based explicitly on Althusser's theory of interpellation, Matt Garite concludes that 'gaming is essentially an aestheticized mode of information processing, and therefore the digital economy's ideal form of leisure.'[65] In Garite's characterization, what is involved is a particularly aggressive process in which 'subjects are interpellated or called upon to (mis)recognize themselves as distinct, autonomous, freely acting individuals,' a general emphasis on player freedom masking the extent to which players are subjected to a narrow range of limits and demands.[66] Missing from many such accounts, however, (although not that of Crogan) is any notion of the 'play' that can be permissible within the confines of the particular tasks set by any game, the space for *paidea*, in which rules and win-states can be ignored or subverted, as well as for more goal-oriented and prescribed *ludus*. The idea that something like a flow-state – where intention and skill come closely together in heightened moments of absorbing gameplay – is blankly mechanical and devoid of emotion seems particularly to miss the point in relation to many such gameplay experiences, in which intense passions are often provoked and vocalized.

Another factor to be considered here is the potential games have to create frustration and anxiety, rather than impressions of smooth, seamless agency, mastery or presence. Playing games can generate negative reactions as well as pleasures – and various dynamically related combinations of the two – which complicates any notion of the implication or interpellation of the player in the kinds of activities structured into gameplay. If games can be seen as engines of interpellation, generally or in more specific contexts, they (and/or their players) do not always function at anything like an optimum level. If 'progress' based on the achievement of mastery is often structured into gameplay, for example, it is not always realized. Progress might remain an ideal to which to aspire in such cases, implicitly maintaining its broader cultural valorization, but it might be a quality from which the player feels excluded rather than into which he or she can be said to be interpellated. Any notion of the 'free will' of the player is also subject to major limitations, the result of game rules and restrictions that pre-determine much of the gaming experience. It is easy, in many cases, to overstate the extent to which the player experience maps closely onto the material structured into gameplay, forgetting the myriad disturbances, interruptions and shortcomings that can interfere with the process – at the level of specific representational material/actions, or at the more abstract level of interaction with the technology. This can apply as much to a game with an explicit ideological agenda as to any other. The experience of a pro-Palestinian playing *UnderAsh* or *Special Force*, for example, can be to reaffirm a state of suffering and/or defeat as much as to assert a possibility of victory over occupying Israeli forces – depending on the level of success enjoyed by the individual player (in the case of the former, technical shortcomings make gameplay rather difficult and frustrating). The act of opposition is enshrined in either case, which is important, but with rather different resonances. Where mastery or success is enjoyed in games, exactly what that implies might also be subject to variance. Does a powerful impression of agency created within a game reinforce broader cultural/ideological notions of agency – or does the pleasure involved lie in some level of acknowledgment of the fact that such agency is, precisely, *not* available in the outside world? A strong measure of caution is always necessary when attributing to games the ability to contribute actively to the ideological shaping of the player.

How particular kinds of investments come to be structured into games can also be understood by more detailed consideration of the contexts in which they are developed and played, both social-cultural and industrial. Much light can be shed in this manner on the emphasis on violent activity found in many games. A number of specific factors help to account for this emphasis, on violence itself and on violence as an ingredient generally more likely to be associated with products aimed at male consumers (according to prevailing gender stereotyping). Stephen Kline, Nick Dyer-Witheford and Greig De Peuter identify a series of conjunctures, the accumulated effects of which have been to encourage this emphasis in many games.[67] The starting point in this account is the combined influence on the development of the first generation of games (examples such as *Spacewar*) of military-industrial funding, hacker experimentation and science-fiction oriented subcultures. Each made a significant contribution to the genealogy of the videogame.[68] To this list might be added the subculture of table-top *Dungeons and Dragons*, a primarily male-oriented sector in which many older game developers were involved.[69] In the move of games out from these relatively closed military-oriented and/or subcultural realms to the domain of commercial entertainment, existing tendencies in game content were reinforced.

The arcade, along with settings such as bars, became the first source of profit from videogames: 'The themes of shooting, violence, and intense competition, present at the very origins of gaming's Pentagon-sponsored inception, at once made the arcades a natural setting for the video game's commercial placement and were amplified in this environment.'[70] Male dominated and already considered socially suspect, as sites of supposed delinquency, arcades contributed to the particular aura surrounding games. It was not inevitable that the games business would capitalize on this quality, however, rather than seek to counter it, to reassure its critics and the parents of potential players, as Kline, Dyer-Witheford and De Peuter suggest. Future developments were to cement a strong emphasis on violence in many prominent titles, however, once the home gaming market was established, along with successive waves of competition between one console system and another and between console and PC.

When Sega challenged the dominance of Nintendo in the early 1990s, the company sought to outflank its rival not just at the level of technology but also in targeting an older audience (15–17 year-olds as opposed to Nintendo's 8–14).[71] A key marker of this distinction was the introduction of a new level of violence in games such as *Mortal Kombat*: 'Upping game violence was integral to Sega's repositioning in the market, and to the production-differentiation strategy it deployed against Nintendo, rejecting the "kiddie" orientation of its rival and marking its own games as excitingly transgressive.'[72] Nintendo offered condemnation, but eventually responded to the commercial success enjoyed by Sega, tacitly boosting the violent content of its own games.[73] By the mid 1990s, when PC games re-entered a market that had been dominated by consoles, 'they did so in a setting where the test and touchstone of their emergent 3-D capacities was in the representation of violent action.'[74] Within existing genres, a pattern developed in which a key mark of differentiation was the elaboration and intensification of violence. Subsequent generations of games consoles, especially Sony's PlayStation and Microsoft's Xbox, continued the process of successively targeting older audiences, a factor that further consolidated potential for the production of violence, among other qualities, in games. Compared with other possible innovations, the creation of greater intensities of violence is a relatively easy, commercially safe and inexpensive way of offering product differentiation within an established genre repertoire. It also has the advantage of selling in transnational markets, forms of violent combat generally requiring little translation across cultural borders. 'All of these factors', as Kline, Dyer-Witheford and De Peuter put it, 'give virtual violence momentum and staying power.'[75]

Heavily violence-oriented gameplay is usually associated with the playing preferences of male gamers, especially adolescent and post-adolescent males. A number of explanations have been offered for this, including the potential appeal of the spectacle/sensation of hyper-masculinity at a time often characterized by gender insecurity. For the game developer and researcher Celia Pearce, the pleasure of such gameplay might also, in this context, be one of sexual sublimation, 'a high-tech outlet for otherwise out-of-control hormonal oscillations.'[76] Female gamers generally prefer other pleasures, Pearce suggests, although this is far from an entirely clear-cut divide. From her own research and testing experience, Pearce offers the following broad 'rules of thumb': males tend to prefer games that involve clear and finite goals such as 'kill-or-be-killed'; women tend to prefer activities that involve assembling, collecting, creating or constructing, favouring open-ended activities with cumulative results and cooperative rather than competitive play.[77] *Pac-Man* was favoured by girls over other arcade games of the 1980s, in this account, because girl players 'preferred collection to shooting as an activity' (the game was designed with appeal to females specifically in mind[78]). *Tetris*, another game historically favoured by female players, 'possesses two highly appealing attributes to women – puzzle solving and assembling.'[79] A similar argument is made by the game designer Sheri Graner Ray, who suggests that a definition that equates games with zero-sum forms of conflict (a clearly defined win/lose equation) tends to ignore the forms of gameplay most likely to appeal to females.[80] Female players, Ray suggests, tend to prefer flexible or variable goals and reward systems, rather than those based on clear-cut win/lose scenarios or high scores. Games based on construction, such as *Sim City*, or on the creation of relationships between characters – *The Sims* – are, on these lines, also likely to be more appealing to many female players than games based on intense competition or under-motivated violent action. The same goes for online role-playing games, in which female players are generally more strongly represented than elsewhere, and in which the central dimension of cooperation and communication with other players might also be expected to appeal disproportionately to women.

Ray cites a number of anthropological and psychological studies to suggest underlying reasons for such gender-based differences in gameplay preferences, including a difference at the level of stimulus–response dynamics.[81] Males, she suggests, tend to respond physiologically to visual stimulus, provided by dimensions such as the increased graphical detail produced in successive iterations of particular games and genres. Female responses, according to this argument, privilege emotional or tactile stimuli that have featured less prominently in most games.[82] The best resource for extending the emotional dimension of games, Ray suggests, is increased emphasis on narrative, including the provision of background context for gameplay activities. Tactile stimulus has been increased though the use of devices such as vibrating controllers and force-feedback (and most substantially with the resources available to arcade games), but, as we saw in Chapter 2, this remains a relatively undeveloped dimension of gaming. Studies suggesting gender-based differences in spatial skills and navigation, with implications for game design, are also cited by Ray. Males, according to this argument, excel at targeting moving objects in an uncluttered field, females at targeting stationary objects in cluttered fields; males prefer to navigate by directions (left, right, etc.), females by the use of landmarks.[83] Whatever their ultimate provenance (deeply rooted gender difference or more recent cultural construction), differences of these kinds provide the basis, Ray suggests, for efforts to design games more likely to appeal to female players. Other studies have indicated more nuanced or less-clear cut distinctions between players on the basis of gender, however, including a suggestion that repeated exposure to gameplay tends to reduce initial differences.[84] The latter point has something in common with our suggestion that contextual factors generally are liable to recede from attention in conditions such as extended or more intensive play.

In general, gaming remains a realm of popular culture dominated by male players. The games industry has usually focused on what soon became established as its core market – relatively young and male – rather than taking what is seen as the risky move of seeking greatly to widen its appeal. The result can be something of a self-fulfilling prophecy: games targeted at young males that attract, primarily if not exclusively, relatively young males. Some developers – a minority – have sought to design games specifically to embody the kinds of play generally thought to be favoured by the under-served female constituency. Examples include mainstream productions, such as Mattel's *Barbie Fashion Designer* (1996), and more alternative interventions. Early attempts to make games appealing to girls 'largely consisted of having female protagonists and making the content nonviolent', but were not generally very successful.[85] The greater success of *Barbie Fashion Designer* is attributed by Kaveri Subrahmanyam and Patricia Greenfield to the construction of gameplay activities that accorded with the preferences of young girls, specifically as an accessory in person-oriented 'pretend' play, based on real-life models and roles and associated with qualities of nurturance (the power of the Barbie franchise was obviously a significant factor, but, as Subrahmanyam and Greenfield argue, other Barbie-related games were not as successful as *Fashion Designer*).[86] The success of *Barbie Fashion Designer*, which sold more than 500,000 copies in its first two months, caught the attention of the games industry, suggesting the commercial potential of a largely untapped market at a time when that for games designed primarily for young boys appeared close to saturation.[87] A number of new, female-owned and staffed developers also came into existence, motivated by both a feminist agenda and a desire for commercial success, including HerInteractive (where Ray was director of product development), Purple Moon, Girltech and Girl Games. A cross-over between these and major industry players such as Broderbund and IBM was created in the form of the Girl Interactive Library (GIRL), which sought to give increased profile to efforts to increase the female game market.[88] Games designed by Purple Moon, founded by Brenda Laurel, include *Rockett's New School* (1997) and related titles based on the life of a girl of the same age as the 8–12 bracket targeted by the company, the chief gameplay activities of which revolve around relationships; 'emotional rehearsal for social navigation', as Laurel puts it.[89] A similar relationship-negotiation basis is structured into *Dead or Alive: Xtreme Beach Volleyball*, a dimension that appears to be targeted clearly at women (in a game the scantily clad visuals of which seem of more obvious appeal to young males); a range of present-giving and other such bonding activities are required if the player-character is to secure volleyball partners. What, exactly, should be produced to appeal to girls or older women has been subject to often heated debate, feminist and commercial imperatives often being difficult to reconcile (Purple Moon soon ran into economic difficulty, despite being financed by the Microsoft co-founder Paul Allen, eventually being sold to Mattel, the bastion of the mainstream/conventional, in 1998). To design games intended to appeal to girls has often been understood as designing games that reinforce female gender stereotypes that might be just as rigid and confining, in their own ways, as the violence-oriented male stereotypes favoured in many existing titles.

Calls for a widening of the horizons of activities structured into gameplay more generally might imply a broadening of their likely appeal on the basis of dominant/conventional gender preferences. Games that allow wider expressions of emotion might, for example, be more likely to appeal to a larger range of female players, as well as opening up the bounds of gameplay in a broader sense. Some games have also been designed to allow a bridging of what often appears to be a wide gender gap, although their appeal also suggests that distinctions on the basis of gender can also be blurred. The bi-modal address of some action–adventure games that feature female heroines was addressed in the previous section, in which the focus was on the level of representations of gender. Many studies of gender issues in games to date have been restricted to this level of analysis (a telling symptom of this shortcoming is a tradition in which the focus is limited to out-of-gameplay dimensions such as cut-scenes or even cover artwork).[90] But games do not operate only at the level of representation. Games are also, as we have stated many times in this book, about activities performed, in a mediated way, within a game-space. We return here to the experience explored in the previous chapters of 'doing' and of 'being-in-the-game-world'. Much analysis has been made of women warriors in film and television, but little that addresses the specific nature of such figures in the game context. The result has been analysis that tends to hinge around issues of gender representation and the 'gaze' at the screen. In games, the issue is made more complex by the fact that players are asked to align themselves, to some extent, and to act through player-characters, a dimension that includes but also goes beyond the bounds of issues of representation.

A number of games utilize women warrior figures established in other media products as a way to increase potential appeal to a female market. *Buffy the Vampire Slayer: Chaos Bleeds* and *Primal* replace the traditional male hero with feisty women characters, but they also include elements that involve meaningful interpersonal relationships, dimensions absent from the raw masculinist individualism of games such as *Doom* or *Far Cry*. To some extent, these interpersonal relationships are built into the narrative elements of the games. In the case of *Buffy* games, a great deal of back-story and character development is provided by the series on which the game is based, as suggested in Chapter 1. Interpersonal relationships are also embedded into the mechanics of gameplay, however. In *Primal*, the lead female protagonist, Jen, is partly dependent on her male sidekick, an animated stone gargoyle named Scree, who acts as her guide and mentor. At certain points in the game the player must switch to playing Scree to undertake tasks that Jen cannot perform. In *Chaos Bleeds*, players not only fight alongside other characters from the series but actively play as them at times, to retrieve various body parts. The structuring of cooperation and friendship into the fabric of gameplay in this manner, extending beyond the dimension of representation, might make the action-adventure/fighting format more appealing to female players.

In both games, the player's task is to master the game controls sufficiently to enable evil to be defeated and the game-story to unfold. Magic plays a significant role in both cases, and can be understood here as having a gendered dimension. The supernatural basis of the games can be understood in the same context as the contemporary flowering of magic-based films and television shows set in the present with central female protagonists, aimed primarily if far from exclusively at a female audience (examples such as *Buffy the Vampire Slayer*, *The Craft* [1996], *Charmed* [1998-] and *Sabrina the Teenage Witch* [1996-2003]). Magic is used in such texts as a way of signifying power, desire and activity within a feminized register in an often positive and empowering way. To some extent this draws on older, more negative and sometimes misogynistic discourses in which female power is associated with witchcraft, but it is recast here in the light of contemporary interest in female-oriented forms of spirituality and power. In the game context of *Primal* and *Chaos Bleeds*, magic extends to the abilities afforded to the player. When playing as Willow, a witch in *Chaos Bleeds*, the player must activate spells through various key-press combinations to defeat evil, rather than using physical fight skills that might be more commonly associated with male characters. This is not simply a negative alternative to physical power, but a way of articulating a form of agency derived from other spheres: bookish study, imagination and the forces of nature rather than body-honing disciplines. Although Jen and *Buffy* use more physical skills, they are both chosen by the 'powers that be' to become champions. The presence of occult powers does not only operate at the level of representation or story – they are also felt directly by the player in terms of regimes of agency and restriction. The player has, in effect, a hands-on experience that in some respects goes beyond that of the character.

That the player might be unable to defeat a monster that the character can potentially vanquish adds a dimension not present in other media. The player might aspire to the status of women warrior, but only be able to achieve it if committed to the task of mastering the game controls (another example of the game work-ethic in action). The dimensions of agency and restriction are personal to the player, therefore, and capable of resonating with such experiences in real life, as well as being aspects of the diegetic universe. This might speak differently to male and female players (and also along different lines such as social class or constructions of race/ethnicity). Part of the back-story to both games is that *Buffy* and Jen have to learn to be efficient fighters. They also face various dilemmas and problems that relate to their identity: specifically the problems that pertain to being a female fighter. Both are presented as struggling with the impact of their new-found strengths: Jen with the meanings of her acquired demonic forms, *Buffy* with the way her power affects her role as a teenage girl interested in boys and clothes. Power is not presented as straightforwardly pleasurable but as a form of 'otherness' that disturbs the order of their 'ordinary' lives (a dimension more rarely seen in games with male protagonists). Players also have to learn to fight in the games, which may represent a steeper than usual learning curve for some female players (likely in general to have less experience of the beat-'em-up form) and might lead to them being regarded with curiosity or suspicion by the male gaming fraternity. Learning to fight in game terms may also provide girls and women with an opportunity to express a type of aggression often repressed in accordance with dominant gender expectations.

The fact that games involve *players* developing game-specific physical and cognitive skills makes them qualitatively different from other media. Does this alter the 'meaning' of the women warrior? At one level, the answer is: yes. The fact that players control the character complicates and fractures arguments about the object-of-the-gaze. But these characters remain constructions of the imagination through which we play (a fact underlined by the magical/fantasy contexts in which the games are set). A player's investment in such characters is likely to be contingent on a number of factors. These might include whether a player is attracted to a character or able to relate to it in one way or another. A wide range of social-semiotic and representational factors might affect a player's relationship with character: body size, race, nationality, hair colour, dress, speech, personal traits. Each may have an impact on the degree to which a player feels comfortable playing in that skin, as suggested in the previous section. A player's particular gaming skills might also be a factor in the nature of the relationship. When things are going well – controlling the character in an accomplished manner – the player might feel empowered and more strongly identified with the character than is possible in the purely imaginary identification that exists in media such as film and television. When things are going badly, however, it is likely that the player will feel distinctly disempowered, frustrated and incapable. The woman warrior in this case might seem a distant prospect for the player. The same can be said of any relationship between player and player-character. Playing as a woman warrior might sometimes afford female players a virtual experience of a kind of liberation and control they are often denied by the gender inequalities and limitations of real life. Yet, this is clearly an unstable experience, one that has constantly to be worked for, in the game, and that is capable of producing frustration.

Female playable characters in games are not always endowed with magically enhanced physical strength. More ordinary-seeming women feature in some survival horror games, for example. When playing as Jill in *Resident Evil* or Heather in *Silent Hill 3*, it is often more expeditious for the player-character to run than to stand and fight, in order to conserve health and limited supplies of ammunition. This might be read in gender-specific terms, seeming to reinforce notions of female weakness or of a characteristically female need to find other solutions to problems they cannot resolve through physical force. A similar strategy is required, but to a lesser extent, if the alternative male player-character is used in *Resident Evil*. As Sara Grimes suggests, however, Jill is physically weaker than the male protagonist, Chris, a fact that influences gameplay options.[91] This makes for some interesting differences in gameplay strategy according to which character is employed, although they remain grounded primarily in very traditional gender conventions. The general tenor of *Resident Evil* and *Silent Hill* is one of vulnerability and dread, in which the relative weakness of player-characters seems appropriate (compared, say, to the rapid and easy dispensing of zombies in *House of the Dead III*). The physical limitation of characters, particularly in the need to avoid certain threats, contributes to the generation of emotional qualities such as fear and suspense. The player-character has to wander around in a state of uncertainty much of the time, wondering what threat might emerge. For Carol Clover, the vicarious experience of abject terror offered by the horror film is gendered feminine, in opposition to forms of masculinity defined by qualities such as autonomy and control. The inclusion of victimized female protagonists in slasher-type films allows male viewers to experience terror vicariously, without any real threat to their gendered identity, she suggests.[92] This kind of gendered terror-economy might also be at work in some games, but the difference, again, is that players actively operate through the player-character and are aware that, with sufficient honing of skills, the threat can be mastered through their own activity. This might, in some cases, be understood as a reassertion of masculine identity, at the level of mastery of the game itself more than mastery of the diegetic in-game situation. For female players, the same process might act as an assertion of mastery, even in the face of what might at first appear to be the weakness of a female-coded protagonist.

The traditionally macho-coded qualities of fighting-based games can be challenged or subverted in various ways, including the foregrounding of interpersonal dynamics in *Primal* and the *Buffy* games. The use in the latter of items such as water pistols (filled with holy water, of course!), brooms and pieces of broken furniture shifts the domain of weaponry – often subject to macho-oriented fetishization – into a more playful and female-coded domestic arena. *Space Channel 5* offers another such gender twist by having the central female character, Ulala, dispose of aliens by dancing them to death, the player being required to press keys in time to the music to complete the process. Gender subversion might also be introduced through player-created modifications and skins, as in the use of emphatically un-macho character patches such as 'Fighter Chicken' and 'Gumby Doll' in *Doom*. Gender transgression also resulted from the unintentional juxtapositions created by the early use of female skins in *Quake*. Software limitations resulted in the mapping of female skins onto what remained the standard-issue macho musculature, the resulting figure having the transgender appearance of what became known as 'frag queens', a quality subsequently embraced by the Psycho Men Slayers clan.[93]

If gender-role assumptions built into games can be subverted, so can many others, in player activities ranging from refusal to abide by dominant 'win-conditions' to the construction of politically oriented mods. Games can be played 'against the grain', although there may be limits to how far this practice can be sustained. If it is possible to play the 'enemy' GLA in *Command and Conquer: Generals*, for example, it is also possible deliberately to subvert the objectives of play as the US. Such activities usually involve play at the *paidea* rather than the *ludus* end of the scale: 'playing around' inside the game rather than playing to win or progress. These can be pleasurable in their own right, as we suggested in Chapter 1, but they are liable to be restricted in scope and lack the dimension of clear-cut challenge structured into *ludus*-oriented gameplay. Subversive forms of play of this kind often involve a testing of the limits, seeing how far the bounds of the meanings structured into the game can be pushed. They often involve deliberate failure: allowing one side to lose a conflict or letting your unconventional Sims die rather than responding to their demands for what the game presents as the more 'normal' satisfactions of suburban-consumer lifestyle. Some games allow more scope for such experiment than others. In some shooters, for example, it is possible to 'frag' officers on your own side (as occurred in some cases in the US forces during the Vietnam war), while others render any such attacks harmless (in the official version of US combat, *America's Army*, as might be expected, any such action is liable to punishment, including being thrown out of the game). A game such as *Civilization* provides considerable scope for 'playing around' or developing counter-factual histories, which might be politically/ideologically motivated; playing as America and deciding to turn the country communist, for example, or playing an Aztec defeat of Spain.[94] The underlying colonial/expansionist dynamic remains in place in such cases, but structured into the game is an ability to play with outcomes and relationships in a manner that has potential to open particular colonial assumptions to question. Massively multi-player online role-playing games are often policed quite strictly to prevent subversion of gameplay. Players found to have hacked into games to gain unfair advantage are likely to have their accounts cancelled. *EverQuest* also employs a language filter to excise swearing, although this can be subverted through the use of minor changes of spelling. Players reported for breaches of rules against racist, sexist or homophobic speech also face cautions or the cancellation of accounts and the forfeit of characters.

Modifications can result in various ways of altering or subverting the meaning structures of games at the levels of representation or interaction, either working on an original or through the creation of new games based on models established elsewhere. The latter would include shooters such as *UnderAsh* and *Special Force*, and a *Civilization III* modification pack including an option to play as Palestine with 'suicide bombers' as a special unit.[95] A British example cited by Katie Salen and Eric Zimmerman is *Backlash*, an anti-racist 're-versioning' of the arcade game *Tempest* (1981): 'Building on the game's existing shoot-or-be-shot structure, *Backlash* transforms the aliens of the original game into comic book renditions of hooded Ku Klux Klan members and uniformed British police officers.'[96] Another example, *Los Disneys*, pitches post-apocalyptic first-person shooter action into the realm of a Disneyland theme park, a patch for *Marathon Infinity* (1996) that allows the player to shoot oversized Disney characters and 'to blast their way through lengthy lines of children and their parents waiting for rides.'[97] One of the best-known mods, the multi-player *Half-Life* variant *Counter-Strike*, which became a commercial product in its own right, has also been subject to subversive modification in the form of 'Velvet Strike', a collection of spray-paint effects that can be used as graffiti on the walls, ceilings and floors of the game. Created after George W. Bush's declared 'war on terrorism', Velvet's Strike's target is, appropriately, a game in which the player chooses the role of 'terrorist' or 'counter-terrorist' – gameplay being much the same, tellingly, in either case. Sprays available for download from the Velvet Strike website range from a variety of 'peace and love' messages, including images of rival terrorists/counter-terrorists embracing, to more pointed commentary on the American invasion of Iraq.[98] A similar post-9/11 feature enabled players of *The Sims* to download antiwar posters for in-game display.[99] The creators of Velvet Strike went on to produce a multi-player *Quake* mod, *Anime Noir* (2003), in which the aim is to meet other player-characters and, instead of shooting them, touch their body parts in what could lead to a number of increasingly erotic in-game moves.[100] Another modification of *Half-Life* is *Escape From Woomera* (2004), a first-person action-adventure game designed to highlight the plight of asylum seekers held in Australia's infamous Woomera detention centre.[101] The game, based on research including interviews with former detainees, invites players to see the world from their perspective, a view largely denied to more traditional media access. This is a good example of using the specific qualities of games – the opportunity to explore a virtual world, into which particular characteristics and behaviours can be modelled – to offer a version of experiences otherwise inaccessible to most potential players.

Some games can also be understood as not inviting themselves to be taken too seriously, building an element of subversion into their own representations. This might be the case with the excessive versions of masculinity or femininity built into some games, as suggested above. *The Sims* can easily be read in this way, as an ironic commentary on consumerist ideology as well as, or instead of, being seen as a celebration of such values. As Kline, Dyer-Witheford and De Peuter suggest, the games industry, like other aspects of popular cultural production, 'has learned that irony is a no-lose gambit, a "have your cake and eat it too" strategy whose simultaneous affirmation/negation structure can give the appearance of social critique and retract it at the same moment – thereby letting everything stay just as it is while allowing practitioners to feel safely above it all even as they sink more deeply in.'[102]

Game cultures and industry

To be understood fully, games have to be situated within the cultures in which they are found, including the wider industrial/economic context. They also have cultures or subcultures of their own, however, as suggested more generally in Huizinga's definition of play, which includes the tendency for play to generate particular play-communities on the basis of 'the feeling of being "apart together" in an exceptional situation, of sharing something important, of mutually withdrawing from the rest of the world' – a quality similar to that invoked in more recent studies of subcultural forms.[103] A subculture is defined in sociological terms by Gary Alan Fine, in a study of fantasy role-playing games, as a group that has 'networks of communication through which common information is transmitted'; a group recognized as such by those outside and by its own members.[104]

16. Gameplay as community: group play screen-shot from *EverQuest*.

Far from all gameplayers would regard themselves as part of a subculture
defined in this manner, particularly those who play games more casually.
Those who invest a great deal of time, money and energy in playing games
are more inclined to identify themselves as part of a distinct category of
'gamers', however. For many regular or hard-core gamers, gaming can
provide a strong sense of identity and might, in some cases, frame the
way they present themselves to others. As Fine notes, a subculture only
develops if there are strong communicative networks among members.
Gaming magazines, websites and chat rooms devoted to gaming are
central to the creation of a gaming subculture in general, and to particular
subcultures related to individual games or genres. The internet looms
especially large in this area, a domain that cuts across national boundaries
and in which gameplayers are particularly likely to be adept because of
the computer-based nature of the medium. These mainly participatory
modes of communication promote a distinctive shared language that
helps to mark gamers off as a subsection of society. Becoming acquainted
with the language of gaming and sharing experiences with other gamers
creates a sense of shared identity and interest.

Gaming subculture is not a unified entity, however. Disputes are common, in a dimension of popular culture in which the values of individualism and competition are often prevalent. Gaming culture is also deeply hierarchical. Game designers are often the most highly venerated. Those with sufficient skill to create interesting modifications come a little way below, followed by highly skilled players such as winners of high-profile competitions, game's masters, those who write walk-throughs, reviewers and beta-testers. More ordinary gamers are usually ranked according to their playing experience. Those who create or modify games come with the status of 'hacking', valued among the computer-literate for qualities such as transgression and demonstrating high levels of control over the digital domain. Experienced players of massively multi-player online role-playing games can accumulate stores of subcultural capital: forms of knowledge and expertise in the particular domain of a game-world on the basis of which they might earn the respect of other players.[105]

Gaming culture has tended to be largely male-oriented, as suggested above, as evidenced by many factors including the predominance of male players at LAN (local area network) events, and the fact that the majority of game designers, reviewers and senior figures such as guild leaders in *EverQuest* are male. Numerous social and historical factors have created this gender imbalance, some of which are considered above. Within the broader gaming subculture are smaller groups focused around individual games (including some, such as the female *Quake* clans cited above, defined on gender lines). This is particularly the case with players of multi-player games: LAN-based or small and large multi-player online games (console or PC). LAN-based competitions often involve contests between teams playing the same game in close physical proximity. In small-group online play, physical proximity is usually surrendered in return for other forms of inter-player familiarity. Massively multi-player games provide scope to play with large numbers from across the world. Clans and guilds are common in such games, creating their own forms of group identity for players who generally have no contact outside the gamescape (it is not uncommon, however, for extra-gamic friendships to result from relationships established in-game). Fine's term 'idioculture' captures a sense of the more localized and idiosyncratic subcultures that can develop within individual games.[106] In *EverQuest*, for example, the various guilds have rather different identities. The SoulDefenders guild (on the Stromm server) advertises itself as a friendly guild that welcomes new players; questions are generally answered in good faith with humour and 'guildies' often help one another. Other guilds are less tolerant of questions and requests for help, in some cases only admitting players with high-level characters. These guilds tend to concentrate more intensely on raids in which newer players might prove a liability. Often a guild's name says much about its particular culture. The social coherence of guilds is based on an in-game history shared between its members. Particular events become features of the collective identity – as in the construction of external-world cultures – and are subject to frequent reference. Any guild that fails to construct an identity and history is likely to disband before long. Rivalries or perceived injustices often create situations in which players from different guilds refuse to play with one another. As Fine notes of Dungeons & Dragons groups, players of multi-player online games often also tease one another, not primarily as a form of denigration but to promote sociability, particularly the case in guilds and smaller groups that fight together on a regular basis.[107] Hierarchies operate within guilds, as elsewhere in gaming cultures, often on the basis of player accumulations of subcultural capital.

If gameplaying has an array of niche cultures, and the broader subculture of self-identified 'gamers', it has also established a place in the much wider landscape of popular culture and entertainment in recent decades. It has, in the process, become the basis of a very large industrial enterprise. The heights of the industry are fought over by a number of big business players, the principal rivalry at the time of writing being between the electronics and entertainment giant Sony and Microsoft, the globally dominant force in computer operating systems. Former heavyweight contenders include Atari (which first demonstrated the potential of games to become big business and became part of the Warner Communications empire in 1976, before falling victim to a major crash that saw much of the games business wiped out in 1983), Nintendo (which effectively resurrected the business after the Atari crash and dominated the industry from the late 1980s, subsequently being forced to accept third place behind Sony and Microsoft) and Sega (challenger to Nintendo in the early 1990s, later abandoning its investments in hardware platforms after a series of disappointments).[108] The console end of the business is well characterized by Kline, Dyer-Witheford and De Peuter as existing since the early 1990s in a state of 'tumultuous oligopoly': dominated by a small number of large companies, but in an unstable fashion, with fierce competition among the key players (unlike, for example, the Hollywood film industry, which is characterized by a more stable form of oligopoly among the major studio-distributors).[109] The stakes are huge, as demonstrated by the billions poured into the development and marketing of the PlayStation 2 and Xbox platforms and their successors. The games industry is not only big corporate business in its own right, but also viewed as a key element in the wider entertainment and communications sector. Microsoft's enormous investment in the development of the Xbox, for example, was motivated by strategic concern about not just the machines on which games would be played (PC or consoles) but about control over what would be seen as the portal for a range of other applications. The PlayStation 2 was sold as a home entertainment centre, capable of playing CDs and DVDs as well as games, seeking to integrate Sony's investment in games with its broader stake in home entertainment electronics. The decision to give the Xbox similar capabilities, plus a broadband internet connection, was part of its rival claim to become a unified home entertainment/ communications centre (a potential built earlier, to a lesser extent, into Nintendo's Famicom/NES, which came equipped with a data point capable of being connected to a modem).

The games industry is viewed by Kline, Dyer-Witheford and De Peuter as an exemplar of the high-technology end of contemporary capitalism, 'information capitalism' as it is termed by Tessa Morris-Suzuki in her study of the Japanese high-tech sector that has played a central role in the global games business.[110] One of the characteristics of this form is the creation of economic sectors based on 'perpetual innovation', in which the threat of falling consumer demand (always a key issue for capitalist systems) is kept at bay by the constant upgrading of products, a process clearly at the heart of a games industry founded on the cyclical production of new generations of consoles or upgraded capacities for PCs. Product cycles are shortened, promising higher rates of profit than the slower cycles associated with traditional manufacturing industries, although at greater risk of instability.[111] If *The Sims* structures a celebration of consumerism into its gameplay, games themselves (as well as games hardware) are quintessentially consumerist products, constantly updated and offering novelties that appear to render existing titles 'out of date' and in need of regular replacement or supplement.[112] Other key factors for Kline, Dyer-Witheford and De Peuter, allied to the above, are the centrality to the games industry of intensive advertising, promotional and consumer-surveillance strategies, designed to build and monitor markets for new games and game systems. This kind of capitalism is often described as post-Fordist, a term used to distinguish regimes based on flexible production and niche-marketing to particular consumer groups from the 'Fordist' process of mass production and mass consumption.[113]

For some commentators, the term post-Fordism has been used to suggest a form of capitalism in which the emphasis is on large numbers of smaller, high-tech or highly consumer-oriented companies: 'In the most optimistic versions of such theory, post-Fordism is portrayed as an era of digital artisanship, based on a multitude of small enterprises, organizing production as high-technology craft-work and forming vibrant community networks of efficient but human-scale business.'[114] Sceptics point out that the chief beneficiaries of the high-tech digital economy tend to be large corporations, new technologies and new ways of organizing production tending 'not in the least to diminish the pull towards concentration of ownership, oligopolies of knowledge, and corporate giganticism of "global image empires".'[115] The games industry, Kline, Dyer-Witheford and De Peuter suggest, can be cited as evidence of both tendencies, although with an overall leaning towards the latter. At the level of platform technologies, especially consoles, corporate oligopoly holds sway. In software, something closer to the vision of small-scale high-tech artisan production can be found, in the shape of the many and changing companies involved in game development. Strong pressures exist, however, to drive the latter in the direction of the former.

The model on which the console business has functioned in recent decades has been one in which hardware and software production are closely integrated. Hardware has become seen essentially as a loss leader, or as only at best a small profit-centre, a phenomenon that dates back at least to the period of Nintendo's dominance in the 1990s. Software is the principal source of profits, sales of which are key to overall profit or loss calculations. Microsoft, for example, initially worked on the basis of a pricing formula that meant for each Xbox to break even, nine games would have to be sold, three of which would have to be in-house productions (licence fees are charged to outside 'third-party' developers, but a larger share of profit is retained from games developed in-house), a goal that had been achieved by Sony during the lifetime of the original PlayStation.[116] At launch, Microsoft expected to lose $87 on each box (a figure increased by after-launch price-cutting). The importance of software to the success of individual consoles was demonstrated by the industry collapse of the early 1980s, a major aspect of which was attributed to the glutting of the market with inferior products. Nintendo learned the lesson in its reconstruction of the industry, maintaining tight control over the licensing of games by outsiders, restricting market competition and making itself unpopular with many game developers in the process.[117] At the same time, corporate-controlled console manufacturers have also sought to court the favour of developers, recognizing the crucial importance of creative design to their business (both Nintendo's Famicom/NES and Microsoft's Xbox were designed to be easy to program for, specifically to make them attractive to developers). The development end of the business has moved inexorably in the direction of larger-scale and more consolidated operation, however, the result of factors such as escalating technological capability and the increasingly marketing-centred nature of the mainstream games business. Game development has moved from its artisanal roots in the work of individual designers, employing limited resources, to become a large-scale industrial enterprise in its own right, the development of a typical game involving a period of some two or more years and budgets running into tens of millions of dollars, far more when marketing and promotional costs are included. The result is, inevitably, a more conservative industry, more likely to stick to familiar genres, formats and franchises, rather than indulging in riskier experiments. A similar problem of largeness of scale exists in the rapidly growing arena of massively multi-player online gaming, in which a different revenue model exists, based primarily on the payment of monthly subscriptions. To run a game of this kind also requires substantial investment, not just in initial design but in the provision of regular patches and upgrades, to keep longer-term players interested, and in maintaining sources of technical support.

The mainstreaming of the games industry is seen by some as a threat to its roots in the kinds of smaller and more particular subcultures considered in the first part of this section. Games aimed at a wider market might generally be expected to be less inventive or to be made more accessible and less difficult to master, reducing their appeal to the hard-core gamer. The nature of gaming as an active process is such that spaces are always likely to exist for alternative practices, however, ranging from the production of less mainstream or 'indie' games to the modification and use of existing titles in ways not envisaged by their producers. Whether or not an independent games sector exists, as anything other than extremely marginalized, remains open to question. There is a big difference, as Eric Zimmerman suggests, between a sustainable independent games sector, on the kind of model associated with independent cinema, and more inward-looking fan-based sub-cultural production.[118] Independent developers have their own 'special interest group' in the International Game Developer's Association (IGDA), which defines an independent developer as one 'that has a substantial amount of control over the development, design, implementation and distribution of their game.'[119] The latter stage – distribution – is especially important and one in which alternative channels are required if indie developers are to reach a market (it was the creation of independent distribution networks that was crucial to the growth of American independent cinema as a substantial alternative to Hollywood). In the games business, mainstream wholesale and retail networks are tightly controlled by dominant industry players.[120] The number of titles stocked by retailers is relatively small, largely restricted to titles in which large sums are invested in marketing and promotion. The situation is much the same as that of major studio control over film distribution, except that there is as yet no equivalent in games retail of the indie-friendly or 'art-house' cinema that exists alongside the Hollywood-dominated multiplex. Instead, like some independent film-makers, advocates of alternative outlets for games have looked primarily to internet distribution. Games can be downloaded from sites such as RealOne Arcade, considered in 2003 to be one of the most important portals available to independent developers, or GarageGames.[121] Sites such as RealOne have some features in common with mainstream game retailing, including a hit-based economy, in which the market is dominated by a relatively small number of top-selling titles, although online distribution generally makes it easier for a larger range of games to be made available, reducing the intense competition for shelf space experienced in retail sales. It also reduces costs of production, promotion and distribution itself, enabling developers to operate at lower levels of investment and to spread their risks across larger numbers of titles. Outlets such as this can be seen as more commercial manifestations of a longer tradition in which games have been made more freely available online in the form of shareware, in which parts of games are released without charge online or on disks provided on the covers of magazines, players being charged to obtain the rest.[122]

Modification of existing games has often proved the most accessible form of alternative development, although this comes with its own restrictions, including the terms of End User License Agreements. The costs of licensing proprietary game-engine code and development tools often stand in the way of indie/alternative development, as Julian Oliver suggests.[123] Licensed usage of established game-engines is expensive (writing in 2003, Oliver suggests a cost of $250,000 for use of the then two-year old *Quake III* engine, plus a payment of a 5 per cent royalty on the wholesale price of the title produced). Existing products are also limited in how far they can be put to entirely new or innovative uses, or in the extent to which source code is made available for analysis of exactly how it functions. Cheaper and sometimes more accessible alternatives exist in the form of open-source materials, however, including freely available game-engines 'not far behind many of the proprietary products available.'[124] The sharing of code and modifications has its roots in early game development, an alternative economy associated more recently with the 'elite' end of hacker/gamer subculture.

The more mainstream the industry as a whole becomes, the more it might be expected to draw on material with dominant social-cultural or political-ideological implications, at the levels of either background context or meanings structured implicitly or explicitly into gameplay. This depends to a large extent, however, on the particular constituencies being targeted. There is no fixed corollary between size of market and the dominant/alternative nature of the material produced. Plenty of games aimed at relatively narrowly defined groups (young males, for example) play on material generally very dominant/conventional in that arena, even if accompanied by qualities such as violence and gore sold on the basis of its 'transgressive' edge. To widen the target group (to include more women, for example) might mean reducing the extent of some forms of dominant/conventional stereotyping (if probably at the cost of introducing others). It remains the case, though, that game content that raises questions about dominant social–political assumptions is more likely to be found in niche products than those which seek to reach a mass market, as is also the case with other media such as film and television, even if the former does not always follow from the latter.

Afterword

From core gameplay mechanics – as procedures that can be abstracted from any kind of context – to readings of their most heavily political-ideological implications, games offer multidimensional experiences. Gameplay takes numerous forms, even if these tend to resolve into a relatively limited number of dominant game-generic regimes, especially in the commercial mainstream. Dimensions such as narrative, genre or other associational contexts can come into and out of play; sometimes as relatively significant elements in the overall experience, sometimes not. Gamescapes are often ripe for exploration, but this, too, can be shaped, limited or constrained in a variety of ways; as can the degree to which an impression of presence is created, of 'being' (in some sense) in the game-world. Qualities such as these are often inter-connected, as we have argued throughout this book, as they are with additional dimensions such as forms of graphical representation, sound design and the intensity of gameplay activities. The gaming experience, in general, is one in which dimensions such as play, representation (including the politics of representation) and immersion – in its various forms – come together into a complex gestalt, the exact nature of which varies, as we have often stressed, from one game or player to another. All possible combinations are impossible to embrace in a work such as this – a limitation, for us, that is also a measure of the richness and multifaceted nature of the videogame as a part of contemporary popular culture.

Notes

INTRODUCTION

1. We use the term 'videogames' in this book to encompass what are sometimes separately described as 'computer games' (a term associated with games played on personal computers) and 'video games' (associated with various console platforms), also sometimes termed 'digital games'.

2. Different sources often give different dates for the release of games. For the sake of consistency, we have generally used dates as given by www.gamespot.com.

3. For a brief sketch of earlier work, see Jonas Heide Smith, 'Computer Game Research 101 – Brief Introduction to the Literature', *Game Research*, December 2002, www.game-research.com/art_computer_game_research.asp; on the prospects for game research as an academic field in its own right, see Espen Aarseth, 'Computer Game Studies, Year One', *Game Studies*, 1, July 2001, www.gamestudies.org/0101/editorial/html.

4. For examples of studies that include such analysis, see Marinka Copier and Joost Raessens (eds.), *Level Up: Digital Games Research Conference*, Utrecht University, 2003, contributions by: Tosca; Klastrup; Engfeldt-Nielsen; Kerr; Ermi and Mäyrä; Halloran, Rogers and Fitzpatrick.

5. Examples include Espen Aarseth, Solveig Marie Smedstad and Lise Sunnanå, 'A Multi-Dimensional Typology of Games', in Copier and Raessens, *Level Up*; Craig Lindley, 'Game Taxonomies: A High Level Framework for Game Analysis and Design', *Gamasutra*, 3 October 2003, www.gamasutra.com/features/20031003/lindley_01.shtml.

CHAPTER 1

1. For a summary of six different definitions of this kind, along with another of his own, see Jesper Juul, 'The Game, The Player, The World: Looking for the Heart of Gameness', in Marinka Copier and Joost Raessens (eds.), *Level Up: Digital Games Research Conference*, Utrecht University, 2003.

2. *Homo Ludens*, 8.

3. Ibid.

4. Ibid. 10.

5. Ibid. 12.

6. *Man, Play and Games*, 9.

7. Ibid.

8. Ibid. 10.

9. Ibid. 9.

10. Ibid. 10.

11. 'What are games made of?', Level Up: Digital Games Research Conference, Utrecht University, November 2003.

12. *Rules of Play: Game Design Fundamentals*, 86–91.

13. 'Playing Research: Methodological approaches to game analysis', Digital Arts and Culture conference, Melbourne, 2003, accessed at hypertext.rmit.edu.au/dac/papers/.

14. *Man, Play and Games*, 27.

15. Ibid. 27.

16. *The Grasshopper: Games, Life and Utopia*, 34, 41.

17. 'Videogames of the Oppressed: Videogames as a means for critical thinking and debate', master's thesis, Georgia Institute of Technology, 2000, accessed at www.jacaranda.org/frasca/thesis/FrascaThesisVideogames.pdf.

18. *Play, Dreams and Imitation in Childhood*, Chapter V.

19. Ibid. 112.

20. 'Videogames of the Oppressed', 18–19.

21. 'Communication and Community in Digital Entertainment Services: Prestudy Research Report', Hypermedia Laboratory Net Series, 2, University of Tampere Hypermedia Laboratory, accessed at tampub.uta.fi/tup/951–44–5432–4.pdf, 14.

22. 'Hearts, Clubs, Diamonds, Spades: Players Who Suit Muds', accessed at mud.co.uk/Richard/hcds.htm.

23.   'Videogames of the Oppressed', 13.
24.   'The Open and the Closed: Games of Emergence and Games of Progression', in Frans Mäyrä (ed.), *Computer Games and Digital Cultures: Conference Proceedings*.
25.   Mactavish, 'Game Mod(ifying) Theory: The Cultural Contradictions of Computer Game Modding', 'Power-Up: Computer Games, Ideology and Play', Bristol, July 2003.
26.   'Know Your Meta-Game', in François Dominic Laramée (ed.), *Game Design Perspectives*.
27.   'A Theory of Play and Fantasy', in *Steps to an Ecology of Mind: Collected Essays in Anthropology, Psychiatry, Evolution, and Epistemology*, 179; see also Brian Sutton-Smith, *The Ambiguity of Play*, 23.
28.   *Homo Ludens*, 10.
29.   *Rules of Play*, 97.
30.   *The Grasshopper*, 41.
31.   See Robert Hodge and David Tripp, *Children and Television: A Semiotic Approach*.
32.   *Toys as Culture*, 62–4.
33.   Ibid. 139–40.
34.   'The Gameplay Gestalt, Narrative, and Interactive Storytelling', in Frans Mäyrä (ed.), *Computer Games and Digital Cultures*, 215.
35.   Ibid. 208.
36.   'Balancing Gameplay Hooks', in Laramée (ed.), *Game Design Perspectives*, 78.
37.   Ibid.
38.   Ibid. 81.
39.   *Rules of Play*, 316.
40.   Aarseth, *Cybertext: Perspectives on Ergodic Literature*, 91.
41.   '2.0 Introduction', in Laramée (ed.), *Game Design Perspectives*, 61.
42.   Ibid.
43.   *Flow*, 4.
44.   For a history of the development and use of the concept of flow, see Csikszentmihalyi, 'Introduction', in Mihaly Csikszentmihalyi and Isabella Selega Csikszentmihalyi (eds.), *Optimal Experience: Psychological Studies of Flow in Consciousness*.
45.   *The Ambiguity of Play*, 34.
46.   Summarized in *Flow*, 48–67.

47.   *Flow*, 74.

48.   'Balancing Gameplay Hooks', 83.

49.   'Beyond Myth and Metaphor – The Case of Narrative in Digital Media', *Game Studies*, vol.1, 1, July 2001, accessed at www.gamestudies.org/0101/ryan/.

50.   For more detail and sources, see Csikszentmihalyi, 'The Flow Experience and Human Psychology', in Csikszentmihalyi and Csikszentmihalyi, *Optimal Experience*, 17–18.

51.   *Flow*, 53.

52.   *Chris Crawford on Game Design*, 43.

53.   *Flow*, 58.

54.   *Homo Ludens*, 10.

55.   *Flow*, 64.

56.   Ibid. 60.

57.   Ibid. 61.

58.   'Pros and Cons of Hit Point Systems', in Laramée (ed.), *Game Design Perspectives*.

59.   'Alternatives to Numbers in Game Design Models', in ibid. 104.

60.   'Pros and Cons of Hit Point Systems', 101–2.

61.   Sue Morris, 'First-Person Shooters – A Game Apparatus', in Geoff King and Tanya Krzywinska (eds.), *ScreenPlay: Cinema/Videogames/Interfaces*, 86.

62.   Gaming can also be more communal, however, with players grouping around a single console to play together, in turn and/or to watch.

63.   For a sketch of its historical roots, see Sutton-Smith, *The Ambiguity of Play*, 175–81.

64.   *Hypertext 2.0: The Convergence of Contemporary Critical Theory and Technology*.

65.   'The Game as Object of Study', Game Cultures conference, Bristol 2001, question-and-answer session.

66.   Murray, *Hamlet on the Holodeck: The Future of Narrative in Cyberspace*; Atkins, *More than a Game: The Computer Game as Fictional Form*; Molyneux, 'Black and White', in Austin Grossman (ed.), *Postmortems from Game Developers*; Littlejohn, 'Agitating for Dramatic Change', *Gamasutra*, 29 October 2003.

67.   'The Gaming Situation', *Game Studies*, vol. 1, 1, July 2001, section 8, accessed at www.gamestudies.org/0101/eskilinen.

68.   For an argument that suggests that this debate has been overstated, as a false opposition, see Gonzalo Frasca, 'Ludologists love stories too: notes from a debate that never took place', in Copier and Raessens (eds.), *Level Up: Digital Games Research Conference*, Utrecht University, 2003.

69.   Juul, 'The Open and the Closed', 324.

70.   Ibid.

71.   Ibid.

72.   Ibid. 328.

73.   Molyneux, 'Black and White', in Grossman (ed.), *Postmortems from Game Developers*.

74.   'Game Design as Narrative Architecture', accessed at web.mit.edu/21 fms/www/faculty/henry3/games&narrative.html.

75.   'Real Interactivity in Interactive Entertainment', in Clark Dodsworth (ed.), *Digital Illusion: Entertaining the Future with High Technology*, 154.

76.   For more on this, see Petri Lankoski, Satu Heliö and Inger Ekman, 'Characters in Computer Games: Toward Understanding Interpretation and Design', in Copier and Raessens (eds.), *Level Up: Digital Games Research Conference*, accompanying CD-ROM, Utrecht University, 2003.

77.   *Chris Crawford on Game Design*, 163.

78.   'A Poetics of Virtual Worlds', Digital Arts and Culture conference, Melbourne, 2003, accessed at hypertext.rmit.edu.au/dac/papers/.

79.   'A Poetics of Virtual Worlds', 107.

80.   A similar opposition is suggested by Atkins, 20.

81.   *Game Design: Theory and Practice*, 219–20.

82.   'In Defense of Cutscenes', in Frans Mäyrä (ed.), *Computer Games and Digital Cultures*, 200.

83.   Rouse, 224–5.

84.   'The Road Less Traveled – The Case for Computer Game Philology', paragraph 5, accessed at playability.de/en/txt/cgpabs.html.

85.   For design-oriented work that stresses the importance of narrative, see, for example, Troy Dunniway, 'Using the Hero's Journey in Games', 'Gamasutra', 27 November 2000, accessed at www/gamasutra.com/features/20001127/htm/dunniway_01.htm, on the importance of pacing; and Joshua Mosqueria, 'World Building: From Paper to Polygons', in Laramée (ed.), *Game Design Perspectives*.

86.   'The Road Less Traveled', paragraph 5.

87.   'The Gameplay Gestalt', 205.

88.   'Beyond Myth and Metaphor – The Case of Narrative in Digital Media', *Game Studies*, vol. 1, 1, July 2001, accessed at www.gamestudies. org/0101/ryan/.

89.   *Hamlet on the Holodeck*, 145.

90.   Campbell, *The Hero with a Thousand Faces*.

91.   'Using the Hero's Journey in Games'.

92.   *The Writer's Journey: Mythic Structure for Storytellers and Screenwriters*.

93.   *Morphology of the Folk Tale*.

94.   *Hamlet on the Holodeck*, 197.

95.   'Games Telling stories? – A brief note on games and narratives', *Game Studies*, vol. 1, 1, accessed at gamestudies.org/0101/juul-gts/.

96.   Ibid. 7–8.

97.   'Game Design as Narrative Architecture', 5.

98.   'Adapting Licensed Properties', in Laramée (ed.), *Game Design Perspectives*, 126.

99.   For a more detailed analysis of the Xbox game version of *Buffy the Vampire Slayer*, see Krzywinska, 'Playing *Buffy*: Remediation, Occulted Meta-game-Physics and the Dynamics of Agency in the Videogame Version of *Buffy the Vampire Slayer*', *Slayage* 8, March 2003, www.slayage. tv.

100. 'Game Design as Narrative Architecture', 4.

101. 'Environmental Storytelling: Creating Immersive 3D Worlds Using Lessons Learned from the Theme Park Industry', *Gamasutra*, 1 March 2000, accessed at www.Gamasutra.com/features/20000301/Carson_ pfv.htm, 2.

102. Ibid. 3.

103. *Hamlet on the Holodeck*, 132.

104. 'World Building: From Paper to Polygons', 68.

105. Ibid. 69.

106. Ibid.

107. *Hamlet on the Holodeck*, 192.

108. 'Approaches to Computer Game Design', in Frans Mäyrä (ed.), *Computer Games and Digital Cultures*; Barthes, *S/Z*, 18–20.

109. 'Approaches to Computer Game Design', 316.

110. 'In Defense of Cutscenes', 201.

111. *Man, Play and Games*, 7.

112.   *Hamlet on the Holodeck*, 144.

113.   'The Gaming Situation', 14.

114.   *Chris Crawford on Game Design*, 30–1.

115.   'The attack of the backstories (and why they won't win)', in Copier and Raessens (eds.), *Level Up: Digital Games Research Conference*, accompanying CD-ROM, Utrecht University, 2003.

116.   Social-cultural issues raised by conventions such as these more generally are addressed in Chapter 4.

117.   kumawar.com.

118.   'Computer Game Criticism: A Method for Computer Game Analysis', in Frans Mäyrä (ed.), *Computer Games and Digital Cultures*, 95.

119.   Karen Littleton, P. Light, R. Joiner, D. Messer and P. Barnes, 'Gender task scenarios and children's computer-based problem solving', *Educational Psychology*, vol. 18, 3, 1998; cited by Simeon Yates and Karen Littleton, 'Understanding computer game culture: A situated approach', in Eileen Green and Alison Adam (eds.), *Virtual Gender: Technology, Consumption and Identity*.

120.   Yates and Littleton, 'Understanding computer game culture', 110.

121.   Konzack suggests a seven-level method for the study of games: hardware, programme code, functionality, gameplay, meaning, referentiality, and socio-culture.

CHAPTER 2

1.   'Allegories of Space: The Question of Spatiality in Computer Games', paragraph 6, accessed at www.hf.uib.no/hi/espen/papers/space/.

2.   A point also made by Bernadette Flynn, 'Languages of Navigation Within Computer Games', Digital Arts and Culture conference, Melbourne, May 2003, accessed at hypertext.rmit.edu.au/dac/papers/.

3.   'The Open and the Closed: Games of Emergence and Games of Progression', in Frans Mäyrä (ed.), *Computer Games and Digital Cultures*.

4.   'The Role of Architecture in Videogames', *Gamasutra*, 9 October 2002, accessed at www.gamasutra.com/features/20021009/adams_02.htm.

5.   A similar point is made by Barry Atkins in *More than a Game*, Chapter 3.

6.   Ernest Adams, 'The Designer's Notebook: Defining the Physical Dimension of a Game Setting'.

7.   Mark Wolf, 'Space in the Video Game', in Wolf (ed.), *The Medium of the Video Game*, 56.

8.   Bartle, *Designing Virtual Worlds*, 278.

9.   The concept of the rhizome, used in this sense, is developed by Gilles Deleuze and Felix Guattari in *A Thousand Plateaus: Capitalism and Schizophrenia*. The rhizome, spreading out in all directions in examples such as bulb and tuber systems, is contrasted with the more hierarchical model of root-and-tree. Diane Carr uses Murray's distinction between solvable maze and tangled rhizome in a comparison between the structures of *Silent Hill* and *Planescape Torment* in 'Play Dead: Genre and Affect in *Silent Hill* and *Planescape Torment*', *Game Studies*, vol. 3, 1, May 2003, accessed at http:/www.gamestudies.org/0301/carr/.

10.   Richard Bartle, *Designing Virtual Worlds*, 28, 100.

11.   An argument made in numerous works including *The Archaeology of Knowledge*.

12.   'A Touch of Medieval: Narrative, Magic and Computer Technology in Massively Multi-player Computer Role-Playing Games', in Mäyrä (ed.), *Computer Games and Digital Cultures*, 268.

13.   '"Complete Freedom of Movement": Video Games as Gendered Play Spaces', in Justine Cassell and Jenkins (eds.), *From Barbie to Mortal Kombat: Gender and Computer Games*.

14.   Joanna Alexander and Mark Long, 'Designing and Developing for Head-Mounted Displays', in Clark Dodsworth (ed.), *Digital Illusion: Entertaining the Future with High Technology*.

15.   See, for example, Christopher Hasser and Thomas Massie, 'The Haptic Illusion', in Dodsworth, *Digital Illusion*.

16.   See, for example, John Vince, *Essential Virtual Reality Fast*, 5–6.

17.   Game manual reproduced at www.world-of-nintendo.com/manuals/nes/super_glove_ball.shtml.

18.   Joanna Alexander and Mark Long, 'Designing and Developing for Head-Mounted Displays', in Dodsworth, *Digital Illusion*.

19.   Ralph Schroeder, *Possible Worlds: The Social Dynamic of Virtual Reality Technology*, 65, 88.

20.   Stephen Clarke-Willson, 'Applying Game Design to Virtual Environments', in Dodsworth, *Digital Illusion*, 232; Clarke-Willson argues, however, for the possibility and virtue of using the third person in VR games.

21.   See Bruce Geryk, 'CAVE Quake Q & A', accessed at www.gamespot/features/cave_quake2/.

22.   See www.c3dnow.com/showcase/products/3/Dcombo.htm.

23.   On the creation of impressions of presence in both traditional and electronic literary texts, see Marie-Laure Ryan, *Narrative as Virtual Reality: Immersion and Interactivity in Literature and Electronic Media*; on the longer tradition of immersive spaces of which contemporary virtual reality can be seen as the latest instance, see Oliver Grau, *Virtual Art: From Illusion to Immersion*.

24.   'Games Telling Stories – A brief note on games and narratives', 17.

25.   *More than a Game*, 75.

26.   'Cyberbeing and ~space', accessed at www.mcc.murdoch.edu.au/ReadingRoom/VID/cybersein.html; see also the account of McHoul's position in Brett Nicholls and Simon Ryan, 'Game, Space and the Politics of Cyberplay', Digital Arts and Culture conference, Melbourne, May 2003, accessed at hypertext.rmit.edu.au/dac/papers/.

27.   'Cyberspace and ~space', numbered paragraph 16.

28.   Ibid.

29.   Bartle, *Designing Virtual Worlds*, 415.

30.   Ibid. 159.

31.   'Immersion, Engagement, and Presence: A Method for Analyzing 3–D Video Games', in Mark Wolf and Bernard Perron (eds.), *The Video Game Theory Reader*.

32.   'At the Heart of It All: The Concept of Presence', accessed at www.ascusc.org/gcmc/vol3/issue2/Lombard.html.

33.   Ryan, *Narrative as Virtual Reality*, 284–5.

34.   Bartle, *Designing Virtual Worlds*, 288.

35.   See Lombard and Ditton.

36.   'A Poetics of Virtual Worlds', Digital Arts and Culture conference, Melbourne, May 2003, accessed at hypertext.rmit.edu.au/dac/papers/.

37.   Bartle, *Designing Virtual Worlds*, 26.

38.   Ibid. 222.

39.   Walton, *Mimesis as Make-Believe: On the Foundations of the Representational Arts*, 11. Walton has been cited by a number of commentators on games and virtual reality, including Marie-Laure Ryan, *Narrative as Virtual Reality*, Lisa Klastrup, 'A Poetics of Virtual Worlds', and Jill

Walker, 'Performing Fictions: Interaction and Depiction', Digital Arts and Culture conference, Melbourne, May 2003, accessed at hypertext. rmit.edu.au/dac/papers/.

40.   Walton, *Mimesis*, 228.

41.   Ibid. 247.

42.   Ibid. 29–30.

43.   In Freud, *On Psychopathology*, 161–193.

44.   Cora Kaplan, 'The Thorn Birds: Fiction, fantasy and femininity', in Victor Burgin, James Donald and Cora Kaplan (eds.), *Formations of Fantasy*.

45.   Elizabeth Cowie, *Representing the Woman: Cinema and Psychoanalysis*, 134.

46.   Ibid. 140.

CHAPTER 3

1.   This and the following detail is from the account given in Kline, Dyer-Witheford and De Peuter, *Digital Play*.

2.   Ibid. 129.

3.   Ibid. 139–40.

4.   www.eidosinteractive.co.uk/gss/trangel/home.html. Accessed 4 February 2004.

5.   *Andrew Rollings and Ernest Adams on Game Design*, 13.

6.   For a sketch of this history, see Aki Järvinen, 'Gran Stylissimo: The Audiovisual Elements and Styles in Computer and Video Games', in Frans Mäyrä (ed.), *Computer Games and Digital Cultures*.

7.   *Andrew Rollings and Ernest Adams on Game Design*, 293–4.

8.   Mark Wolf and Bernard Perron include graphics in a list of the four 'most fundamental' elements of the videogame, alongside algorithms, the interface and player activity; 'Introduction', *The Video Game Theory Reader*, Wolf and Perron (eds.), 14–15.

9.   *The Video Game Theory Reader*, 53.

10.   See Andrew Mactavish, 'Technological Pleasure: The Performance and Narrative of Technology in *Half-Life* and other High-Tech Computer Games', in King and Krzywinska (eds.), *ScreenPlay*.

11.   For more on the technical aspects of these processes see www. GameDev.net.

12.   For the definitive account of this kind of process, including videogames

among a wider range of media, see Jay David Bolter and Richard Grusin, *Remediation: Understanding New Media*.

13.   'Great Game Graphics... Who Cares?', Game Developer Conference (GDC), 2003, video accessed at www.gamasutra.com/features/20030409/rubin_01.shtml.

14.   *Rules of Play*, 145.

15.   For a more detailed model of how non-verbal communication can be used to increase the expressivity of game characters, see Tomi Kujapää and Tony Manninen, 'Supporting Visual Elements of Non-Verbal Communication in Computer Game Avatars', in Marinka Copier and Joost Raessens (eds.), *Level Up: Digital Games Research Conference*, Utrecht University, 2003.

16.   'Storytelling in Computer Games', in François Laramée (ed), *Game Design Perspectives*, 277.

17.   'Great Game Graphics'.

18.   Ibid.

19.   'Game Graphics Beyond Realism: Then, Now, and Tomorrow', in Copier and Raessens (eds.), *Level Up: Digital Games Research Conference*, accompanying CD-Rom, Utrecht University, 2003.

20.   We are grateful to David Bessell for his advice on the use of sound effects processing in the game.

21.   *Trigger Happy: The Inner Life of Videogames*, 65–6.

22.   *Designing Virtual Worlds*, 240.

23.   For a fuller account of this process, see Rollings and Adams, 258–9.

24.   Ibid. 371.

25.   Ibid. 396.

26.   Ibid. 383.

27.   *The Nature of Computer Games: Play as Semiosis*, 3–6, 20.

28.   See Olli Sotamaa, 'All the World's a Botfighter Stage: Notes on Location-based Multi-User Gaming', in Frans Mäyrä (ed.), *Computer Games and Digital Cultures*.

29.   See Geoff King, *Spectacular Narratives: Hollywood in the Age of the Blockbuster*, Chapter 4.

30.   Accessed via www.gamespot.com.

31.   *Knowing Audiences: Judge Dredd, It's Friends, Fans and Foes*, 146.

32.   On the role of such effects as indicators of presence in games, VR and other media, see Matthew Lombard and Theresa Ditton, 'At the

Heart of It All: The Concept of Presence', section titled 'The Effects of Presence'.

33. *Man, Play and Games*, 23.

34. Ibid. 23.

35. *Chris Crawford on Game Design*, 62.

36. Ibid. 66–7.

37. For a useful account of the latter, relation to Hollywood cinema, see Richard Dyer, *Only Entertainment*.

38. For more on suspense in games, see Aaron Smuts and Jonathan Frome, 'Helpless Spectators: Generating Suspense in Videogames and Film', *Text Technology*, forthcoming.

Chapter 4

1. By ideology here, we mean meanings at the social or cultural level that have specifically political implications, often taking the form of presenting particular meanings that favour particular social-economic groups as if they were of more general, universal or 'natural' provenance.

2. Available at www.newsgaming.com.

3. Available at underash.net.

4. See 'Special Notice' on the game's web pages, at www.specialforce. net/english/important/htm.

5. Tom Loftus, 'God in the console: Looking for religion in video games', MSNBC News, 20 August 2003, accessed at www.msnbc.com/ news/954674.asp?Osi=-&cp1=1.

6. See Walter Holland, Henry Jenkins, Kurt Squire, 'Theory by Design', in Mark Wolf and Bernard Perron, *The Video Game Theory Reader*, 27. Games-to-Teach has since been replaced by the Education Arcade project (www.educationarcade.org).

7. See James Paul Gee, *What Video Games Have to Teach Us About Learning and Literacy*.

8. For a brief outline of some such differences, see Andreas Lange, 'Report from the PAL Zone: European Games Culture', in Lucien King (ed.), *Game On*.

9. For a very similar reading, see Barry Atkins, *More than a Game*, 61.

10. Ibid. 59.

11. Ibid.

12.   'A Touch of Medieval: Narrative, Magic and Computer Technology in Massively Multi-player Computer Role-Playing Games', in Frans Mäyrä (ed.), *Computer Games and Digital Cultures: Conference Proceedings*, 258.

13.   Ibid. 259.

14.   Umberto Eco quoted in Christopher Frayling, *Strange Landscapes: A Journey Through the Middle Ages*, 179. Eco lists a number of other categories but these two apply most pertinently to the neo-medieval in games.

15.   For indicative interviews with gamers of neo-medieval paper-based D&D games that support this claim, see Gary Alan Fine, *Shared Fantasy: Role-Playing Games as Social Worlds*.

16.   Eco in Frayling, 7.

17.   The extent to which such figures dominate games can be overstated, however. A content analysis study of 130 games by Jeffrey Brand, Scott Knight and Jakub Majewski in 2002 found that only 10 per cent had characters with unrealistic, hyper-masculine or sexualized bodies, 80 per cent of which were male; 'The Diverse Worlds of Computer Games: A Content Analysis of Spaces, Populations, Styles and Narratives', in Marinka Copier and Joost Raessens (eds.), *Level Up: Digital Games Research Conference,* Utrecht University, 2003, accompanying CD-ROM, 10.

18.   Susan Jeffords, *The Remasculinization of America*.

19.   For more on this aspect of these and other games, see Sheri Graner Ray, *Gender Inclusive Game Design: Expanding the Market*, 19–20.

20.   Ray, *Gender Inclusive Game Design*, 23–5.

21.   Helen W. Kennedy, 'Lara Croft: Feminist Icon or Cyberbimbo?: On the Limits of Textual Analysis', *Game Studies*, vol. 2, issue 2, December 2002, 2; accessed at www.gamestudies.org/0202/kennedy.

22.   Diane Carr, 'Playing Lara', in King and Krzywinska (eds.), *ScreenPlay*, 178.

23.   Carr, 'Playing Lara', 171.

24.   Richard Dyer, *White*, 2.

25.   Donald Bogle, *Toms, Coons, Mulattoes, Mammies and Bucks: An Interpretive History of Blacks in American Films*; Frantz Fanon, *Black Skin, White Masks*.

26.   The first game to offer a choice of avatar gender and race, according

to Ray, was *Ultima VII Part Two, The Serpent Isle; Gender Inclusive Game Design*, 27.

27.   Sue Morris, personal communication.

28.   *Hamlet on the Holodeck*, 89.

29.   *Chris Crawford on Game Design*, 383–94.

30.   'The Microserfs are Revolting: Sid Meier's Civilization II', *Bad Subjects*, 45, October 1999, accessed at eserver.org/bs/45/stephenson.html.

31.   'The Microserfs are Revolting'.

32.   *Andrew Rollings and Ernest Adams on Game Design*, 324.

33.   For an account that makes some direct connections between games and colonial-era American mythology, see Mary Fuller and Henry Jenkins, 'Nintendo and New World Travel Writing: A Dialogue', in Steven Jones (ed.), *Cybersociety: Computer-Mediated Communication and Community*.

34.   Among other writings about the game, see the account in Stephen Kline, Nick Dyer-Witheford and Greig De Peuter, *Digital Play*, 275–9, and Miguel Sicart, 'Family Values: Ideology, Computer Games & *The Sims*', in Copier and Raessens (eds.), *Level Up: Digital Games Research Conference*, Utrecht University, 2003, accompanying CD-ROM.

35.   'Family Values', 8–9.

36.   *Chris Crawford on Game Design*, 402.

37.   'Virtual Real(i)ty: *SimCity* and the Production of Urban Cyberspace', *Game Research*, July 2002, accessed at www.game-research.com/art_simcity.asp.

38.   Louis Althusser, 'Ideology and Ideological State Apparatuses', in *Lenin and Philosophy and Other Essays*, 170–76. Althusser's approach has been widely criticized, both within and outside Marxist-oriented critical circles, especially for the absolute nature of the determining power attributed to ideology, from which no freedom is allowed other than for a Marxism characterized as 'science'. His concept of interpellation is used here for its broader and more suggestive qualities, rather than in quite such restrictive terms.

39.   Another area in which this approach has been controversial, used by some in a manner that exaggerates the capacity of any such medium fundamentally to 'position' or 'shape' the viewer, rather than to contribute to a broader range of influences.

40.   *Black Hawk Down*, 'Official Manual' supplied with the game, 31.

41. Shenja van der Graaf and David Nieborg, 'Together We Brand: America's Army', in Marinka Copier and Joost Raessens (eds.), *Level Up: Digital Games Research Conference,* Utrecht University, 2003.

42. Ibid. 329.

43. *Virtuous War: Mapping the Military-Industrial-Media-Entertainment Network,* 14.

44. Ibid. 164.

45. Ibid. 15.

46. The now–classic source is Baudrillard's *Simulations.*

47. Grossman, *On Killing* and, with Gloria DeGaetano, *Stop Teaching Our Kids to Kill: A Call to Action Against TV, Movie & Video Game Violence.*

48. For an extremely cogent analysis of the various factors involved in a case such as the Columbine High School shootings in Littleton, Colorado, one of the key reference points in recent debate about violent game 'effects', see the testimony provided by Henry Jenkins to the US Senate Commerce Committee which considered the issue in May 1999, available at www.senate.gov/~commerce/hearings/0504jen.pdf.

49. *On Killing,* 113.

50. For useful critical commentary, see Martin Barker and Julian Petley (eds.), *Ill Effects: The Media / Violence Debate.*

51. Gerard Jones, in *Killing Monsters: Why Children Need Fantasy, Super-Heroes, and Make-Believe Violence,* argues that childhood play involving guns or other weapons is widespread, children in all cultures developing fantasies of projecting destructive power across space to knock down large opponents as part of their ways of imaginatively dealing with anxiety or disempowerment; 48.

52. 'Violence and the Political Life of Videogames', in Lucien King (ed.), *Game On,* 27.

53. 'It's no videogame: news commentary and the second gulf war', in Copier and Raessens (eds.), *Level Up: Digital Games Research Conference,* Utrecht University, 2003.

54. The BFG (big fucking gun) is the biggest and most powerful weapon available in the *Doom* and *Quake* games.

55. *Killing Monsters,* 11.

56. A similar argument, in relation to children's developing sense of what is and is not 'real', is made in relation to television programming by Robert Hodge and David Tripp, *Children and Television: A Semiotic Approach.*

57.   *Killing Monsters*, 101. Bruno Bettelheim's *The Uses of Enchantment* and Melanie Klein's work on children's play reach similar conclusions. Bettelheim argues that fairy tales offer children scenarios through which they can project their own conflicts – repressed or otherwise – with parents and siblings. Klein found that very young children symbolized latent resentments and aggressions in their imaginative play. In an essay on play, Bettelheim makes an argument very similar to that of Jones, suggesting that children can work through and master difficulties and anxieties through play and that parental concern about shooting games is a function more of adult anxieties about aggression than anything directly related to the experience provided to children ('The Importance of Play').

58.   *Killing Monsters*, 142.

59.   'Ideology and Interpellation in the First-Person Shooter', in Ronald Strickland (ed.), *Growing Up Postmodern: Neoliberalism and the War on the Young*.

60.   Ibid. 114.

61.   Ibid. 117.

62.   Sutton–Smith, *Toys as Culture*, 64–7.

63.   'The Experience of Information in Computer Games', Digital Arts and Cultures conference, Melbourne, 2003, accessed at hypertext.rmit. edu.au/dac/papers/.

64.   'Civilization and Its Discontents: Simulation, Subjectivity, and Space', accessed at www.duke.edu/~tlove/civ.htm.

65.   'The Ideology of Interactivity (or, Video Games and the Taylorization of Leisure)', in Marinka Copier and Joost Raessens (eds.), *Level Up: Digital Games Research Conference*, Utrecht University, 2003, accompanying CD-ROM, 10.

66.   'The Ideology of Interactivity', 6.

67.   *Digital Play*.

68.   Ibid. 85–90.

69.   Gary Alan Fine, *Shared Fantasy*.

70.   *Digital Play*, 91.

71.   Ibid. 130.

72.   Ibid. 133.

73.   Ibid. 134.

74.   Ibid. 250.

75.   Ibid. 251; on the issue of the ease of developing violent games, see also Celia Pearce, 'Beyond Shoot Your Friends: A Call to Arms in the Battle Against Violence', in Clark Dodsworth (ed.), *Digital Illusion: Entertaining the Future with High Technology*.

76.   'Beyond Shoot Your Friends', 211.

77.   Ibid. 215–16.

78.   Steven Kent, *The Ultimate History of Video Games*, 141.

79.   'Beyond Shoot Your Friends', 214.

80.   *Gender Inclusive Game Design*, 42.

81.   Ray relates many of these differences to earlier human cultures, including familiar arguments about the needs of males as 'hunters' as opposed to the roles of women as child-bearers and nurturers. How far any such differences might be rooted in notions of 'primordial' human gender-roles, or might be the outcome of more specific, arbitrary or more recent cultural constructions, reinforced through process of socialization, remains subject to much debate.

82.   *Gender Inclusive Game Design*, 54.

83.   Ibid. 68–9.

84.   See Yasmin Kafai, 'Video Game Designs by Girls and Boys: Variability and Consistency of Gender Differences', in Justine Cassell and Henry Jenkins (eds.), *From Barbie to Mortal Kombat: Gender and Computer Games*, 92–3. For further consideration of gaming qualities likely to appeal to female players, see Cornelia Brunner, Dorothy Bennett and Margaret Honey, 'Girl Games and Technological Desire', in Cassell and Jenkins. In a small-scale study by Aphra Kerr, women players listed sports and racing titles as well as *Grand Theft Auto III*, conventionally seen as male-oriented, among their favourite titles; 'Women Just Want to Have Fun – A Study of Adult Female Players of Digital Games', in Marinka Copier and Joost Raessens (eds.), *Level Up: Digital Games Research Conference,* Utrecht University, 2003.

85.   Kaveri Subrahmanyam and Patricia Greenfield, 'Computer Games for Girls: What Makes Them Play?', in Cassell and Jenkins (eds.), *From Barbie to Mortal Kombat*, 48.

86.   'Computer Games for Girls', 65.

87.   Justine Cassell and Henry Jenkins, 'Chess for Girls? Feminism and Computer Games', in Cassell and Jenkins (eds.), *From Barbie to Mortal Kombat*, 14–5.

88.   Cassell and Jenkins, 'Chess for Girls', 16–7.

89.   'An Interview with Brenda Laurel (Purple Moon)', in Cassell and Jenkins (eds.), *From Barbie to Mortal Kombat*, 124.

90.   Studies such as these tend to use a 'content analysis' methodology, in which fixed elements of content are counted and tabulated, rather than including any consideration of gameplay activities themselves. For an example that focuses exclusively on cut-scenes, see Jeroen Jansz and Raynel G. Martis, 'The Representation of Gender and Ethnicity in Digital Interactive Games', in Marinka Copier and Joost Raessens (eds.), *Level Up: Digital Games Research Conference,* Utrecht University, 2003. Jansz and Martis argue that introductory cut-scenes provide 'an adequate summary of the game, its purpose and content' (264), which we would argue is simply not the case if a full understanding of games *as games* is to be achieved. They cite a number of earlier examples of such studies, in two of which, including E.F. Provenzo's *Video Kids: Making Sense of Nintendo*, the analytical data is limited to cover illustrations. The conclusions of these studies suggest a trend towards increasing numbers of female leading characters, to the point of equality with male characters in Jansz and Martis.

91.   Sara M. Grimes '"You Shoot Like a Girl": The Female Protagonist in Action-Adventure Video Games', 6.

92.   Carol J. Clover, *Men, Women and Chainsaws: Gender in the Modern Horror Film*, 51–64.

93.   Katie Salen and Eric Zimmerman, *Rules of Play: Game Design Fundamentals*, 560–2.

94.   See Stephenson, 'The Microserfs are Revolting', and Sybille Lammes, 'On the Border: Pleasure of Exploration and Colonial Mastery in *Civilization III: Play the World*', in Marinka Copier and Joost Raessens (eds.), *Level Up: Digital Games Research Conference,* Utrecht University, 2003.

95.   Lammes, 'On the Border', 128.

96.   *Rules of Play*, 562.

97.   Ibid.

98.   www.opensorcery.net/velvet-strike.

99.   Cindy Poremba, 'Patches of Peace: Tiny Signs of Agency in Digital Games', in Copier and Raessens (eds.), *Level Up: Digital Games Research Conference,* accompanying CD-Rom, Utrecht University, 2003.

100.   Brad King and John Borland, *Dungeons and Dreamers: The Rise of Computer Game Culture from Geek to Chic*, 217.

101.   See escapefromwoomera.org.

102.   *Digital Play*, 277.

103.   *Homo Ludens*, 12. For the classic study of popular subculture, see Dick Hebdige, *Subculture: The Meaning of Style.*

104.   Fine, *Shared Fantasy*, 26.

105.   For a useful study of subcultural capital in a different arena, see Sarah Thornton, *Club Cultures: Music, Media and Subcultural Capital.*

106.   *Shared Fantasy*, 123.

107.   Ibid. 59–71.

108.   For a useful general account of the history of the games business, see Steve Kent, *The Ultimate History of Video Games*; also see Kline, Dyer-Witheford and De Peuter, *Digital Play.*

109.   *Digital Play*, 171.

110.   Ibid., Chapter 3; Morris-Suzuki, *Beyond Computopia: Information, Automation and Democracy in Japan.*

111.   See *Digital Play*, 66–7, for more sources of this analysis.

112.   Brian Sutton-Smith suggests a similar reading of commercially-produced toys more generally; *Toys as Culture*, 187–9.

113.   The concept of 'post-Fordism' has been contested, however, and subject to much debate, some of which is summarized by Kline, Dyer-Witheford and De Peuter, 62–6; it is best used in relation to particular sectors of the economy (and, some would argue, the wider society) rather than to suggest wholesale change across the board.

114.   *Digital Play*, 170.

115.   Ibid. 171.

116.   Dean Takahashi, *Opening the Xbox*, 185.

117.   See David Sheff, *Game Over: Nintendo's Battle to Dominate Videogames.*

118.   'Do Independent Games Exist?', in Lucien King (ed.), *Game On.*

119.   'Independent Game Development SIG', www.igda.org/indie/.

120.   For more detail on how this process operates, in the particular case of the launch of Nintendo's NES in the United States, see Sheff, *Game Over*, 151–2.

121.   On this and the following detail in relation to RealOne, see Brian Hook, 'Indie Interview – David Nixon – The Real Deal', IGDA website, www.igda.org/indie/interview_nixon.htm.

122.   For a radical call for such alternative, lower-cost sources of distribution, and a polemical critique of the existing games business, see 'The Scratchware Manifesto', available at www.the-underdogs.org/scratch. php.

123.   'Developers in Exile: Why Independent Game Development Needs an Island', Digital Arts and Culture conference, Melbourne, May 2003, accessed at hypertext.rmit.edu.au/dac/papers/.

124.   'Developers in Exile', 158.

Select Bibliography

Note: multiple entries from edited collections cited in the notes are not generally included in this bibliography.

Aarseth, Espen (1997) *Cybertext: Perspectives on Ergodic Literature.* Baltimore: Johns Hopkins University Press

Aarseth, Espen (1998) 'Allegories of Space: The Question of Spatiality in Computer Games', available at www.hf.uib.no/hi/espen/papers/space/

Aarseth, Espen (2003) 'Playing Research: Methodological Approaches to Game Analysis', *Digital Arts and Culture* conference, Melbourne, available at hypertext.rmit.edu.au/dac/papers/

Adams, Ernest (2002) 'The Role of Architecture in Videogames', *Gamasutra*, 9 October, available at www.gamasutra.com/features/20021009/adams_02.htm

Adams, Ernest (2003) 'The Designer's Notebook: Defining the Physical Dimension of a Game Setting', *Gamasutra*, 30 April, accessed at www.gamasutra.com/features/20030430/adams_01.shtml

Atkins, Barry (2003) *More than a Game: The Computer Game as Fictional Form.* Manchester; New York: Manchester University Press

Barker, Martin and Julian Petley (eds.), (2001) *Ill Effects: The Media/Violence Debate.* London: Routledge. 2nd Edition

Barthes, Roland (1975) *S/Z.* New York: Hill and Wang

Bartle Richard (1996) 'Hearts, Clubs, Diamonds, Spades: Players Who Suit Muds', accessed at mud.co.uk/Richard/hcds.htm

Bartle, Richard (2004) *Designing Virtual Worlds.* Indianapolis: New Riders

Bateson, Gregory (2000) 'A Theory of Play and Fantasy', in *Steps to an Ecology of Mind: Collected Essays in Anthropology, Psychiatry, Evolution, and Epistemology*. Chicago: University of Chicago Press

Bettelheim, Bruno (1987) 'The Importance of Play', *Atlantic Monthly*, March, accessed via www2.roguecc.edu/earlychild/pfarster/HDFS226/assignments/assign6.html

Bolter, Jay David and Richard Grusin (2000) *Remediation: Understanding New Media*. Cambridge: MIT Press

Brunner, Cornelia, Dorothy Bennett and Margaret Honey (1998) 'Girl Games and Technological Desire', in Justine Cassell and Jenkins (eds.), *From Barbie to Mortal Kombat: Gender and Computer Games*. Cambridge: MIT Press

Caillois, Roger (2001) *Man, Play and Games*. Urbana, Chicago: University of Illinois Press

Campbell, Joseph (1968) *The Hero with a Thousand Faces*. Princeton: Princeton University Press, 2nd Edition

Carr, Diane (2002) 'Playing Lara', in Geoff King and Tanya Krzywinska (eds.), *ScreenPlay: Cinema/Videogames/Interfaces*. London; New York: Wallflower Press

Carr, Diane (2003) 'Play Dead: Genre and Affect in *Silent Hill* and *Planescape Torment*', *Game Studies*, vol. 3, 1, available at http:/www.gamestudies.org/0301/carr/

Carson, Don (2000) 'Environmental Storytelling: Creating Immersive 3D Worlds Using Lessons Learned from the Theme Park Industry', *Gamasutra*, 1 March, available at www.Gamasutra.com/features/20000301/Carson_pfv.htm, 2

Cassell, Justine and Henry Jenkins (eds.), (1998) *From Barbie to Mortal Kombat: Gender and Computer Games*. Cambridge: MIT Press

Cassell, Justine and Henry Jenkins (1998) 'Chess for Girls? Feminism and Computer Games', in Cassell and Jenkins (eds.), *From Barbie to Mortal Kombat: Gender and Computer Games*. Cambridge: MIT Press

Copier, Marinka, and Joost Raessens (eds.), (2003), *Level Up: Digital Games Research Conference,* Utrecht University Press

Craig, Lindley (2002) 'The Gameplay Gestalt, Narrative, and Interactive Storytelling', in Frans Mäyrä (ed.), *Computer Games and Digital Cultures Conference Proceedings*. Tampere: Tampere University Press

Crawford, Chris (2003) *Chris Crawford on Game Design*. Indianapolis: New Riders Publishing

Crogan, Patrick (2003) 'The Experience of Information in Computer Games', *Digital Arts and Culture* conference, Melbourne, available at hypertext. rmit.edu.au/dac/papers/

Csikszentmihalyi, Mihaly (2002) *Flow: The Classic Work on How to Achieve Happiness*. London; Sydney; Auckland; Johannesburg: Rider

Csikszentmihalyi, Mihaly and Isabella Selega Csikszentmihalyi (eds.), (1988) *Optimal Experience: Psychological Studies of Flow in Consciousness*. Cambridge: Cambridge University Press

Der Derian, James (2001) *Virtuous War: Mapping the Military-Industrial-Media-Entertainment Network*. Boulder: Westview Press

Dodsworth, Clark (ed.), (1998) *Digital Illusion: Entertaining the Future with High Technology*. New York: ACM Press

Dunniway, Troy (2000) 'Using the Hero's Journey in Games', *Gamasutra*, 27 November, available at www/gamasutra.com/features/20001127/htm /dunniway_01.htm

Eskilinen, Markku (2001) 'The Gaming Situation', *Game Studies*, vol. 1, 1, section 8, available at www.gamestudies.org/0101/eskilinen

Fine, Gary Alan (1983) *Shared Fantasy: Role-Playing Games as Social Worlds*. Chicago: Chicago University Press

Flynn, Bernadette (2003) 'Languages of Navigation Within Computer Games', Digital Arts and Culture conference, Melbourne, available at hypertext. rmit.edu.au/dac/papers/

Frasca, Gonzalo (2000) 'Videogames of the Oppressed: Videogames as a Means for Critical Thinking and Debate', Master's thesis, Georgia Institute of Technology, available at www.jacaranda.org/frasca/thesis/ FrascaThesisVideogames.pdf

Friedman, Ted (undated) 'Civilization and Its Discontents: Simulation, Subjectivity, and Space', available at www.duke.edu/~tlove/civ.htm

Fuller, Mary and Henry Jenkins (1994) 'Nintendo and New World Travel Writing: A Dialogue', in Steven Jones (ed.), *Cybersociety: Computer-Mediated Communication and Community*. London: Sage

Gee, James Paul (2003) *What Video Games Have to Teach Us About Learning and Literacy*. New York: Palgrave

Grossman, Austin (ed.), (2003) *Postmortems from Game Developer*. San Francisco; New York; Lawrence: CMP Books

Grossman, Dave (1995) *On Killing*, Boston: Little, Brown

Grossman, Dave and Gloria DeGaetano (1999) *Stop Teaching our Kids to Kill:*

A Call to Action against TV, Movie and Video Game Violence. New York: Crown

Hodge, Robert and David Tripp (1986) *Children and Television: A Semiotic Approach*. Cambridge: Polity Press

Holland, Walter, Henry Jenkins, Kurt Squire (2003) 'Theory by Design', in Mark Wolf and Bernard Perron (eds.), *The Video Game Theory Reader*. New York; London: Routledge

Huizinga, Johan (1955) *Homo Ludens: A study of the play element in culture*. Boston: The Beacon Press

Järvinen, Aki, Satu Heliö and Frans Mäyrä (2002) 'Communication and Community in Digital Entertainment Services: Prestudy Research Report', Hypermedia Laboratory Net Series, 2, University of Tampere Hypermedia Laboratory, available at tampub.uta.fi/tup/951-44-5432-4.pdf

Jenkins, Henry (1998) '"Complete Freedom of Movement": Video Games as Gendered Play Spaces', in Justine Cassell and Jenkins (eds.), *From Barbie to Mortal Kombat: Gender and Computer Games*. Cambridge: MIT Press

Jenkins, Henry (undated) 'Game Design as Narrative Architecture', available at web.mit.edu/21 fms/www/faculty/henry3/games&narrative.html

Jenkins, Henry (1999) 'Testimony before the U.S. Senate Commerce Committee', available at www.senate.gov/~commerce/hearings/0504jen.pdf

Jenkins, Henry (2001) 'The Game as Object of Study', *Game Cultures* conference, Bristol, question-and-answer session

Jones, Gerard (2002) *Killing Monsters: Why Children Need Fantasy, Super-Heroes, and Make-Believe Violence*. New York: Basic Books

Juul, Jesper (2001) 'Games Telling Stories? – A Brief Note on Games and Narratives', *Game Studies*, vol. 1, 1, accessed at gamestudies.org/0101/juul-gts/

Juul, Jesper (2002) 'The Open and the Closed: Games of Emergence and Games of Progression', in Frans Mäyrä (ed.), *Computer Games and Digital Cultures Conference Proceedings*. Tampere: Tampere University Press

Juul, Jesper (2003) 'The Game, The Player, The World: Looking for the Heart of Gameness', in Copier and Raessens (eds.), *Level Up: Digital Games Research Conference*. Utrecht University

Kennedy, Helen (2002) 'Lara Croft: Feminist Icon or Cyberbimbo?: On the Limits of Textual Analysis', in *Game Studies*, vol.2, 2, available at www.gamestudies.org/0202/kennedy

Kent, Steven L. (2001) *The Ultimate History of Video Games*. California: Prima

King, Brad and John Borland (2003) *Dungeons and Dreamers: The Rise of Computer Game Culture from Geek to Chic*. Emeryville, California: McGraw Hill/ Osbourne

King, Geoff and Tanya Krzywinska (eds.), (2002) *ScreenPlay: Cinema/Videogames/ Interfaces*. London: Wallflower Press

King, Lucien (ed.), (2002) *Game On: The History and Culture of Videogames*. London: Laurence King.

Klastrup, Lisbeth (2003) 'A Poetics of Virtual Worlds', *Digital Arts and Culture* conference, Melbourne, available at hypertext.rmit.edu.au/dac/papers/

Klevjer, Rune (2002) 'In Defense of Cutscenes', in Frans Mäyrä (ed.), *Computer Games and Digital Cultures Conference Proceedings*. Tampere: Tampere University Press

Kline, Stephen, Nick Dyer-Witheford and Greig De Peuter (2003) *Digital Play: The Interaction of Technology, Culture and Marketing*. Montreal: McGill-Queen's University Press

Kücklich, Julian (undated) 'The Road Less Traveled – The Case for Computer Game Philology', available at playability.de/en/txt/cgpabs.html

Kurtz, Andrew (2002) 'Ideology and Interpellation in the First-Person Shooter', in Ronald Strickland (ed.), *Growing Up Postmodern: Neoliberalism and the War on the Young*. Lanham: Rowman & Littlefield

Landow, George P. (1997) *Hypertext 2.0: The Convergence of Contemporary Critical Theory and Technology*. Baltimore: Johns Hopkins University Press

Lange, Andreas (2002) 'Report from the PAL Zone: European Games Culture', in Lucien King (ed.), *Game On: The History and Culture of Videogames*. London: Laurence King

Laramée, François (ed.), (2002) *Game Design Perspectives*. Hingham: Charles River

Littlejohn, Randy (2003) 'Agitating for Dramatic Change', *Gamasutra*, 29 October, available at www.gamasutra.com/features/20031029/littlejohn_pfv.htm

Littleton, Karen, P. Light, R. Joiner, D. Messer and P. Barnes (1998) 'Gender Task Scenarios and Children's Computer-Based Problem Solving', *Educational Psychology*, vol. 18, 3

Lombard, Matthew and Theresa Ditton (1999) 'At the Heart of It All: The Concept of Presence', available at www.ascusc.org/gcmc/vol3/issue2/ Lombard.html

Mactavish, Andrew (2002) 'Technological Pleasure: The Performance and

Narrative of Technology in *Half-Life* and other High–Tech Computer Games', in King and Krzywinska (eds.), *ScreenPlay: Cinema/Videogames/Interfaces*, London: Wallflower Press

Mactavish, Andrew (2003) 'Game Mod(ifying) Theory: The Cultural Contradictions of Computer Game Modding', *Power-Up: Computer Games, Ideology and Play* conference, Bristol

Mäyrä, Frans (ed.), (2002) *Computer Games and Digital Cultures Conference Proceedings.* Tampere: Tampere University Press

McHoul, Alec (undated) 'Cyberbeing and ~space', available at wwwmcc. murdoch.edu.au/ReadingRoom/VID/cybersein.html

McMahan, Alison (2003) 'Immersion, Engagement, and Presence: A Method for Analyzing 3-D Video Games', in Mark Wolf and Bernard Perron (eds.), *The Video Game Theory Reader.* New York; London: Routledge

Miklaucic, Shawn (2002) 'Virtual Real(i)ty: *SimCity* and the Production of Urban Cyberspace', *Game Research*, July, available at www.game-research.com/art_simcity.asp

Molyneux, Peter (2003) 'Lionhead Studios: *Black and White*', in Austin Grossman (ed.), *Postmortems from Game Developer.* San Francisco: CMP Books

Morris, Sue (2002) 'First–Person Shooters – A Game Apparatus', in Geoff King and Tanya Krzywinska (eds.), *ScreenPlay: Cinema/Videogames/Interfaces.* London: Wallflower Press

Morris-Suzuki, Tessa (1988) *Beyond Computopia: Information, Automation and Democracy in Japan.* London: Routledge

Murray, Janet (2001) *Hamlet on the Holodeck: The Future of Narrative in Cyberspace.* Cambridge: MIT Press

Murray, Janet (2003) 'What are Games Made of?', in Copier and Raessens (eds.), *Level Up: Digital Games Research Conference*, Utrecht University

Myers, David (2003) *The Nature of Computer Games: Play as Semiosis.* New York: Peter Lang

Oliver, Julian (2003) 'Developers in Exile: Why Independent Game Development Needs an Island', Digital Arts and Culture conference, Melbourne, available at hypertext.rmit.edu.au/dac/papers/

Piaget, Jean (1962) *Play, Dreams and Imitation in Childhood.* London: Routledge

Poole, Steven (2000) *Trigger Happy: The Inner Life of Videogames.* London: Fourth Estate

Provenzo, E. F. (1991) *Video Kids: Making Sense of Nintendo.* Cambridge: University of Harvard Press

Ray, Sheri Graner (2004) *Gender Inclusive Game Design: Expanding the Market.* Hingham: Charles River

Rollings, Andrew and Ernest Adams (2003) *Andrew Rollings and Ernest Adams on Game Design.* Indianapolis: New Riders

Rouse, Richard (2001) *Game Design: Theory and Practice.* Texas: Wordware

Rubin, Jason (2003) 'Great Game Graphics… Who Cares?', Game Developer Conference (GDC), video available at www.gamasutra.com/features/20030409/rubin_01.shtml

Ryan, Marie-Laure (2001) *Narrative as Virtual Reality: Immersion and Interactivity in Literature and Electronic Media.* Baltimore: Johns Hopkins University Press

Ryan, Marie-Laure (2001) 'Beyond Myth and Metaphor – The Case of Narrative in Digital Media', *Game Studies*, vol. 1, 1, available at www.gamestudies.org/0101/ryan/

Salen, Katie and Eric Zimmerman (2003) *Rules of Play: Game Design Fundamentals.* Cambridge: MIT Press

Schroeder, Ralph (1996) *Possible Worlds: The Social Dynamic of Virtual Reality Technology.* Boulder: Westview Press

Sheff, David (1993) *Game Over: Nintendo's Battle to Dominate Videogames.* London: Hodder & Stoughton, abridged edition, 1999

Sikora, Drew (2002) 'Storytelling in Computer Games', in François Laramée (ed) *Game Design Perspectives.* Hingham: Charles River

Stephenson, William (1999) 'The Microserfs are Revolting: Sid Meier's Civilization II', *Bad Subjects*, 45, October, available at eserver.org/bs/45/stephenson.html

Suits, Bernard (1978) *The Grasshopper: Games, Life and Utopia.* Toronto: University of Toronto Press/Boston: Nonpareil, 1990

Sutton-Smith, Brian (1986) *Toys as Culture.* New York: Gardner Press

Sutton-Smith, Brian (1997) *The Ambiguity of Play.* Cambridge: Harvard University Press

Takahashi, Dean (2002) *Opening the Xbox.* Roseville: Prima

Tanguay, Daniel and Brent Boylen (2002) 'Adapting Licensed Properties', in François Laramée (ed.), *Game Design Perspectives.* Hingham: Charles River

Thompson, Clive (2002) 'Violence and the Political Life of Videogames', in Lucien King (ed.), *Game On: The History and Culture of Videogames.* London: Laurence King

Vince, John (1998) *Essential Virtual Reality Fast.* London: Springer-Verlag

Walker, Jill (2003) 'Performing Fictions: Interaction and Depiction', Digital Arts and Culture conference, Melbourne, available at hypertext.rmit.edu.au/dac/papers/

Walton, Kendall (1993) *Mimesis as Make-Believe: On the Foundations of the Representational Arts.* Cambridge: Harvard University Press

Wolf, Mark (2002) 'Space in the Video Game', in Mark J. P. Wolf (ed.), *The Medium of the Video Game.* Austin: University of Texas Press

Wolf, Mark and Bernard Perron (2003) (ed.) *The Video Game Theory Reader.* New York: Routledge

Yates, Simeon and Karen Littleton (2001) 'Understanding Computer Game Culture: A Situated Approach', in Eileen Green and Alison Adam (eds.), *Virtual Gender: Technology, consumption and identity.* New York: Routledge

Zimmerman, Eric (2002) 'Do Independent Games Exist?', in Lucien King (ed.), *Game On: The History and Culture of Videogames.* London: Laurence King.

Index